Blackboard Tyranny

Blackboard Tyranny

Connaught Coyne Marshner

ARLINGTON HOUSE·PUBLISHERS
NEW ROCHELLE, NEW YORK

P10 9 8 7 6 5 4 3 2 1

Book Design by Pat Slesarchik

Manufactured in the United States of America

Library of Congress Cataloging in Publication Data

Marshner, Connaught Coyne, 1951–
  Blackboard tyranny.

  Includes bibliographical references and index.
  1. Public schools—United States. 2. Home
and school—United States. 3. Education and state
—United States. I. Title.
LA217.M34   379.73   78–8696
ISBN 0–87000–402–6

To my father and mother,
who gave me my first typewriter;
and my husband,
without whose understanding
this would never have been finished.

Contents

Acknowledgements		9
Foreword by Hon. Robert K. Dornan,		
Member of Congress		11
1	What Went Wrong?	15
2	The Education Establishment	40
3	Uncle Sam Steps In	89
4	Federal Tyranny	127
5	Fighting Within the System	158
6	Guidelines for Parent Activists	227
7	Alternatives Public and Private	264
8	Around and Out of the System	291
Notes		323
Index		343

Acknowledgements

I wish to thank Dr. Onalee McGraw, and Lawrence Uzzell of the Heritage Foundation, for their encouragement and assistance; and Richard Odermatt, librarian of the Heritage Foundation, for his invaluable job of "information storage and retrieval."

Foreword

As a parent of five children, I spend lots of time worrying about my children's education. As a Congressman, I find myself worrying about the whole nation's education. Sometimes, I think my generation had an easy time of parenthood, compared with the burdens on today's young parents. We were raising our children in postwar affluence, in a society that still held, at least nominally and publicly, to basic principles of a Judeo-Christian social order.

Today, American society is hard on parents. Not only does the ZPG mentality scorn parenthood, but irresponsible government fiscal policies are making parenthood a state of sacrifice and financial risk. Uncontrolled inflation is a monstrous cruelty to the aged, but it is also a handicap to parenthood. Saving is almost impossible, and circumstances render domestic thrift almost futile. If a young father tries to earn some extra money, he must do so at the cost of his time with his family. And an appallingly large number of mothers find they must work in order to make ends meet. Which luxury will parents give their children: new clothes or their own time? Such a choice should not be necessary in our nation, but, tragically, it is.

11

And it is part of a vicious cycle: the more parents must work, the less time they can spend with their children; and the more time children spend at school, the less time they want to spend at home. Parents find themselves with less and less control over their children's activities and education. Here again, government fiscal habits cause more trouble—public schools are at the forefront of the big-spend delirium.

It seems an inverse ratio exists between the measurable achievements of students and the number of dollars spent on them, and illogical though it be, educationist lobbies use that argument to get more money from Washington. If the high cost of public schools were a guarantee of quality, parents would gladly shoulder the burden—American parents are unmatched in their willingness to pay for what they believe will help their children. But the secret is out: huge public education budgets do not buy the kind of education hard-working parents want for their children. Instead, money is spent on training children for a "new society" or a "new world," even when such dreams directly conflict with parental values. Many dollars from local budgets find their way into the coffers of the nation's strongest, most organized pressure group—the education lobby, which unashamedly declares that the one proper place for parents is in voting for bond issues.

In sum, parents are being asked to finance their enemies, and worse, to fund the so-called "educational" programs that are designed to make families obsolete, such as the notorious MACOS curriculum. (See Chapter 4.)

There is worse tyranny: parents who try to get their children a good education under private auspices find themselves paying double—assuming, of course, that they manage to scrape up the money for the necessarily high costs of private education, and assuming that the private schools have not already swallowed the doctrines that make public education unacceptable.

I'm sorry I paint a grim picture. Nevertheless, it is an accurate one. Parents from all over the country, knowing my concern, tell me the same thing. Now, Connaught Coyne

12

Marshner has painstakingly documented all these problems with education, and likewise documented her findings as to the source of the problems. But this book is more than a catalog of errors; it is a CARE package for beleaguered parents, full of practical suggestions, both short- and long-range, for the defense of traditional values and family integrity, and the improvement of education for all children.

Concerned parents have known for years that something was wrong with American education. It wasn't until 1974 that the media discovered this, thanks to the drama of the Kanawha County (West Virginia) textbook battle. But the ranks of concerned parents are growing rapidly. Millions of young parents are just beginning to cope with the schools. These young parent activists need an orientation manual, an action program, to help them coordinate their efforts and promote their cause. I think this book is that manual, and I welcome it as ammunition in the battle for American education, for America's children.

Robert K. Dornan
Member of Congress

1

What Went Wrong?

A high school graduate sues the San Francisco Unified School District because he finds out, after graduating, that he is still reading at a fifth-grade level. In 12 years of education no teacher had indicated he was below par. His lawsuit gains him nothing, however, because the appeals court says that state law does not cover his case.[1]

The School of Journalism of the University of Wisconsin at Madison finds that more than one-third of its applicants are unable to meet minimum requirements for spelling, grammar, and word usage.[2] These are the future arbiters of the English language, no less.

A new vocational-education high school in Alexandria, Virginia, is constructed with microwave anti-intrusion devices to scan the rooms and halls, closed-circuit TV to watch the roof, and an intercom system to listen for unusual noises. The few windows in the school are of sturdy plastic. Library books have tiny circuits in them to sound an alarm if smuggled out of the library. All the security devices in the school are connected with a central switchboard, which has a direct line to police headquarters. It cost extra to build this security system, but school officials feel the initial outlay was cheaper than repairing the damages that would occur without the system.[3]

In the academic year of 1974–75, public schools in Kanawha County, West Virginia were closed by civil disorders that erupted when parents protested the use of dirty textbooks. A local newspaper, which favored the new books, found that 70 percent of the community opposed their adoption. Nonetheless, the school board voted 4–1 to reaffirm the purchase. A minister and five other persons were indicted in connection with the bombing of two schools. They were indicted not by the county, or even by the state of West Virginia, but by the U. S. government. The bombed property belongs to the Kanawha County Board of Education, but that body receives federal financial aid, so the federal government assumes jurisdiction.[4]

Some time later Representative Norman Lent, a Republican from New York, became aware of a textbook dispute in the Island Trees School District, in his constituency. Some of the disputed books were the same that caused trouble in West Virginia. Congressman Lent decided to print excerpts from the books in the *Congressional Record,* trusting that if high schoolers were expected to read them, mature, sophisticated members of Congress would hardly find the passages embarrassing. Congressman Lent was informed by the Joint Committee on Printing that the material would not be printed in the *Record* because congressional rules prohibit profanity, obscenity, and extreme vulgarity in that public document.[5] What is good enough for public schoolchildren is not acceptable for lawmakers, apparently.

In South Saint Paul, Minnesota, a high school custodian blew the whistle on the militant lesbian text *Our Bodies, Ourselves,* which had been bought without any review at all for a class on "Parent-Child Relationships."[6]

In Butte, Montana, after perhaps as long as two years, the school board ordered a halt to the practice of shutting retarded children in a coffin-size box as a form of "behavior modification."[7]

A New York City widow objected to having her seven-year-

16

old son taught the "look-say" method of reading. She kept him home to teach him phonics. The board of education charged that the child was neglected, deprived of peer-group association, and that the mother, a high school graduate, was unfit to teach him. Queens Family Court Judge Moskoff found that the mother was qualified to teach her son, ruled that the peer-group association factor was "not relevant," but nonetheless ruled that the child was "neglected" according to the meaning of the New York Education Code. She was forced to reenroll the child in school.[8]

In upstate New York a family objected to sex education courses for six of their nine children. When measures to excuse the children from the classes failed, the parents kept them home. Suddenly the six children were forcibly taken away and farmed out to foster homes. Only a barrage of publicity and a sympathetic, clever lawyer created enough pressure to bring the family back together.[9]

These are the dramatic cases. Some of them are well known. But most of the time, when the education establishment tramples on parental prerogatives, the incident never hits the newspapers or reaches the courts. Many of these cases—and they surely number in the millions—are not even recognized by the parents for what they are. Mothers have long observed that after the first child starts school, the rest of the family starts catching more colds and flus. But other forms of disease are not so evident.

What about the personality traits that start developing? What about the dissatisfaction with family rules and routines? What about boredom with learning, loss of curiosity about ideas and the world at large? Why do children suddenly begin to complain about responsibilities toward little brothers or sisters? Why do they resent doing accustomed chores? Why does off-color language or unfamiliar slang suddenly crop up in a child's conversation?

As childhood yields to preadolescence and adolescence, and the condition gets worse, parents are told that these symptoms indicate normal stages of maturation. But when a mother is told by her high schooler, "You don't know what's right and wrong for me," or "You don't really care about me," she knows in her heart that it is something more than youthful *Sturm und Drang* that is causing the anguish. It is not biologically mandated for human offspring to turn against their parents. But all the kids on the block are acting the same way, so Mrs. Middle America figures she must be oversensitive . . . until something provokes her to take a closer look at her children's public schools.

The New Illiterates

Despite educators' efforts to ascribe inordinate responsibility to vague "social trends," parents are starting to see a connection between their children's unaccountable abnormal behavior and the schools. But this relation is hard to pin down. When a fifth grader cannot read a "Peanuts" comic strip, however, his condition indicates that the school that was supposed to teach him to read has objectively failed. As parents investigate why the schools have not taught their children to read, they stumble upon larger and worse failures.

Language instruction has been deteriorating for a couple of generations. Look-say was common by the 1950s; by the 70s phonics was rare. By the 70s teachers no longer talked about reading and writing; they talked about "language arts" instead, a subtle but revealing semantic shift.

The look-say method of reading was invented in the 1800s as a means for teaching deaf-and-dumb children how to read. Rev. Thomas Gallaudet found that children could memorize a vocabulary of about 50 words without learning letters—but these were children with no concept whatsoever of language. Normal children came (and still come) to school with a vocabulary of thousands of words. Why it should be assumed that the same principles of learning would apply to both groups of children defies logic. Nonetheless, the man who authored the

18

first Dick-and-Jane primers, published in 1930 by the Scott-Foresman Company, died a millionaire. A curious observation: that 1930 edition taught 68 sight words in 39 pages. The 1951 edition taught 58 words in 172 pages.[10] Obviously, something wasn't working. But educators were not about to admit that.

Parents could tell that making children guess at the meaning and pronunciation of words was not a wise strategy. Guesses are right only so often, and after a few years of low guessing averages, a child is likely to give up trying. Besides, the readers designed for the "controlled vocabulary" child are notoriously dull. After all, what can be said with 58 words or less?

Time was, after a child had learned to read he went on to literature, drama, public speaking, and composition. As things are now, such refinements are reserved for the very few. Millions of youngsters, unable to read works of quality, are bored, hostile, and unresponsive to discipline, and some even resort to violence to release their frustration. The typical junior and senior high school language-arts books try to appeal to minimal student interest by being "multiethnic" and by dealing with sensational topics (sex, drugs, crime, suicide). The limited text is lavishly illustrated. Teaching "strategies" stress student discussion: Was Pablo right to steal? How would you feel if somebody did that to you? Have you ever felt like hitting somebody? Why? What did you do? It is an easy slide from group discussions and hot-air sessions into tampering with privacy and interfering with personal values.

One typical teaching strategy is the game "Finishing a Story." The National Education Association (NEA) publishes two volumes for use in the classroom, *Unfinished Stories* and *More Unfinished Stories*. An NEA flyer advertising these volumes for sale lauds their "real-life appeal . . . their adaptability" and "their flexability" *(sic)*. It is a pleasing irony that the NEA should succumb to its own product, illiteracy.

Nor is English alone. Anyone who has watched a teenager try to add up a column of figures knows why there are so many poorly balanced budgets in the nation: finger counting and counting out loud were never outgrown. In response, teachers allow kids to bring in electronic calculators to help them solve problems. The Maryland chapter of the National Association for the Advancement of Colored People has asked the state legislature to forbid the use of such calculators—on the grounds that "disadvantaged" students can't afford them and that they discourage pupils from doing the work mentally.[11] The National Science Foundation launched the so-called new math on its merry course some years ago. A substantial consensus of teachers now admits that it turned out to be a dismal failure. But does the National Science Foundation admit it? Hardly. And the NSF continues planning new ways to teach other sciences.

Historian Henry Steele Commager, an establishment liberal, gave a speech to the Society for College and University Planning in 1976. He started out with the unchallenged axiom that colleges are today what high schools were 50 years ago. Now, he asked, where do we go from here?[12] His assumption is right on target. During the 1930s a typical vocational curriculum—*not* an academic curriculum—required two years of a foreign language, one year each of algebra and geometry, as well as the standard years of history and English, and the strictly vocational courses.[13] What vocational diploma today would even contain a foreign language, or anything more difficult than general math? One excuse offered for the inadequate teaching of American youth is that so many of them are poor; they come to class hungry and tired; they are unable to study because they live in crowded quarters; their families move frequently. The plight of most children during the Great Depression was much worse. Yet "there is no evidence of widespread illiteracy among the twelve-year-olds who went through the . . . primary schools during the Great Depression, nor is there any evidence that large numbers of these children could not handle simple mathematics."[14] The army of World War II, at least, found most young men of the Depression era to be well educated enough for its purposes,

20

something that cannot be said of the army of the 1970s, which has lower standards to begin with.

Of course, all these comparisons rest on objective standards: achievement tests, grade-level determinations, and the like. Realizing that their claims of professional capability are exploded by the standardized test results, educators vigorously seek to debunk them. The International Reading Association, for example, resolved at its 1975 meeting that "there can be no expectation that all students in a given grade achieve at the 'grade level' for that grade. . . . The level of reading achievement for any given student is an individual matter. . . ."[15]

Other educators seek to excuse the record of objective failure with sociological cliches: "It may well be that [the low scores] are more indicative of our culture than the artificially high scores of the 1940s and 1950s when testing results represented a smaller, more selective, more affluent sector of society."[16]

One psychologist suggests a genetic factor in the decline of achievement test scores.[17] Another psychological team tries to please the Zero Population Growth crowd by coming up with research "proving" that large families have caused the drop in scores.[18] The College Board Advisory Panel on Score Decline was formed in 1976 to try to find reasons for the steady 12-year fall in student performance. Meantime, an independent research group based in Chicago did a four-month study of the standardized tests themselves and concluded that the drop in scores cannot be explained away by inadequacies in the testing procedure. These researchers feel that student achievement has slipped even more than the scores indicate.[19]

Educationists may hem and haw, and researchers may speculate, and Lord knows what historians will end up recording, but the typical concerned American parent has a pretty good idea what has caused the problem: lack of discipline, lack of study, teachers unprepared in the subject matter and unconcerned about mastery of content, social promotion policies, subjective grading systems, and in general too much pedagogical faddism. And these are precisely the aspects of modern education that parents most frequently complain about.

What Is "Modern Education"?

Hardly a school district is exempt from the plagues of "modern education." An unkind irony is that the "best schools in the area" are usually the first and worst afflicted, even though, or perhaps because, many parents have moved into the district and paid higher taxes just so their children can take advantage of the supposedly superior program. What does it mean, the "best schools in the area"? Who usually makes that claim? Realtors, for one. They hear it from the school district's public relations man. Usually it is synonymous with saying, "We spend more money per child than other districts." The suppressed premise there is that more money yields better results, for whatever variety of suggested reasons. Sometimes the statement runs, "More of our graduates go on to college than those of other districts in the area." But anyone who knows how college admission standards have declined, and in some states disappeared, realizes that the boast is hollow.

The public relations officer may claim that "this district is up to date: our teachers are very professional"—they average 15 hours of in-service training a year, 60 percent have graduate degrees in training, 34 percent do graduate work during the summer, and so on. "We are preparing your child for the busy, sometimes confusing, world beyond school," a district administration office propaganda piece might read. "While basic skills have their place, perhaps more important in today's changing world is the adaptability that comes from knowing who you are and knowing where you belong in the human community. . . ."

What does all this mean? It means that this district is snugly in bed with the education profession at its trendiest. It means that learning who John Keats was, and why acids neutralize

22

hydroxides, and what happened at Sarajevo, and what *pi* means is of incidental importance in this district's preparation of children for "life." The National Education Association has never blushed to admit that it regards teachers as "clinicians" rather than transmitters of a cultural heritage.

It is not exactly news that progressive education—and much of today's public education is the progressive education of 25 to 40 years ago—fails to teach the time-honored academic lessons to students. More than two decades ago parents were criticizing what was then called the "new education" because it wasted their children's time and did not teach them what their parents, college instructors, and employers thought they should know: "While neo-pedagogues palaver more and more about the 'real needs' of youngsters, the pupils are learning less and less about the arts of word and number, the history and literature, the science and the esthetics, and the rest of the painfully accumulated culture of this harassed civilization."[20]

In 1951 a meeting of the National Education Association devoted itself to defending the new education. At the time, the NEA turned to standardized tests to buttress its position. Results from 1928 were compared with results from 1950 in selected districts, and the most encouraging thing that could be said was not very reassuring: "A twelve-year record . . . indicates that the pupils there are performing at approximately their level of capability" (whatever that means). In another district, "In reading, arithmetic, and composite scores, the percentage of pupils making average or higher scores is similar."[21] What had the NEA spokesman actually said? Merely that scores on any given test will always fall into high, average, and low categories.

Students in school around 1951 would fall between ages 33 and 45 today; since the great decline was only beginning in the 1950s, it is not too surprising that some 60 percent of citizens that age have enough basic arithmetical and literacy skills to function in a job and manage a family. Nor, sadly, is it surprising that of the 18–29 age group, products of a more thoroughgoing "modern education," only 49 percent have

23

the minimal functional skills.[22] Popular magazines, news broadcasts, in fact all the mass media, publicize the sad fact of growing illiteracy. Yet the nation that considers itself the greatest and best educated in the world (because its citizens average 15.2 years of formal schooling, more than in any other nation in the world)[23] has not risen in wrath to demand improvement in the supposedly greatest public school system in the world.

A few centuries ago children were sent to school because their parents and their society believed they had to learn to read the Bible in order to escape going to Hell. Whatever else might be said for that theory, it was effective motivation. Later the public schools were expected to train up a self-supporting, independent, and capable citizenry, so that the young republic would develop soundly. But about the time the frontier closed, along came John Dewey, with his romantic notions left over from the French Enlightenment (which he seasoned with a smattering of biology, philosophy, and politics), to redefine the purposes of American public education. He summed it up in one word: democracy. "The schools were to be democratic, and to produce a democratic social order."[24]

Who was accusing the United States of being a class-divided, hierarchical, undemocratic society? Hardly anybody then, although such charges have multiplied since the schools set out explicitly to teach democracy. To Dewey, democracy was far more than a form of representative government, which already existed. For him, it was a paradigm of an ideal society, a complete social "lifestyle" if you will, in which all men are equal, respect each other, and do not compete. A representative government will give its public schools carte blanche to further true democracy, and thus give them free rein to change society in subsequent generations. Democracy, according to Dewey, is admittedly an ideal, but one toward which society should constantly grow, such growth being the purpose of education itself.

If the purpose of schools is to grow toward an ideal democratic social order, then naturally content will have to be

24

deemphasized and social attitudes made the object of attention. For one thing, knowing Latin sets one "equal" man apart from another "equal" man who does not know Latin. The desire to excel and the striving for knowledge put a premium on self-reliance, which is undemocratic because it does not allow room for a group to interact. A social order is produced when people behave in a certain way: traditional education was not sufficient to incline behavior in the direction that Dewey selected. So Dewey's followers (and he has had many disciples who were and are no credit to him) began to pay more attention to their students' behavior, and the motivating factors of values and attitudes, than to their intellectual development. As the end of education became more and more amorphous, the means became more and more specific.

The affective aspects of education had to be given as much attention as, if not more than, the cognitive elements. Behavior modification became inevitable as a purpose of education and has been practiced quite universally:

> Since the early 1960s, the application of behavior-modification principles in classroom settings has developed at an extremely rapid pace. Almost every public school near a large city or a university center has at least one behavior-modification program.
>
> Sometimes these programs are supported by federal agencies . . . but more and more projects are being developed independently by teachers or administrators. . . .[25]

Content—facts, concepts, and other objective pieces of information—was shunted aside. Expensive assistance here was provided by the federal government. What local school board would have been willing or able to fund such innovations as these:

• Operation Bruce: 77 potential dropouts are helped to select, carry out, and evaluate their own curriculum, the

25

academic aspects of which are limited to half-days.

• Institute for Political and Legal Education: outside "trainers" come into the classroom to "inform" students on lobbying and campaigning. Then students intern in local and state agencies, and finally undertake "projects" in their own communities. (Providing this free labor for radical politicians is called social studies, and replaces mere history and geography.)

• Washington, D.C.: 10th through 12th graders join with their teachers to set their goals for the year. Together they develop "curriculum packages," which are later distributed to other schools; teachers learn to "share responsibility for learning with the class."[26]

• Compton, California: at the cost of more than $1 million a computer system is installed that will give over 19,500 individual lessons a day, automatically selecting questions and grading answers.[27]

Compared with this kind of experimentation, a mere class on human sexuality seems quite academic and tame. A word about sex education. Sex educators like to appear as if they were harassed by the "radical right," which they see as spoiling their chances to rescue young America from "medieval" standards of sexual conduct. In at least one case the concerned parents had the court on their side: a federal district court in Michigan ruled that a Michigan law prohibiting the teaching of birth control in public schools does *not* infringe a teacher's right of free speech.[28] In response to this sort of public reaction against sex education, "population education" is being presented as an alternative, perhaps in the hope that the global scope of the problem to be discussed will lend academic respectability to it. The disguise is thin, as evidenced by the following passages from a single speech by Dr. Louis Hellman of the National Center for Family Planning Services, a project of the U.S. Department of Health, Education, and Welfare:

> Population education is not an attempt to present
> sex education under a disguise, nor is it a subterfuge
> to introduce ideas concerning sexuality, abortion,
> or the use of contraception. . . .

> Population education must deal with the family,
> responsible parenthood, and sexuality. . . . Such
> sensitive issues as abortion and sex education and
> contraception to minors cannot be turned aside as
> not germane.[29]

From time to time sex-lobby researchers announce that they
have just discovered that astoundingly large percentages of
American parents want their children taught sex in school.
Such convenient statistics should be taken with more than a
few grains of salt, and probably anybody who knows their
source regards them skeptically. At any rate, all the statistics
in the world should not change the moral conviction of one
parent who is trying to preserve in his home, and inculcate in
his child, the Christian or Judaic ethic of proper use of sexual
faculties.

American education has always been subject to fads. But
today's fads of behavior modification and values clarification,
in their multifarious disguises, are more damaging than yester-
day's fads, which focused on method and downplayed educational content. If a child failed to learn to read, that was most
unfortunate; but if a child is taught that everyone hates him,
he may commit suicide. It has happened. Therefore, parents
must refuse to cooperate with today's psychologically oriented
fads as long as the damage is being perpetrated.

Some fads will pass. The U.S. Office of Education, for example, not long ago spent $1.8 million to discover that many
popular innovations, such as team teaching, open classrooms,
paraprofessional aides, and some individualized instruction
techniques, make little difference in student achievement.[30]
Experienced teachers might have predicted that finding; most

parents reached the same conclusion after about four weeks of hearing how the new practice was working in the classroom; and students probably thought the whole thing was a game all along. But the education establishment, having hatched the egg, is not inclined to disown it. The expenditure of nearly $2 million of public money to demonstrate the contentions of common sense may at most convince a few academicians. It is up to the public to use the results of that research to convince the politicians.

Education As Social Reform

Meanwhile, the whole concept of education as social reform is thriving. In 1933 the Progressive Education Association proclaimed that education "should aim to foster in boys and girls a profound devotion to the welfare of the masses, a deep aversion to the tyranny of privilege, a warm feeling of kinship with all the races of mankind, and a quick readiness to engage in bold social experimentation."[31] Eleven years later the Progressive Education Association had changed its name to the American Education Fellowship, and had modified its rhetoric a little bit, now defining education as "that process of learning and living by which the child becomes an understanding adult citizen with a strong concern for the development of a world in which free men can and will act together . . . for the common good."[32]

Whether today's inner-city schools are a shining testimony to the success of education geared to teach children to "act together for the common good" is open to debate. What is not open to debate is that the children, victims of several generations of progressive education in its various incarnations, are illiterate, ignorant, uncultured, undisciplined, immoral, and irreligious—in short, uncivilized. Some progressives argue that all those adjectives describe a wonderfully liberated way to live, and wish that American children showed more of those "qualities." But not Mr. and Mrs. Middle America.

28

Of course, not every child educated in the public schools for the past 35 years can be described this way. Why not? Because, thanks be, most children in the past 35 years have grown up in a family environment. The influence of the schools was mitigated by parental influence. But the generation now coming up will finish high school with 12,000 hours of classroom teaching behind them, and 15,000 hours of television viewing.[33] If instead they had spent 15,000 hours with parents and other adults, the prospects might not be so grim for the continuation of Western civilization.

The 12,000 classroom hours are not reassuring either. For example, the typical unit on the Eskimos in elementary school used to consume a day or two of geography class, and consisted of general descriptive information, adequate for most children's needs and interest span. Then it became desirable for children to construct styrofoam igloos in order to have a "real-life relationship" with the Eskimos. Parents thought it was silly, but they provided the styrofoam and sometimes built the silly igloo for their child to take to school. But the people who had to build styrofoam igloos when they were in school think it is a little worse than silly when *their* children are expected to learn the social customs of Eskimos and discuss in class the relative merits of leaving decrepit grandmothers alone on an ice floe to die or bringing them along with the tribe.

Similarly, ancient history used to consist of facts, with appropriate illustrations in the textbook, of pyramids, the Nile, and so on. Some geography would be included in the unit, some politics (e.g., why Hammurabi's law code is remembered), maybe a little sociology (e.g., the religious motivation behind the pyramids), or a little language and literature (e.g., the Rosetta stone and its significance), but that was enough to convey a fundamental grasp of the significance of the ancient river-valley civilizations.

How does a typical lesson in today's ancient history class run? It discusses at great length the miserable position of the Egyptian slaves, how exploited they were, how they had no

29

rights and no means of redressing grievances. They are likely to be compared to medieval serfs. Besides being ideological and negative, this approach encourages false comparisons between quite diverse civilizations. Or the students will hear the story of King Solomon's adjudication of the two women claiming the baby, and a story will be related about Johnny, whose teenage unwed mother put him up for adoption when he was born, the result being that he was raised in middle-class comfort; but now his mother has gotten married and wants him back. At this point the students are invited to play King Solomon and decide what to do with Johnny. This is called making history relevant to today's world. It is also called "clarifying students' values," and in many classrooms the two cannot be separated.

Parents who want their children to learn something would call this kind of history lesson nonsense, at best. If they said so to the principal, however, they would be called disruptive.

> We are impatient with the schools which lay all stress on reading and writing, suspecting them to rest upon the assumption that all knowledge and interest must be brought to children through the medium of books. Such an assumption fails to give the child any clue to the life about him, or any power to usefully or intelligently connect himself with it."[34]

Sounds familiar, does it not? It was said in 1902 by Jane Addams of Hull House fame, who was complaining about the failure of public education to teach the immigrant and slum children anything "useful." Her cry was enthusiastically echoed, first by the social welfare pioneers, and then by the progressive educators. Indeed, the history of progressive education in this country is largely the old story of throwing the baby out with the bathwater. Some useful educational innovations were introduced: home economics classes, shop training for boys, for example. No doubt both were needed in the slums; in fact, they still are. But today's slums languish under the logical extension of progressivism: the schools are afraid to teach students *anything.*

For the professional educators, preserving Western civilization has long since ceased to be one of the purposes of education; the progressivists hope to teach our children a "quick readiness to engage in bold social experimentation" instead. The sad truth is that our society has been complaisant about this nonsense for a long time. As far back as 1937 the Progressive Education Association could say:

> It is evident . . . that the tendency to be avowedly experimental is gaining ground. To "experiment with children," to "experiment with taxpayers' money," are not the crimes they used to be. "Radical notions" may safely be incorporated in the instructions of a city superintendent to his corps of principals and teachers, or in the public pronouncement of a state commissioner. . . .[35]

And in 1937 educators did experiment with children and with the taxpayers' dollars. Just as they do today.

Historians of American education note that the progressive-education movement appeared to suffer a deathblow when Sputnik went up, and that a reaction set in, with the public demanding objectively measurable performance from the educational system. College became a status symbol that everyone wanted. In the 1950s most colleges had not yet wholly adopted the progressive ideology, but still expected content mastery both for admission and for graduation.

In 1955, amid cries of "right-wing plots," the American Education Fellowship quietly folded. Why, then, do we wake suddenly in the 1970s to find ourselves in a situation that would please the progressivists beyond their fondest dreams?

Consider for a moment how the original progressive educators got their start—in social work. Education as social work, as a tool to better the lot of the unfortunates of our world: it

31

seemed like a good idea. The notion never really died after Jane Addams. The concept became popular because it was adopted by a few active "professional educators" who had great impact on the direction of their nascent "profession." The people who ran the normal schools adopted the ideals of progressivism; the professional association, the National Education Association, strongly advocated progressivist reforms; the U. S. Office of Education, "confined by law and tradition to diffusing information and statistics . . . also became a prime propagator of progressivism."[36] And, most of all,

> At the state level newly professionalized departments of education sponsored a plethora of publications . . . as well as conferences, institutes, and seminars designed to put . . . teachers and administrators in touch with the latest pedagogical thought. Needless to say, progressive ideas and practices were widely disseminated, with state aid and favor as the reward for interested localities.[37]

If education were conducted in a free market, progressivism *might* have faded away in fact as it did in appearance after its failures were discovered in the mid-1950s. Parents *might* have insisted that their children learn the multiplication tables, and know who Hannibal was, and what Louis Pasteur discovered, for teachers in public schools were then acutely aware that they *had* to respond to parental demands. But the hope never materialized. What happened between the mid-1950s and the mid-70s to restore progressive educators' control of American public education? What gave progressive education in all its guises a renewed lease on life?

What happened was the Elementary and Secondary Education Act of 1965. It came out of Washington, D.C., naturally. The political verbiage about how this was the most vital piece of legislation ever signed, a watershed for American education, a point of no return, and all the rest, turned out to be quite accurate. None of that language necessarily means that the legislation was *good* for American education, take note.

The particulars of the legislation and its practices will be examined in detail later on. Sufficient for now to note that the federal government, which had been creeping up on education for several decades, now leaped boldly into the arena with armfuls of money to give to the "professionals." And those professionals just happened to be the progressives, who dutifully came crawling out of the woodwork. The money, naturally enough, proved addictive, and the education lobby kept it flowing.

Federal aid does funny things to people. The experience of Terrel Bell, U.S. commissioner of education in the early 1970s, is typical. Says Bell:

> I came here feeling that education was almost exclusively a state responsibility. My view has shifted to where I feel education is vital to what this country is trying to accomplish, and it is the prime instrument for attaining our ideals. Congress and the federal statutes can no longer defer to the states and say "you take the lead." The federal government must guarantee certain rights, and in doing so, it should specify the ends of education and provide the financial support to meet those ends.[38]

Terrel Bell, a Mormon from the heartland of the nation, came to Washington with a sensible notion of education and succumbed to the whole messianic delusion that the goddess of education can reach down her hand and provide the nation with all that its heart desires—as long as the federal government specifies the desires and provides the funding.

That delusion quickly turns into a nightmare. For one thing, specifying the ends of education gets the government into the business of specifying the means as well. And isn't it totalitarian when government makes decisions like that, in the first place? Americans are told the public controls its public schools —have civil service bureaucrats become synonymous with local self-government? For the government to specify means and ends of education from kindergarten through postgraduate or lifelong career training, still omits some crucial years.

Education begins in the bassinet, and the federal government rapidly finds itself specifying goals from that point forward. Even before Jimmy Carter was inaugurated President, his Vice President's pet scheme was again being dressed up and paraded before the nation: an HEW study proposed elaborate national policies to "help" American children by meddling in their family lives. This was the culmination of a long-standing concern of government—and educators—that families were coming between the professionals and the children whose future they wanted to form. Federal day care, child advocacy, and income redistribution are only part of this social reform proposal that masquerades as educationally essential. The public rejected all former incarnations of Walter Mondale's idea for half a decade, but that was before Mondale was Vice President. Helping children "within the context of their family lives" means intervening in the family in one way or another to tell parents how to rear their children; it could easily come to mean more than that. Parents can see this; they don't want Uncle Sam rocking the cradle—not in *their* house.

It is bad enough that the federal government has been in the child-care business for years: by 1976 there were over 60 federal programs that contributed to early-childhood and child-care programs.[39] And each program, of course, was regulated by federal guidelines. One such guideline, mandated by Congress in 1972, called for Head Start programs to increase their quota of handicapped children to at least 10 percent of their total enrollment. Two years later HEW reported to Congress that, sure enough, 10.1 percent of Head Start enrollees had been diagnosed as handicapped. One enterprising researcher set about to see just how this miracle of efficiency had been accomplished. It was simple. There was not much special recruitment of handicapped children; already-enrolled children were simply rescrutinized and labeled handicapped.[40] That's easy enough to do: if you look closely enough at anybody, you're likely to find something about him that would qualify as a "handicap," whether physical, social, emotional, or mental. The only problem is that a Head Start child labeled "handicapped" for the convenience of meeting a federal quota must live with that tag for the rest of his life.

One commentator has noted that the "screening of children barely past toddlerhood may be one of the nation's growth industries."[41] Fifteen years ago nobody had heard of something called "learning disability"; by 1975, at least five million children in America were considered "learning disabled." What does it mean? Nothing, except that the child in question is different from most children. Sometimes money may be available for training special children, which furnishes an incentive to "identify" these children. And again, they must bear the burden throughout the rest of their school career of being classified as "learning disabled." They get the jaundiced eye from every teacher they encounter. Children at the opposite extreme—those who are very bright—are not free, either; they, too, are objects of federal concern. For quite a while federal programs for the gifted were handled through the Office of the Handicapped, a bizarre coincidence that says something about the fate of anyone unfortunate enough not to be "average" in a "democratic" educational system.

Partly because lifestyles differ from family to family, many children are *not* average. But federal programs are being devised to bring divergent family lifestyles into a more standard pattern. Parenthood education is the wave of the future, and federally funded pilot programs are under way in 1,815 public schools. Spending too much time with one's parents is bad. It can produce a nonaverage child. So the educationists have come up with such highly touted innovations as running schools on a year-round basis—claiming, of course, as justification that it will save parents money in taxes, and neglecting to mention the discouragement to family togetherness implicit in some of the schemes. Programs like this are well under way, usually with federal assistance.[42]

Is anything sacrosanct? No—except perhaps the respectability of the education establishment, which cogitates about the problems of the world and blithely charts the ways and means, through public education and with public money, to remold the world nearer to its heart's desire.

Hopeful Signs

Prospects are not all dismal, however. Parents are not bereft of common sense. They are taking notice of education, and forming opinions on how to improve it, and mapping their own strategies to try to bring it back into line with its traditional functions. Starting from a local base, as all grassroots movements must, concerned parents are realizing that to cure the ills of modern education is going to take years and is going to require work at the state and national levels of government.

Every year, the Gallup polling organization conducts a national survey of attitudes toward public education in America. Financed by the Charles Kettering Foundation, the survey has been a regular feature of the educational scene since 1969. The questions vary somewhat from year to year, but the overall picture is quite revealing: the American public is becoming more critical of its schools, and it has specific suggestions for improvement.

The 1969 poll, for example, asked what was the biggest problem the public schools faced. Twenty-six percent of respondents listed discipline as the number one problem.[43] A comparable question in 1976 asked what would do the most to improve the quality of public school education: 50 percent said "enforce stricter discipline" and 51 percent said "devote more attention to the teaching of basic skills."[44] Another 1976 question asked, "Should all high school students be required to pass a standard nationwide examination in order to get a high school diploma?" To which 65 percent of the American public assented.[45] In light of other responses, this figure should be taken as a demand for objective standards, rather than as a desire for a federalized educational system. Another

1976 question asked, "Do you believe that a decline in national test scores of students in recent years means that the quality of education today is declining?" Fully 59 percent of the nation said yes.[46] So much for the educationists who quibble about the value of objective standards.

The common sense of the public was apparent in another question, designed to gauge favorable or unfavorable response to a list of suggestions for cutting school costs. Seventy-two percent of the public favored reducing the number of administrative personnel; 52 percent favored reducing the number of counselors on the staff; a notable 36 percent favored cutting out 12th grade and covering in three years what is now taught in four.[47] Educators contend that counselors and administrators do not take up a significant proportion of school budgets; but the public instinct is sound in recognizing those positions as the most dispensable.

The education establishment watches the Gallup polls very closely, seeking guidance for future public relations programs. Parent groups can use the same polls to impress upon their local board members and their legislators the legitimacy of their complaints.[48] If a mother feels discipline is inadequate in her son's school, it is not because she is a crackpot, although if she tries to remedy the situation someone is bound to call her that. A parent who believes that declining standardized-test scores tell us something is not old-fashioned or elitist—59 percent of the nation is getting the same message. In short, the findings of the Gallup poll can lend weight to many particular local complaints about public education, because chances are, those local problems are cropping up elsewhere.

The contention of this book is that parents are an interest group, just as much as longshoremen or firemen. In fact, parents are more powerful than any other lobby because of their potential influence on the next generation of voters. And their rights are not mere legal creations, like the "rights" of civil servants. Parents' rights come from God by way of the natural law; the existence of the family unit presupposes parental

37

rights; continuation of civilized society presupposes the existence of the family unit.

Yet parents' rights are often ignored, scorned, and violated by the American public education system. Educators and education bureaucrats, who specialize in making ordinary people feel insignificant, seek to intimidate the parent who asserts his God-given rights. Parents know their own children better than does any teacher, or counselor, or psychiatrist. Years of college courses cannot replace a parent's knowledge of his child, and of what is good and bad for that child. A parent's right to decide the direction of his child's life is a *sovereign right,* as long as the child is subject to his parent. Educators have no business creating dissatisfaction with and rebellion against parental wishes.

American parents come in all races, creeds, political affiliations, social classes, occupational categories, and in every other subdivision imaginable. Because of this diversity, parents as parents have been slow to organize themselves as a single interest group. Until recently, the need has not been imperative to do so. But a child is educated only once. If he does not learn what he should during that period, he may never correct the deficiency. A child grows up only once, and if his formation is poor he can be ruined, and ruined permanently.

The duties of parenthood are many, and they are time consuming, demanding, and difficult. Political activism is not usually considered part of parenthood. But if parents—rather than government bureaucrats—are to guide their children's lives, political activism must be added, and added now, to the burdens of parents in the 1970s.

This book will suggest some—not all possible, but some— guidelines for political action in behalf of parents' rights. Because effective political action depends on accurate information, I shall also attempt to provide essential background on the source of the problems in American education.

I believe that effective action can be taken within the American system of government to ameliorate the problems of the public schools. Whether enough problems can be eliminated, or sufficiently remedied, for the school system to merit the endorsement of parents again is debatable. One thing is certain: whatever gains are made through the political system must not be taken for granted. Protecting parental victories will require constant vigilance.

Many parents have already decided that the public school system is unsalvageable. I do not pronounce that verdict, but merely entertain it. Private education and family education may be the only acceptable recourse for some concerned parents. Nonetheless, we know that millions of American youngsters will continue to be victimized by the public school system; and by abandoning the fight to improve that system, or to make it feasible for children to be educated outside that system, we may be abandoning the future of those millions as well. Consider the following metaphor: If a ship is sinking, it is small comfort to stand on the shore and watch your friends bailing for dear life. At least, if you set your own children, your primary responsibility, safely on shore, and then return aboard to pump out as much water as you can, when the ship does sink your own conscience will be easy because you did everything you could. And there is always the chance, after all, that the ship may not sink, thanks to your efforts.

American public education is that ship. The efforts of concerned parents and concerned citizens will decide whether it sinks or floats. Since the cargo aboard that ship is the nation's future, that is no small challenge.

2

The Education Establishment

What did the Elementary and Secondary Education Act do? It provided ever expanding amounts of money to the public education establishment, to do all the things educators previously could not afford to do. Prior to ESEA, the financing of education was a local concern, and local bond issues had to be defensible and practical. Insofar as state money had a role, it was subject to the same conditions. Federal money was easier to procure: for one thing, citizens find it harder to argue about federal taxes. The Internal Revenue Code is beyond the comprehension of most people—including some judges and tax lawyers. So federal taxes can be raised with less difficulty than local ones. Also, federal grants for education could be procured with rhetoric alone. ESEA encouraged educators to experiment, with the assurance that they would not be responsible for the results (in fact, to this day, no federal grant for education has ever required evidence of progress or improved student learning).

Who Is the Establishment?

Not all educators were invited to this banquet, however. Only those with proper club memberships, the "professionals in good standing," would be considered for the programs available. Under the sanctimonious guise of protecting the public from quackery, great emphasis was put upon ensuring "professional" dominance of federally sponsored programs. In so doing, ESEA assured the professional public education establishment, which had never ceased to be progressive in sympathy and training, of a permanent lease on life. Protected from public disfavor by the federal dole, and enjoying automatic respectability from the same source, educational theorists and strategists created their own little greenhouse for educational and social innovation. Education as social engineering became practicable, because it did not have to be defended to those who were paying the bills.

In Washington, D.C., as in most state capitals, the education establishment is a bureaucracy, a lobby, and a pressure group. In local districts it is generally the professional administrative staff, whose advice the school boards seek and follow. In teachers' colleges—the primary agents of homogenization—the establishment is the committee that sets course requirements and the director of the placement office. To the nation's opinion-makers, the education establishment is a respectable, even revered, "profession."

What is meant by the education "profession"? This term is somewhat amorphous. Authors of textbooks on how to be a professional educator list three essential characteristics that make an occupation a profession:

1. It must provide a unique and essential social service.
2. The practitioner must have had a prolonged education.
3. There must be professional autonomy.[1]

The authors will then explain how in education the third condition is gravely deficient; and the second, while present, is not very satisfactory; yet they speak of an education "profession." Likewise with propagandists for the establishment: they give their demands and their programs an air of infallibility by alluding to "professional" expertise, "professional" skills, "professional" standards.

This definition of a profession bears some examination, but more pertinent is how the education establishment meets even its own criteria for professionalism.

It is obvious that doctors provide a unique and essential service for society. Likewise the trained officer corps of the armed forces, or ministers of a legitimate church. The law is traditionally a profession, and in our society lawyers are indeed essential—the definition says nothing about the benefits to society of the services provided. But teachers?

Granted, it is necessary for the young to be taught and to be civilized. But what is so extraordinary about the process of teaching that a special class of citizenry is required to do it? Parents are teachers; older siblings are teachers; the old man next door, the priest in the pulpit, the geese flying overhead —all could be considered teachers because children learn something from them. Children learn how to eat, how to listen, how to pay attention, how to speak the language, how to act appropriately, and yes, how to read and compute in the same natural way, if someone is willing to teach them. Having attained those last several proficiencies, a person is equipped to teach himself vast amounts of almost anything that interests him. Most people will agree that the most valuable things they learned in life were learned outside school, technical skills in areas like the sciences and the law generally excepted.

But does the organized teaching profession agree with this common sense? Of course not, because then it would not be performing a "unique and essential social service." Rather, the profession says,

> Teaching is a highly complex endeavor involving ever greater techniques and never-ending knowledge of the highest order. . . . Teaching requires continuous education relevant to the needs of the practitioner. . . . Teaching assumes the need to have

a supportive staff of specialists for the teacher to draw upon at all times for assistance. . . . Teaching assumes the inextricable relationship between the conditions in which children attempt to learn and a teacher to teach, and success in these endeavors.[2]

The amazing thing is not that such a description was written, but that it is not laughed to scorn. Of course, the self-interested parties who stand to benefit by accepting such a series of assumptions will swallow it whole. Notice how the description just quoted provides for "prolonged education," believed to be a hallmark of professionalism. Not only is the teacher nothing short of heroic for undertaking such a "highly complex endeavor"; he must be backed by a "supportive staff of specialists"—if doctors have laboratories and nurses, by golly, teachers must have labs and aides as well.

College graduation did not become a prerequisite for public school teaching until the heyday of reform after the Civil War. In that same period state certification and licensure made their appearance. But even certification and licensure were a gesture more than anything else—until the state bureaucracies were established shortly thereafter. When the state departments of education were established and given supervisory and enforcement powers, things began to happen. Bear in mind that these bureaucracies were dominated and run by the progressive-education enthusiasts. It was only to be expected that the office would be used to advance progressivism.

These progressives became educational policymakers. They were the "experts" whose advice was offered to legislatures, commissions, and propagandists. They urged further professionalization of teaching; meanwhile they created a captive clientele through enactment and enforcement of compulsory-attendance laws. They also perpetuated their own jobs by guaranteeing public financial support of their agencies, programs, and training institutions (normal schools or colleges).

Doctors do not require every person in the nation to patronize their services under threat of criminal prosecution. Because they perform an essential service, most people voluntarily seek them out. One wonders what kind of a "profession" education is when its clients must be provided, and its fees paid, by force of law. Clearly, the public is not especially anxious to avail itself of these supposedly "unique and essential" services, or there would be no need for coercion to "sell" the services. This is not a profession. This is an interest group, no different in most respects from the electrical workers or meatcutters.

After all, education in the United States is big business: in one way or another, it involves about one-third of the total population.[3] There are parents and students, obviously, nursery school through graduate school. There are also teachers, librarians, administrators, school board members, trustees, and nonprofessional school staff. Behind them are state and federal bureaucrats, managers, grant administrators, researchers, statistics gatherers, computer programmers, and so on. In the private sector are architects, publishers, audiovisual creators and producers, stationery suppliers, food vendors, bus drivers and bus manufacturers, science-lab equipment suppliers, and on and on. To include all these supportive and tangential businesses in an overall financial figure would be impossible. Suffice it to say that the livelihood of millions depends indirectly on the education industry, just as that of millions depends directly on it.

Direct educational expenditures, both public and private, at all levels, came to about $120 billion per year as of 1975–76, or approximately eight percent of the gross national product.[4] More than three-fourths of that is public money, extracted from citizens through taxation, which is to say, involuntarily contributed. The involuntary aspect of it is significant: goodwill is not enough to pay all the salaries, even if goodwill toward the massive education establishment were a fact.

Does the public really want to spend, spend, spend, to support education with such prodigality? Hardly. Anyone, even the credentialed professionals, can tell that the financing of education is the one political issue that most concerns citi-

44

zens at the local level.[5] And if the federal income tax were broken down according to what amount went to which government program, and the citizens were allowed to say yes or no to each, chances are the lavish educational schemes would get vetoed. To keep the supply of money coming in, the education establishment must exert pressure at all pertinent points, where taxes are voted, collected, and spent. The fact remains: eight percent of the nation's gross national product is spent on public education. How does this happen?

The Establishment: An Interest Group

Behold, an interest group, exercising its influence at the local school district level, in state capitols, in the halls of the United States House and Senate, in the offices of executive-branch appointees and bureaucrats, and in the courts of the nation.

There are 16,561 local school districts in the nation (as consolidation continues, that number decreases steadily), so there are probably as many local teachers' associations, affiliated with one of several such national organizations. To be sure, some districts may have no teachers' association, while others may have three of varying importance in the district. There are far more than 50 state teachers' associations, which is not surprising when one takes into account the diversity of organizations and the number of national territories. And these are only the teachers-as-teachers' associations. There are also the subject-matter associations; for example, the National Council for Social Studies, the Music Teachers National Association, the National Association of Biology Teachers, the National Council of Teachers of English.

Then there are the special-factor interest groups: the National Alliance of Black School Educators, the National Association for Environmental Education, the National Catholic Education Association. And not only teachers have interest groups. There are also the National Association of State

45

Supervisors of Distributive Education, the National Association of Elementary School Principals, the National School Board Association, the National Association of State Boards of Education, the Council of Chief State School Officers—these and more represent all aspects of middle- and upper-level management.

All the above listings are mere samplings. Since this book will not consider the problems of higher education, the plethora of higher-education and teacher-education interest groups has been overlooked altogether. Also beyond consideration are the interests indicated by such organizations as the National Association of Educational Broadcasters, the National Audio-Visual Association, and the National Student Lobby. Nor should it be forgotten that seemingly unrelated organizations also have an interest in education, like the Mid-Continent Railway Historical Society, the National Council on Family Relations, the National Recreation and Park Association, and the National Safety Council.

Needless to say, not all these groups are equally influential. Some of them don't even try to influence legislation or policy, but confine themselves to advancing their subject matter or gathering their facts. About 250 or 300 groups are sufficiently concerned about the national future of their cause to maintain offices in Washington, D.C. These are the ones to watch.

Even among the Washington, D.C., groups some are effective and some are not. No one should be surprised that the following are among the most successful: American Federation of Labor–Congress of Industrial Organizations (AFL-CIO), National Education Association (NEA), National Association for the Advancement of Colored People (NAACP), American Federation of Teachers (AFT), National School Board Association (NSBA), and Committee for Full Funding of Education Programs.

The AFL-CIO is effective as a pressure group for education quite independently of its affiliated union, the AFT. With 14 million organized members around the country, the AFL-CIO has more clout than any other single association in the nation

—as Jimmy Carter appreciated very well on November 2, 1976. Although bread-and-butter issues have traditionally concerned the AFL-CIO most, the social issues, of which education is primary, have been receiving more attention of late.

The NAACP also does not limit its concerns to education, but makes it a high priority. The Legal Defense and Educational Fund, particularly, is of historical importance because of the landmark civil rights and education lawsuits it has brought. In the fall of 1976, NEA and AFT both joined to help NAACP raise the $1.5 million it needed to pursue some non-school-related litigation in Mississippi that the NAACP claimed could endanger its continued existence.[6]

The Committee for Full Funding (originally, Emergency Committee for Full Funding) came into being in 1969 when it became apparent that President Nixon was more concerned about fiscal responsibility than about the demands of the education lobby. In a show of good organizational sense and good discipline, the NSBA, the NEA, and the AFL-CIO joined together to pursue something wanted by all: full appropriation of authorized federal funds for education. On other issues these organizations may differ; their willingness to cooperate for the sake of one mutually beneficial goal demonstrates a great strength of the education establishment, a characteristic often lacking among local and national groups that try to balance the impact of the educationists.

Of the NEA and the AFT there is much to say. Both are teachers' associations. The NEA is older (founded in 1857, and holder of a federal charter since 1906, whereas AFT began in 1916). The NEA is the largest professional organization in the world, with about 1.8 million members, if one counts members through affiliated state associations, to AFT's 450,000 members. Both associations burgeoned after World War II, perhaps in a delayed response to the social ideas of the 1930s and clearly in response to low teachers' salaries during inflationary times.

The NEA has the larger budget, about $34.5 million, to AFT's less than $10 million. The NEA has a staff of 700 (most of them members of an AFL-CIO–affiliated union, the Communications Workers of America) in its D.C. office, while AFT's bureaucracy is much smaller. AFT has several dozen national organizers, whereas NEA has 11 regular regional offices and aims eventually to have one UniServe organizer for every 1,200 members. Theoretically, NEA membership is open to any professional educator, regardless of rank. However, the American Association of School Administrators loosened its ties with NEA in 1973 and other management-level groups did likewise, as NEA militance assumed an undisguised antiadministrator bias. The AFT constitution prohibits membership by principals or anyone higher.

AFT is an affiliate of the AFL-CIO; NEA has numerous affiliates of its own, in three categories. NEA departments are the closest connected, with their entire memberships also belonging to NEA. These are: Association of Classroom Teachers, American Driver and Traffic Safety Education Association, Department of Rural Education, and Department of School Nurses.

Affiliate organizations are in the next degree of closeness: they promote NEA, but only their officers must be members. There are 17 national affiliates:

> National Council of Administrative Women in Education
> National Association for Public School Adult Education
> National Art Education Association
> Department of Audiovisual Instruction
> American Association of Elementary/Kindergarten/Nursery Educators
> National Association of Elementary School Principals
> American Association for Health, Physical Education, and Recreation
> Home Economics Education Association
> American Industrial Arts Association

48

Journalism Education Association
National Council of Teachers of Mathematics
Music Educators National Conference
National Retired Teachers Association
National Council for the Social Studies
Association for Student Teaching
National Association of Educational Secretaries
Association for Supervision and Curriculum Development

Then there are the associated organizations, which are more independent than the other two categories. Among the associated organizations are:

National Business Education Association
Association for Educational Data Systems
Council for Exceptional Children
American Association for Higher Education
National Training Laboratories Institute for Applied Behavioral Science
American Association of School Librarians
National School Public Relations Association
National Science Teachers Association
National Association of Secondary School Principals
American Association of School Administrators
Speech Association of America

These lists read like a rollcall of all the respectable bodies of educators in the nation. Is it any wonder that a "respectable professional educators' organization" hardly ever says anything that doesn't sound like something that has already been said? Is it any wonder that the pronouncements of various professional associations sound rather like variations on the same tune?

The record of both NEA and AFT deserves some examination. AFT has always been a union, avowedly reformist, never pretending to be a "professional association," since it was first granted its charter by the American Federation of Labor. George Meany has paid the AFT a high compliment: "There is no more militant organization in the labor movement than this one. And I like that."[7] AFT's record of support for liberal causes is impeccable.

In 1954 AFT filed an *amicus curiae* brief in the landmark school desegregation case, *Brown v. Board of Education.* In the early 1960s it operated "freedom schools" in areas of the South that had closed their schools rather than bow to the Supreme Court's desegregation order. In 1966 the NEA tried to salvage its reputation on racial concerns by getting the American Teachers Association, a 32,000-member independent organization of black teachers, to merge with it.

In the late 1960s the NEA began to embrace the militance it had previously avoided when it was an educators' association "vested by the public with a trust and responsibility requiring the highest ideals of professional service."[8] A strong internal influence was the urban educators, who became a vocal and visible faction urging greater social and political activism. Also, in 1961 NEA had lost an election to represent New York City teachers in collective bargaining, and lost to the AFT union, the United Federation of Teachers. The AFT quickly stuck a few more feathers in its collective-bargaining cap—Detroit, Philadelphia, Boston, Chicago, among others—and NEA, seeing the direction of the future, resolved not to lose the competition by being too respectable. By 1970 the mood of the NEA leadership had changed completely, and concern for helping teachers do a better job took a back seat to liberalization of welfare benefits for members and agitation for social change, both in the name of improving education and improving society through education.

What NEA Wants

NEA is a political animal. Its policy positions demonstrate this. Every year, at the annual Representative Assembly (never to be held, by the way, in a state that has not ratified the Equal Rights Amendment), NEA votes on a series of resolutions. For each session of Congress a legislative program is drawn up in Washington, enumerating NEA's major demands. The short shrift given to educational concerns in these documents is striking.

Bimonthly, NEA publishes *Today's Education,* which features a regular column by the NEA president. These remarks, along with most other articles in the journal, give a clear sense of general and specific political and social positions. Each even-numbered year the National Education Association Political Action Committee (NEAPAC) gathers a war chest, which is given away to legislators and aspiring legislators deemed to share the NEA point of view. In 1976, for the first time, NEA endorsed a presidential candidate, who, it so happened, won the election. Most of NEA's congressional and senatorial candidates were similarly blessed by Fate.

The following are typical standing resolutions, endorsed by the 1975 Representative Assembly. The number in brackets indicates the year in which the resolution was first adopted.

> • A–5. The National Education Association urges the establishment of a cabinet-level U.S. Department of Education [1969].
> • B–7. The National Education Association seeks general federal support for the whole of public elementary and secondary education. It believes that federal monies must be expended solely for public education. . . . Federal funds must be allocated without federal control for expenditure and be suballocated by state education agencies. . . . The association will oppose any bill which includes provision in federal legislation to provide funds, goods, or services related to the instructional process for nonpublic schools or nonpublic school students [1969].
> • C–2. The association believes that teachers and other professionals should evaluate supervisory and

administrative personnel and school board members [1969].

• D–2. The National Education Association believes that decisions on which school learning experiences and techniques will develop a student's talents are best made by a teacher who knows the learner. . . . Teachers must select instructional materials without censorship. . . . The association urges its affiliates to seek the removal of laws and regulations which restrict the selection of a diversity of instructional materials or which limit educators in the selection of such materials [1969].

• D–4. The National Education Association believes that academic and professional freedom is essential to the teaching profession. Controversial issues should be a part of instructional programs when judgement of the professional staff deems the issues appropriate to the curriculum and to the maturity level of the student . . . [1969].

• E–4. The National Education Association shall provide leadership in teacher retirement and believes that a retirement program for teachers includes . . . automatic cost-of-living benefits in local, state, and national systems . . . retirement housing facilities for teachers . . . teachers' contributions and benefits that are not subject to federal income taxation . . . [1969].

• E–5. The National Education Association believes that . . . it may be necessary to give preference in the hiring, retention, and promotion policies to certain racial groups or women or men to overcome past discrimination [1969].

• E–11. . . . The association denounces the practice of keeping schools open during a strike. . . . [1969].

• H–1. The National Education Association believes it is imperative that full integration of the nation's schools be effected. The association recognizes that acceptable integration plans will include affirmative action programs and a variety of devices such as geographic realignment, pairing of schools, grade pairing, and satellite schools. Some arrangements may require busing of students in order to comply with established guidelines adhering to the letter and spirit of the law . . . [1969].

• H–4. The National Education Association believes that all citizens should be free to reside in the communities of their choice. Local affiliates should lead in breaking down barriers that limit this freedom [1969].

• H–5. The National Education Association . . . supports the proposed Equal Rights Amendment to the U.S. Constitution. . . . The association urges governing boards and education associations to eliminate discriminatory practices against women in employment, promotion, and compensation. Personnel policies must include maternity leave; paternity leave; leave for adoption of a child; child-care leave; and professional leave . . . [1969].

• H–6. The National Education Association is committed to the achievement of a racially integrated society. . . . To be effective citizens, individuals must be trained and aided in developing strategies and expertise that will enable them to operate effectively in a democratic society [1969].

In this wide range of standing resolutions, what has the association endorsed? More bureaucracy, more federal aid (aid that specifically discriminates against private or religious education), teacher (not parent or community) evaluation of school boards and administrators, teacher (not parent or community) say-so on "learning experiences and teaching techniques" and "instructional materials" and "controversial issues." It starts to sound like a partnership of federal government and public school teachers to run the lives of

American children—never mind the existence of the parents.

Also endorsed are luxurious retirement programs for teachers, as if society's immense debt of gratitude to them could never be repaid; quotas in hiring; school lockouts; and every forced integration tactic, including busing. Common sense might hint that teachers, who have to live with the difficult and sometimes perilous consequences of forced busing, would restrain their enthusiasm for it. Common sense has little place in ideological orgies, however. The association has further endorsed open housing, though the relation of that to education is tenuous, and the ERA, with its logical consequence of expanded and costly leave policies for fathers and mothers. Finally, it has issued a sweeping endorsement of civil rights activism, culminating in a call for training students in political action ("strategies and expertise that will enable them to operate effectively in a democratic society"). What the NEA has in mind is obviously something more than the citizenship education supposedly given to all American boys and girls in their public school classrooms and auditoriums. The precise intent of the rhetoric is open to speculation, but a good guess is that the NEA hopes to raise millions of teenage shock troops to campaign for its favorite radical-liberal politicians.

Enough for the standing resolutions of the association since 1969. The association also comments on topics of more immediate interest. Some examples from the 1975 Representative Assembly:

> • 75–1. The National Education Association believes the following programs and practices are detrimental to public education and must be eliminated by the united teaching profession: performance contracting, voucher plans, and evaluations by private, profit-making groups.
> • 75–2. The National Education Association recognizes the interdependence of all peoples and urges that the United States make every effort to strengthen the United Nations. . . .

54

• 75–4. The National Education Association believes that the cost of public welfare should be assumed by the federal government and that the federal welfare program should be based on standards of human dignity.

• 75–7. The National Education Association believes that voucher plans . . . could lead to racial, economic, and social isolation of children and weaken or destroy the public school system. The association urges the enactment of federal and state legislation prohibiting voucher feasibility studies and the establishment of voucher plans and calls upon its affiliates to seek from members of Congress and state legislatures support for this legislation.

• 75–8. . . . The association believes educators must teach the facts of world hunger . . . and help students develop the capacity and the commitment to resolve these problems.

• 75–10. The National Education Association believes that, in the process of adjusting to new limits on national energy resources, a priority rating for schools as energy consumers must be secured.

• 75–11. The National Education Association believes that sex education that provides children and youth with information appropriate to their age is basic to healthy, well-adjusted mental attitudes. It also believes that the public schools must assume an increasingly important role in providing this instruction and that teachers must be qualified to teach in this area. The association urges that . . . classroom teachers who teach the courses be legally protected from irresponsible censorship. The association urges its affiliates and members to support . . . sex education programs, including information on birth control and venereal disease.

• 75–16. The National Education Association believes that basic student rights include: the right to free inquiry and expression; the right to due process; the right to freedom of association; the right to freedom of peaceful assembly and petition; the right to participate in the governance of the school, college, and university; the right to freedom from discrimination; and the right to equal educational opportunity. . . .

• 75–19. The National Education Association urges the enactment of federal legislation to assist state and local communities in providing child-care services, including childhood development programs. . . . The National Education Association urges its affiliates to seek legislation that would insure the implementation of early childhood programs primarily through the public school system.

• 75–30. The National Education Association believes that when federal funds are to be used on a local level for specific instructional programs, the recognized bargaining agent must be involved in the development of such programs and must approve such programs prior to implementation.

• 75–31. The National Education Association encourages the inclusion of the role of unions in the social studies curriculum. It seeks the adoption of textbooks that depict the role of unions in the social studies curriculum. It seeks the adoption of textbooks that depict the role of American labor in the development of our free institutions.

• 75–37. The National Education Association insists that a professional salary schedule for faculty members should . . . provide a starting salary of $15,000 for a qualified beginning teacher with a bachelor's degree and advance to $34,500 with a master's degree or equivalence within 10 years . . . include a cost of living adjustment, based upon consumer price index, which is in addition to regular pay scale and payable to the employee.

• 75–43. . . . The association will also develop guidelines for action leading to prevention of verbal abuse or harassment of educators and other school personnel by any individuals. Educators must take the responsibility to call attention to such cases so that appropriate action may be taken.

• 75–52. The National Education Association supports legislation for reform of the social security laws to eliminate discrimination based on sex or marital status.

• 75–55. The National Education Association strongly encourages the elimination of group standardized intelligence, aptitude, and achievement tests to assess student potential or achievement until completion of a critical appraisal, review, and revision of current testing programs.

• 75–59. . . . The association requests that presidential appointments of federal education officials be made only after screening and approval by a panel of professional educators established by the association's board of directors.

A few items from the "New Business" of the 1975 Representative Assembly deserve mention:

The NEA's absolute top legislative priorities shall be: (a) winning a collective bargaining bill for teachers everywhere in the nation and (b) reforming school finance so that the federal government contributes at least one-third the cost of public education . . . [1975–15].

Because of the disproportionate outlays of public funds appropriated to the national defense budget and public education, the National Education Association strongly endorses a reduction of the defense budget; such reduction to be applied directly to the funding of public education [1975–35].

The NEA supports the desegregation of the Boston schools and favors whatever legal steps are necessary to enforce Judge Garrity's order . . . [1975–19].

The Representative Assembly directs that a continuing unit of the NEA investigate, report on, and monitor the attacks on the American public education system which endanger academic freedom; prepare materials and programs to assist local and state associations to anticipate and thwart such attacks; and publicize nationwide in various media the history of and need for academic freedom in a democracy [1975–30].

On contemporary issues, then, where does NEA stand? Nearly every position is inflationary: federal takeover of welfare, federal child care, incredible salary scales for teachers, broadening of social security benefits, federal collective-bargaining law. Many positions, if put into practice, would thwart community or parental control over schools: NEA condemns performance contracting, private evaluations, and voucher plans or experiments; demands legal protection for sex education; supports a sweeping list of student rights; and wants teacher unions involved in carrying out federal curriculum programs. NEA believes it should have a veto over federal appointments, and maintains a "continuing monitor" of "attacks on the American public education system," by which the educationists mean anything from parent-group flyers protesting behavior-modification programs to legislative proposals to assist private education.

Nor does the NEA lack an awareness of international relations; recall the resolutions "recognizing the interdependence of all peoples" and urging education about and commitment to the problems of world hunger. America's defense budget,

NEA implies, is excessive. Study of the role of unions is encouraged: but is there a word about the free enterprise system? The self-interest of the education business is not forgotten: schools are to be given priority in fuel rationing; educators are to be protected from "harassment" (parent criticism?) and from "irresponsible censorship" (who defines "irresponsible"?).

Once parents discover where the nation's largest professional education association stands, they can only wonder whether their children have a chance of receiving an unbiased education from teachers who belong to it.

The NEA legislative program for the Second Session of the 94th Congress, the most recent at this writing, is largely a recapitulation of these positions, with the notable addition of "national health security" as an area of NEA concern. The other concerns are:

- "provision of collective bargaining rights to all teachers and other public employees"
- substantial increase in federal financing of public education
- extension and expansion of vocational and career education programs
- improvement of retirement programs for all teachers and other employees
- revision of copyright laws

There are no surprises there. What is interesting, in the 1976 legislative program, is NEA's justification for getting involved in noneducational issues:

> NEA believes that a significant part of the education process takes place outside the traditional school structure and that NEA has a responsibility to see that the other influences experienced by students of all ages are conducive to healthy development of the individual within a just and humane society.

59

The National Education Association does not limit its oversight of education to formal schooling; rather, because all of
life is education (a sound principle in itself, literally understood), the NEA has decided it has an appropriate and justified
interest in controlling *all of life*. That is what is necessary, after
all: to see that only influences "conducive to healthy development . . . within a just and humane society" are allowed.
Within such a framework, is there any legislation, social reform, international question, physical or biological phenomenon, or thought in the mind of man, that is not the subject of
NEA's "responsibility"? The word "totalitarian" might seem
libelous to the NEA, but the paragraph cited above indicates
beyond question that NEA feels responsible for the "totality"
of man's existence. To claim that much territory, the National
Education Association presumes mightily.

NEA Political Tactics

So much for the political goals of the National Education
Association. What about the means to achieve these ambitious
ends? It is not in vain that NEA president John Ryor made
threats like this one:

> NEA leaders all over this country must serve notice
> that we either get the kind of funding that will do
> the job for kids and protect the jobs of teachers, or
> we'll institute an accountability system of our own
> —and many of those same politicans will be outside
> the legislative halls trying to get back in, just like the
> quarter of a million teachers who sought but
> couldn't find jobs in our public schools this fall.[9]

In general, the educational-political complex is very sophisticated. There is no better proof than the results. Of course,
local district-level organization depends so much on local issues and local leadership that generalizations are risky.

60

At the state level there is more to talk about. When the professional association gets angry, its wrath is terrible to behold, as was the case in New Jersey in 1973. Carl Marburger, a bona fide liberal, was nominated for a second term as commissioner of education. In his first term he had pleased the education establishment by working for racial balance and expanding state authority over districts with poor local management. Apparently he was a man of consistent principles, however, for he also did a few things to try to rein in the New Jersey Education Association's growing influence—a big mistake. After a very dramatic last-minute campaign, Marburger's nomination was defeated by one vote. Later, Marburger became the first chairman of the National Citizens' Committee for Education, which works in its own way to channel parental concern into forms acceptable to the establishment.

New Jersey is a well-organized NEA state, as the $5 million annual NJEA budget might indicate. NJEA represents approximately 90 percent of the state's teachers.[10] The Michigan Education Association has an even larger budget, some $8 million per year, and also has a full-time staff of 125.[11] This staff has provided leadership for some of the association's national militance: Michigan Education Association executive director Terry Herndon in 1973 became NEA's executive director, and former Michigan Education Association president John Ryor was elected NEA's president in 1975.

California's NEA affiliate is the California Teachers Association (CTA). It charges dues of $105 annually from its members, this in addition to annual NEA dues of $30. CTA is well known for its political involvement, which was perhaps goaded on by CTA's failure to defeat Max Rafferty as commissioner of education in 1962. By 1968, when Rafferty ran for the Senate against Alan Cranston, CTA had learned enough to defeat Rafferty by 351,000 votes, giving Cranston 53 percent of the total. CTA also makes a habit of jumping into local school board races with financial assistance and advice. In 1974 CTA made $327,000 worth of intrastate campaign contributions.[12]

Since the late 1960's NEA has been actively encouraging teachers to get involved in politics. This is a far cry from the 1950s, when an NEA poll found only 23 percent of members believing that teachers should be actively involved in politics. An estimated 414 educators held state legislative office in 1973, and the trend seems to be up.[13] Forty-nine states have teachers' political-action committees tagged onto the professional NEA affiliate, but bearing different names. Catchy acronyms like VOTE (Vote of Teachers for Education) and ABC (Association for Better Citizenship) are typical.[14] The childish names should not deceive the unwary: an estimated $3 million was raised for political activism in 1972 by teachers' political-action committees.[15]

The National Education Association Political Action Committee (NEAPAC) was formed in 1972 and had time to distribute only about $30,000 that year. It was money carefully spent, however: 128 out of 165 supported House candidates, and 12 out of 19 Senators were elected. The grateful recipients of this aid recognized full well the implications:

> My election is a victory for teacher power. Before the teachers began to help me, I was a two-to-one underdog. Now, thanks to an army of teachers who knocked on thousands of doors and made thousands of phone calls, I have won by more than 33,000 votes. This victory is a victory for education.[16]

Thus spoke Senator Claiborne Pell (D–R.I.), who had indeed been a probable loser until the teachers organized behind him. It was the least they could do for a friend—after all, Pell is the chairman of the Senate Subcommittee on Education. He is up for reelection in 1978, by which time he should have been able to get ESEA extended and enlarged for another four years.

Congressman Bill Hathaway (D–Maine) managed to attach an amendment adding $363.8 million to the education budget of fiscal year 1973. When Hathaway ran for the Senate shortly thereafter, NEAPAC gave him the "additional punch which was absolutely vital in the final stages of the campaign."[17]

Nothing succeeds like success, so in 1974 NEA spent about $700,000 in conjunction with its affiliates, which spent some $500,000 more on federal candidates independently[18] and about $3.5 million on federal, state, and local campaigns combined.[19] In 1974, 247 of 310 liberal friends of education were elected as the notoriously left-wing class of '74 swept into Washington. Most of the class returned in 1976, thanks to NEAPAC's $630,000 and the $3 million or so that was spent by state and local affiliates.[20]

Supposedly, of course, these state and local affiliates spend their money separately and independently, without collusion. Thus, federal election laws allow the national PAC and each local PAC to contribute up to $5,000 to each candidate in each election (primary and general count as separate elections for donation purposes). NEA and most other unions take advantage of this loophole in the law and encourage a proliferation of so-called separate organizations and affiliates. The Federal Election Commission had prepared a regulation for the fall 1976 elections to bring union affiliates under one roof for purposes of campaign contributions, but thanks to vigorous NEA and union lobbying, that regulation was prevented from taking effect.

Also prevented from becoming effective was another FEC regulation that would have prevented NEA from using its "negative checkoff" system to raise its political action warchest. By law FEC regulations have to be submitted to Congress for 30 legislative days before they become effective, in case Congress wishes to rewrite them. The proliferation and negative checkoff regulations went to Capitol Hill on August 3, 1976, but Congress adjourned on October 2, with just one or two of the 30 legislative days left before the regulations would have become binding. Since there was much unfinished business, as there usually is in the last days of a Congress, that was truly a rush to adjournment.

The negative checkoff is unique among the coercive measures NEA uses on its members. When AFT collects money from its members for political contributions, the members either authorize specific payroll deductions or make voluntary contributions personally to the Committee on Political Education (COPE), which adds AFT's $400,000 or so to its already overflowing coffers. NEA is much more sophisticated, at least in 19 states: it adds $1 to the regular payroll dues deductions of its members (thanks to union-bargained contracts which allow such arrangements). Thus, NEA has the money before the teacher knows it is missing, for all practical purposes. Oh, to be sure, if some member objects strongly enough to this dictatorial technique, he can ask for a refund. That means his name goes on record, and with a union like NEA, few can afford to be known as noncooperators. And for one insignificant dollar, when demanding its return might consume one-third of its value anyway, few are about to go through a "hassle" to demand their right freely to contribute money for political causes. So vast amounts of political money are raised, painlessly and at hardly any cost to NEA.

Even liberal Common Cause finds NEA's negative checkoff a little excessive. Common Cause filed a formal complaint against NEA with the Federal Election Commission, charging it was collecting political contributions as a condition of union membership.[21] The complaint was filed on October 22, 1976, about 10 days before the election, and Common Cause no doubt knew the FEC was powerless at that point, so it was able to preserve its public reputation for fairness without really causing serious trouble for its ideological bedfellow, the NEA.

Shrewd indeed was NEA in preventing those FEC regulations from going into effect in 1976; considering the outcome of the 1976 presidential elections, it is unlikely such strict measures will be tried again by the appointees of a White House brought into office with the help of teachers' and other union political action groups from coast to coast.

NEAPAC, by the way, for a while shared its director with NEA proper. Stanley McFarland was director of both NEA-

PAC and of the NEA's Government Relations Department. He allegedly received no pay for his NEAPAC job, and if asked would also have denied that his PAC work was done on Government Relations time. It would be illegal for NEA to pay him for political action work.

NEA, remember, is tax-exempt. Until 1970 it was a 501(c)(3) organization, an educational, nonpolitical association, under the Internal Revenue Code. By 1970, however, NEA's collective-bargaining and lobbying activities could not escape the notice of even an IRS inclined to look elsewhere for violations. So NEA became 501(c)(6), a business-league-type organization. The change was really overdue: since 1950 NEA had been among the top 20 or 30 registered lobbies in terms of money spent to influence Congress.[22] With the 501(c)(6) status, the organization is still permitted tax exemption, and endures no prohibition against lobbying. Members may deduct their dues (NEA's main income source) as professional expenses, but gifts are not tax-deductible, nor may tax-exempt foundations (for example, Ford Foundation, Carnegie Endowment) make gifts to it. To sidestep this inconvenience to its foundation supporters, NEA established another "separate" organization, the National Foundation for the Improvement of Education, which is completely pure and 501(c)(3).

> We are not in the business to buy politicians, because those who are for sale are not worth the price. But because of our size and resources we are expected to be on hand when good men and women . . . seek office and afford them every possible opportunity to run a good campaign.[23]

This statement from the director of IMPACE, Minnesota's statewide teacher political arm, summarizes well the attitude probably held by rank-and-file NEA members.

While there is no doubt that the top echelon of membership and the leadership of the organization are conscious, ideological liberals or left-wingers, there is equally little doubt that the

65

majority of the 1.8 million members claimed are probably as politically oblivious as Americans at large. They join NEA because they are required to in order to get a contract, or because it is the thing to do, or because they like the life insurance or mutual fund or homeowners' insurance or buyers' club that they qualify for if they are members. As with any organization, most people join because they are interested not so much in the organization as in some personal benefit to be gained. Chances are, they don't follow very closely the publications they automatically receive, and don't pay much attention to the routine housekeeping business they do for NEA. When once every couple of years they are asked to run phone banks or go door to door for a candidate, chances are they don't think too much about it. They may even like the opportunity it gives them to feel involved in an election. Perhaps this analysis errs by giving too much benefit of doubt to the rank-and-file NEA membership, but I should emphasize that this passage refers primarily to the ordinary teacher. By definition, an officer in a local affiliate, or an organizer, or a delegate to the Representative Assembly, is not an "ordinary teacher." Perhaps with the wider establishment of UniServe, the ordinary teachers of the nation will become more radical and what has just been said will no longer apply. Time will tell.

The UniServe program, begun in 1970, is an ambitious plan for nationwide grassroots organizing. Presently accounting for between 20 and 25 percent of national NEA's budget, UniServe is an indication of what to expect in the future. Its goal is to provide a regular staffer in the field for each 1,200 teacher-members, with salary paid half by the national organization and half by a combined state-local effort. These staff members will be trained in negotiation and grievance procedures, political action, public relations, and other things deemed essential to advancing the education profession. They will be a reliable channel for quick, effective mobilization of troops for a chosen cause. In the first three years, 500 local associations asked to participate, so the program promises to be popular. With that high a ratio of staff to members, the typical characteristics of a bureaucracy may emerge, which in turn might lessen the capability for decisive action. However, NEA has a record of preserving its effectiveness in the face of top-heavy staff.

The Union Makes Us Strong

Not all the influence exerted by the "organized profession" is overtly political. In 1975 the United Federation of Teachers of New York City exercised a little fiscal influence: it decided to use its retirement funds to purchase $150 million worth of bonds issued by the Municipal Assistance Corporation. This was at the time New York City was in peril of defaulting, and it was a good civic gesture by Albert Shanker. Since the City Teachers Retirement System controls assets of about $2.8 billion, accumulated over almost 60 years, it was not a very risky venture (though its merits as an investment are something else again).[24]

This action demonstrates a distinct advantage of unionizing: many small amounts of money can be contributed more or less painlessly to make up a large, comforting sum, of which everyone is pleased to feel a part. In this respect, unionization makes large-scale influence—and large-scale political activity—possible.

Of more direct concern to union members are the bread-and-butter issues—the material benefits. One of the oldest and truest union benefits has been the saving of jobs. Teacher unions have a strong record in this regard: student populations at all levels have been going down since 1971, but teacher populations are actually going up. In the 1975–76 school year, for example, 2.46 million teachers were employed, according to the NEA, .5 percent more than the year before.[25] This, remember, was during a year of high inflation and national unemployment. The average salary for classroom teachers that year was $12,524, some 7.4 percent more than the previous year.[26] This, during a time of national recession.

Demands for smaller classes and larger paychecks are, of course, a regular part of the bargaining at contract time. And the unions often enjoy special side benefits during the bargaining sessions. For example, in Detroit, the Detroit Federation of Teachers (DFT) uses the Detroit Board of Education's internal mail system to distribute its union notices, bulletins, memos, newsletters, and what-have-you free of charge to all the schools and offices in the district. This is a fairly common practice, but the U.S. Postal Service is becoming alarmed and has issued an advisory letter to the Detroit schools, while reviewing a similar case elsewhere.[27]

Usually, the union wins the right to have the school board collect dues for it through automatic deduction from the paycheck. One of the penalties imposed in 1976 on New York City's UFT by the New York Public Employment Relations Board as a result of an illegal walkout was a 14-month suspension of automatic dues checkoff. Union officials estimated it would cost them $750,000 to collect the dues themselves.[28] Which shows that a good chunk of what the citizens of New York pay for "education" does not, in fact, go to teaching children how to read and write. But then, the same UFT had saved the taxpayers $31 million in 1975 because there is a fine of two days' pay for every day a public employee is on strike.[29]

Not all states have enacted such strong laws against strikes by public employees, but even if they did, their effectiveness would still be open to question. During the 1975–76 school year there were 203 teacher strikes, 137 by NEA affiliates and 61 by AFT affiliates.[30] In the summer of 1976 NEA executive director Terry Herndon predicted even more strikes for the 1976–77 school year,[31] but by September NEA had changed its tune and was suddenly saying it didn't expect strikes to exceed those of the previous year.[32] Why the shift? Presumably, it was felt that NEA could gain a little public sympathy by not sounding too threatening; after all, there are still more parents than teachers, and parents vote, too.

Already back in 1973–74 teachers were striking more than other state and local government employees, according to the

Census Bureau, which also noted significantly that teachers were more organized than other public employees, with (at that time) some 72 percent in one collective-bargaining unit or another.[33] The connection between the high level of union organization and the high level of strikes is far from coincidental, as a recent study by the Public Service Research Council has found.[34] NEA has stated that the percentage of teachers actually covered by collective-bargaining agreements may be higher than that 72 percent, but the organization continues to demand a federal collective-bargaining statute. The 95th Congress, at least in its 1977 session, was reluctant to grant NEA's request.

It is a continual thorn in the side of NEA and AFT that 20 states have right-to-work laws. Along with the AFL-CIO, the American Federation of State, County, and Municipal Employees (AFSCME), and the International Association of Fire-Fighters, NEA is a part of the Coalition for American Public Employees (CAPE), another separate legal entity (that is, a separate fundraising and political action group) dedicated expressly to the goal of obtaining passage of a national collective-bargaining statute.

As of 1976, the right-to-work situation provided an occasion for rivalry between the two big teachers' unions. AFT claims superior membership in the right-to-work states, attributing its success to its own more aggressive, militant image. NEA was very embarrassed in 1975 when the Alabama Education Association, its affiliate, narrowly rejected a motion of support for collective-bargaining legislation in that right-to-work state. The AEA made sure that the resolution passed next time around, in 1976, but by then the resolution had less political impact than it could have had a year earlier.[35]

Another professional organization of teachers, the National Association of Professional Educators, is definitely *not* a union. Though only a few years old, NAPE shows a good growth record, thanks to its forthright appeal to teachers who object to working in a closed shop. NEA sent staffer Dick Dashiell to NAPE's 4th Annual Convention in 1976, after which he prepared an 11-page report for NEA. Quite predictably, he steered away from substantive issues and confined himself to ridiculing the conventioneers for their unsophisticated ways. Dashiell felt superior because he belonged to a larger and richer organization. It is significant that NEA thought it necessary to alert its state and local affiliates to the threat of this upstart organization; evidently, NEA fears that NAPE is effective. And anything that fosters diversity among educators is anathema to NEA.

What Happened to Local Control?

Somewhere in all this there still remain local school districts, legally at least, which, according to textbook descriptions, have the final say-so in educating America's children. What, in practice, remains of local control?

If a family moves from Nebraska to Maine, and then to Texas, it finds teachers in all places sounding the same and schools offering and promoting more or less the same programs. A student in teacher's college would find remarkably little variation among the education departments at a Seven Sisters school, a large state university, and a little state college (Troy State in Alabama might be an exception, because Max Rafferty is dean there). The practitioners of education are homogenized—in their training, their outlook, their subsequent professional development. They are taught to look only to approved sources for pronouncements on the merits and demerits of any given issue or position. In turn, these educators tend to standardize the schools in which they are employed and the students whom they teach. And through it all, the ordinary public is told it cannot understand the complicated concerns of education.

A time-honored bureaucratic tactic for self-aggrandizement and perpetuation is the "we/they" dichotomy. "They" are the great unwashed, those outside the profession. Laymen are not supposed even to think of telling doctors how to treat their patients. If professional educators had their way, parents would not even think of telling teachers what, or how, to teach their children. The reliance on jargon, the obscurity with which controversial issues are discussed, the continual revision of terminology, as well as the not-so-subtle disapproval of too much public concern, are all part of the dichotomizing strategy of the bureaucracy and the professions.

In those long-ago days when the schoolteacher spent a few weeks in every family's home, parents didn't need to worry too much about school, because they knew the teacher personally. If they weren't satisfied with his performance, it wasn't difficult to talk to the other parents who had a hand in the decisionmaking, and send the fellow packing if necessary. In more recent decades, too, parents felt confident in the operation of their children's schools, and justifiably confident. They had little need to interfere, and so, unless extraordinary circumstances dictated it, they did not. It was a workable arrangement, sensible and practical for its time.

It worked as long as the public schools deserved the confidence thus placed in them. After the alarms and excursions of the 1950s the American public was lulled to sleep, and the educators became protective and defensive, though none the less progressive. And suddenly in the 1970s the nation awoke to find that it had not been paying enough attention to its children's education. Too much trust and too much complacency toward better organized and self-conscious teachers have cost many parents their children. And only now is the public starting to notice what has happened while it dozed, and paid the ever increasing bill.

It is understandable, though not necessarily desirable, that the citizens most conversant with public education generally are parents of public school children. Parochial school parents follow parish politics more closely than other parishioners, which is only to be expected. A common defense against parent criticism of some educational scheme is, "Well, the rest of the public doesn't seem to care. Don't you think perhaps you lack objectivity?" But naturally most of "the public" doesn't care—most of "the public" doesn't stand to have its child's life ruined by this particular innovation, or that program. The great challenge to the concerned parent is to awaken the "rest of the public" and to make it easier for the "rest of the public" to get involved in public education.

Established policies discourage wide citizen involvement in the running of the public schools; whether intentionally or accidentally cannot be said. For example, school board elections are usually required to be nonpartisan. A Democrat or Republican precinct chairman who might get interested in the school board race if a member of his party were running does not have that special incentive. School board elections are almost always off-elections, held at some odd time during an ordinary year, when citizens in general are paying little attention to electoral politics. Also, terms on the school board tend to run long: six years is not unusual. Even if a controversy should develop over an individual board member, it may be years until the public has a chance to express its disfavor by denying that member's bid for reelection. Few problems are interesting enough and compelling enough in this age of crises to hold popular attention for the sustained period necessary to effect change.

Researchers have found five educational issues of perennial concern to citizens in general: (1) school tax rate; (2) building and expansion programs; (3) bond issues to support the expansion programs; (4) school budget; and (5) teachers' salaries. This list coincides with most of the issues the public ever has a chance to vote on—one wonders, if parents had the chance to vote on criteria for teacher selection or contract renewal, or on introduction of experimental programs, whether there might be some big differences in public education. As it is, educators can point to the predominance of pocketbook issues as evidence of the basic stinginess of the public where education is concerned, and as evidence of lack of other interest. A taxpayer might point to the fiscal irresponsibility of educators where the public is concerned, but because taxpayers have no local, state, and national associations to promote their cause, they usually go unheard.

There are a few hopeful signs, however. The founder of the Business and Professional Peoples' Alliance for Better Textbooks of Kanawha County, West Virginia is a grandfather whose own children long ago finished college. Yet Elmer Fike's interest in education has stayed high because, as a businessman, he is acutely aware of the failure of schools today to graduate employable students. Parents who fight the good fight for their own children often find that private schools offer better education, free from pressures on the youngsters because of their parents' activism. Too, as battles drag on year after year, the children whose futures were at stake when the fight started have often finished school. To their credit, parent activists are more and more staying in the fight even after it ceases to hold a compelling personal interest. The base of concerned citizen interest seems to be broadening.

The Local School Board

An NEA inquiry around 1960 found that the public education system in Indianapolis had been effectively removed from public control for more than three decades. The very nominations to the Board of School Commissioners were controlled for over 30 years by a self-appointed citizens committee of less than 200.[36] Limitation of public access is not so obvious in most places, of course.

Nonetheless, one wonders why anybody would want to be on the school board anyhow. After all, what power does a school board have? Can it decide who is hired and fired? Not always. Federal regulations stipulate racial and sexual quotas; state laws may define the weight given to seniority if layoffs are ordered; local unions and associations may wring agreements out of school boards that reduce evaluation of teachers to technicality and formality; state laws limit the selection of teachers to those who hold state certificates.

Can a school board set a salary schedule? Not really, once collective bargaining has entered the picture. In many areas minimums are set by the state also. Can a local board enforce discipline in the schools? Not effectively, since the U.S. Supreme Court has manacled discipline with laborious procedural details; not since the Court overrode a school board that tried to require the Pledge of Allegiance from pupils (*West Virginia State Board of Education v. Barnette,* 319 U.S. 624); and not since dress style was declared a constitutional right (*Tinker v. Des Moines School District,* 393 U.S. 503). Small blessing: the Supreme Court has not pronounced yet on whether one's hairstyle is also a constitutional right.

Can a local board respond affirmatively to parent and community wishes for acknowledgement of God? Hardly, since the U. S. Supreme Court has banned released time (*McCollum v. Board of Education,* 333 U.S. 203), has banned Bible reading (*Abington Township School District v. Schempp,* 374 U.S. 203), and has banned school-sanctioned prayers (*Engel v. Vitale,* 370 U.S. 421).

What *can* a local school board do?

To some extent, it frequently can select textbooks—following professional recommendations, usually, and sometimes within state-set limits, or with federal money. But it cannot order the removal of books from a school library, or at least dare not try, since the Ohio Civil Liberties Union won a 1976 decision from the 6th District U.S. Court of Appeals forbidding the Strongsville, Ohio board to do just that.

A local board can set goals for professional educators and for the bureaucracy within the district on such matters as adult education, vocational programs, library expansion, and the like. In some cases it can influence curriculum, by bringing in sex education, for example, or establishing a free-enterprise course. In all cases, a local board can receive local, state, and federal money (unless it is being punished for something), spend the same, and ask for more.

74

This reads like a puny list of powers for what is supposed to be the primary controlling body of American public education. The plight of local school boards, however, is not unlike the plight of other local bodies: three men on the Garfield, New Jersey, City Council voted no to a $65,000 hot-lunch program and for their audacity were sentenced to 45 days in jail and fined $300.[37] The hot-lunch program had been court ordered. So who really decides public school policy? (Hint: unelected judges do not qualify as the public, in this writer's opinion.)

Nonetheless, the school board as an institution continues to exist. Perhaps someday it might regain its former significance. Even in its debilitated condition, it can do some constructive things. (The possibilities will be discussed later.) But it must be admitted that the school board, as a political entity, brought upon itself many of its own troubles by so readily relinquishing authority to the "professional staff."

Right after World War II there were about 100,000 school districts in the country; in 1976 there were around 16,000. In the same period, school enrollment more than doubled, from 6,000,000 to 15,000,000 (in 1974).[38] Clearly, there has been consolidation and, therefore, centralization. It may make for cost-efficiency, which indeed was one of the strongest selling points of the whole idea, but it also encourages bureaucracy, which means disregard for local standards and practices and preferences, and standardized rather than individualized decisions.

The first predictable thing was about the first thing that happened: teachers banded together for job security. If a district is too large to allow for individual decisions to be made about hiring and firing, then for efficiency's sake, impersonal standards have to be set and followed; once that happens, teachers are going to demand a voice in setting and following those standards. Having successfully promoted their interest on that score, educators will seek to promote their interest in other areas as well. And teacher interest is synonymous, partic-

75

ularly in recent times, with political organization, which tips the scales in many local elections.

To return: the textbook prototype is that control of education rests with the local district school board, which is elected by all citizens to represent the parents and citizens of the area. The board is supposed to represent parent and public interest and at the same time further education. Following this prototype hypothetically for a mythical Middle American town, one sees it breaks down almost immediately. Consider the office of superintendent of schools. True, the superintendent is generally hired by the board. After clearing that hurdle once, however, he discovers that the task of satisfying his employer is relatively easy (Middle America, recall, is our focus, not the troubled urban areas). The "Super" has a staff of assistants, to whom he delegates tasks, and whose advice he himself usually follows. Sometimes this staff is "his"; often he inherits it. Almost always, the professional staff consists of former teachers. The cult of professionalism is so advanced that the members of the board of education, "mere" laymen, have come to regard themselves as ignorant and perhaps even stupid where the "highly complex" subject of education is concerned. They willingly accept the interpretations of the educationists and assume, without the least cynicism, that the educators represent the true and the good. To compound the problem, the tenure of superintendents may predate the tenure of new or young board members, who must then overcome shyness stemming from a sense of inferiority or ignorance before they question the superintendent.

Suppose the superintendent comes before the board with a request, his budget proposal, which includes a new curriculum program, a couple of new counselors, an outreach plan for deprived children, and improvements in the gym facilities. Because the superintendent is believed to have the good of the children at heart and, furthermore, to be in a position to know what's good for them, his word is usually taken without question. His fundamental assumptions are seldom contested.[39] When the time comes to buy new textbooks, and someone

76

must make a decision from among the hundreds available, thank goodness for the professional staff selected by the superintendent! Committees can be set up, spiced generously with the professional opinion and expertise of willing educators in the field, to decide these issues (the willing educators in the field, it never seems to be noted, are usually the ambitious ones, which means they are progressive, because to make a good impression on those who can advance your career, you almost always must give the flavor of novelty). Usually, then, the school board accepts the decisions of its own committee. And by this time, that budget is pretty big.

Then comes time to consider teacher issues. The board now deals directly with the teachers—the militant profession has elbowed the administrator into a neither-fish-nor-fowl position in the negotiations. The teachers probably want the same things the superintendent wants: new programs, improved facilities, more counselors, and so on. But they also are likely to want more money, lighter teaching loads, more parking spaces, better health insurance benefits, and, say, the right to demand that all teachers hired in the future must join the professional association. Now, most of these demands cost money. The teachers' representatives—sometimes homegrown, sometimes, if the spoils look good enough, imported from an NEA or AFT stable for the occasion—like true bargainers, do not think beyond their own demands and the demands of their constituents. The board is under somewhat more pressure, because its members know that if they displease the public too much they may not be reelected. They also know that if they please the public too much and in the process displease the educationists too much, they may not get reelected. The latter threat carries more weight, because the public is not organized to defend its multifarious interests, whereas educators, whose interests are more uniform, are highly organized.

And so a bargain is reached by the teachers and the board: a new contract is drawn up. And the public gets the bill for both the administrative requests and the teacher requests. A growing number of districts around the country are faced with another sticky wicket: their administrators belong to the American Federation of School Administrators, an AFL-CIO affiliate union—which is not part of the American Federation of Teachers. About 1,300 districts have administrators belonging to one union or another.[40] This trend is symptomatic. Administrators recognize that no one is clearly in control of the situation. Superintendents don't run the show, school boards don't, the public doesn't—so who does?

Should the public happen to complain about the bill presented to it after all the bargaining is over, the administration and the teachers are likely to rise to the occasion as a united professional front, knowing what's best for the children. Before the common enemy—the tightfisted public—the front is solid.

And the board of education? Where did the board of education get lost in the midst of all this? It is still there, pointing sheepishly to the teachers and the professional staff, saying it was just trying to follow their advice and to do what they said was best, and just trying to be fair to everybody, et cetera.

The story of Kanawha County, West Virginia shows how powerless a board of education can be in its own right. Although the board took the heat from the public for purchasing those new textbooks that provoked such strenuous objection, the board in fact bought the books on the advice of its professional committee. Then it had to defend itself for taking that "professional" advice. In at least this respect, the Kanawha County board got what it deserved: the self-protective bureaucratic we/they tactic backfired. Whereas it had once felt comfortably superior to the uncultured hillbillies, the board was now despised by the very people it had previously patronized.

From the larger education establishment's point of view, the most alarming aspect of the whole West Virginia dispute was the wave of sympathetic responses it set off. Textbook protests broke out in districts all over the country. Not that these were not occurring before 1974—indeed they were—but the na-

78

tional press paid them no attention. Comparing textbook disputes to busing, NEA patiently pointed out that both have "been a continuing target of extremist attack . . . in Kanawha County and . . . similarly targeted protests in other parts of the country."[41] Taken aback by the public's outspokenness, the education establishment assumed a "highly sophisticated, well-organized right-wing extremist group"[42] was behind it all. What better way to discredit the legions of concerned West Virginia parents? Elsewhere, NEA tried to make the case that textbook protests were evidence of an "organized national movement whose members spearhead protests against unpopular textbooks in communities across the country."[43]

Claims of right-wing conspiracies, by the way, have been the standard tactic used by NEA for more than 25 years to escape blame when its projects have displeased the public. But then, it is another characteristic of bureaucracies to attempt to dismiss their critics as irresponsible minorities.

Professional Self-Governance

The "organized profession" has come up with yet another strategy to emasculate what control is left with local school boards. Called professional self-governance, it means that teachers should make every decision that affects them as teachers. What decisions? Bluntly put, everything from who gets a license to teach to what the schoolday routine will be.

Americans have long been demanding some kind of accountability from public education, making the establishment decidedly uncomfortable. The party line nowadays seems to be that educators cannot be held accountable until the profession is recognized by law as self-governing. But there are ample contributions to the public record indicating that the education establishment views any program of accountability as by definition antiprofessional and hostile. Nevertheless, educators do realize that the public wants to feel important somehow or other in the educational process, so the following line of rhetoric has been adopted:

> It is pure myth that classroom teachers can ever be held accountable, with justice, under existing conditions. The classroom teacher has either too little control or no control over the factors which might render accountability either feasible or fair.[44]

So says Helen Bain, former president of the NEA. However, she then went on to indicate that if certain minimal conditions were met, the question of teacher responsibility for educational results might become a legitimate one. Four characteristics are essential to professional self-governance, according to Mrs. Bain.

1. *Authority over issuing, suspending, revoking, and reinstating the legal licensure of educational personnel.*[45] This authority now resides, in most cases, in the state department of education, which in turn follows certain statutory guidelines. Even if a "fully professional teaching profession" were to set up a commission to lend an air of impartiality to its licensure decisions, one can be quite sure no public interference in the form of legislative oversight would be tolerated. Standards would be set by the state's professional association. Period.

Leave aside the thorny question whether that association would be the NEA or the AFT. In 45 to 48 states it would most likely be the NEA affiliate. The state organization, filled with the heady wine of self-governance, would probably turn straightaway to its national office for assistance in details. One can be confident that the bureaucrats in the national office would have foreseen this eventuality and prepared a draft of guidelines, suitable for adoption or adaptation by each state. Remember, a local board of education does not have the right to hire an uncertified teacher. Teacher control of certification would further limit the choice of the local boards, to say nothing of the choice of parents, who might want educators not enslaved to a party line.

What sort of criteria might be expected if the teachers handled certification? Standardized tests, presently a significant factor in licensing decisions, would fall quickly into disuse. The National Teachers' Exam draws no demarcation between passing and failing; acceptable minimum scores vary from state to state. And, besides, the NTE is like the college boards—it's a standardized test. Educators *all* know that those are unfair by definition, according to today's fashion. Never mind that most intelligent people are likely to feel the NTE is infinitely easier to score well on than, say, the SAT or the GRE.

Without the NTE scores to go on, what objective criteria might be used? It would be hard to find any. Grades from college courses are similarly suspect. The B.A. by itself might be a criterion, provided it had a sufficient number of education courses behind it. And then, to ensure continuing "professional development," the B.A. might be superseded by requirement for an M.A. after perhaps seven years of teaching. One can safely surmise that a good deal of emphasis would be put on education in education, even as it is today in many areas, because that's an efficient, indeed maybe the only way to feed educationist notions to practicing teachers.

Prospective teachers' attitudes toward teaching would have to be watched closely if professional self-governance were the order of the day. The "profession," remember, is a calling to social service, so clearly a candidate should not regard teaching as merely a means to support his family (there is little danger that many public high school teachers are likely to feel genuine dedication to instilling knowledge). A written statement of purpose might be required, as an index to the candidate's sincerity, dedication, goals, worldview, human sensitivity, and so forth. Thus, anyone with dangerous ideas about individualism or national sovereignty or disciplined behavior could be spotted at the beginning of his career. Since the self-governing profession could also suspend and revoke licenses, the career of such an extraordinary individual would most likely be short.

Then there would be the peer evaluation. After all, doctors decide which of their colleagues to certify and which to distinguish by granting membership in honorary societies. But doctors, one might recall, possess certain information and knowledge that laymen do not share. Educators like to think their science is arcane too. Several years ago it was noted that teachers were reluctant to evaluate each other;[46] however, aggressive personalities sometimes scruple little about doing just that, and it is the aggressive individuals who are pushing the whole self-governance crusade and therefore would take charge should the dream be realized. Informal blackballing is common enough, as many teachers could relate; but why make it into an institution?

2. *Authority to establish and administer standards of professional practice and ethics for all educational personnel.* Standards of professional practice could be anything from membership in a trade union (as it is already, for all practical purposes, in some areas) to belief in interdependence of nations as a moral principle to be conveyed to students. Standards of professional ethics might be defined as anything from preserving confidentiality about student violations of the law to not giving surprise quizzes. Or sensible standards might be established, which would be largely unobjectionable.

The point, however, is that teachers in public schools are, like it or not, *public servants,* and basic justice says that he who pays the piper calls the tune. Teachers have no superior ethical endowments that make their whims deserving of public respect and acceptance. To the contrary, since the children they influence and control are not their children in any sense whatsoever, there are compelling reasons for the parents of those children to have a say in setting the standards and ethics of their teachers.

In 1975 Kathleen Sullivan, a teacher in the small town of Union Center, South Dakota, was fired because she was shacking up with her boyfriend, in full public view, and making no pretense of embarrassment in front of her students. When Miss Sullivan appealed, the South Dakota U. S. District Court upheld the firing—a surprising verdict, but thoroughly commendable.[47] A similar set of circumstances in a larger city, or in a typical suburb, would not have had such a satisfactory ending; in fact, cases can be found where the opposite disposition of the case was made. In Union Center, South Dakota, population under 500, public control of public education is more than a memory. A fully self-governing profession would not tolerate such foreign control; under professional self-governance, Kathleen Sullivan would probably never have been fired.

3. *Authority to accredit teacher-preparation institutions.* This is logical enough from the educationists' point of view. It is not very far from the actual practice. True, states do exercise their accreditation powers, but usually on the recommendation of the state department of education, which usually is staffed by former teachers. And there are regional or national accreditation bodies that play a role. Those associations are scarcely hostile to the education establishment; they are not even foreign, since many of their field men and their own decisionmakers are former educators themselves.

4. *Authority to govern in-service and continuing education for teachers.* Logical enough also. Although access to, and preparation for, the profession may be controlled, once teachers are on their own in a classroom, they may find themselves thinking independently, or succumbing to the influence of parents, or demonstrating too much common sense and not enough appreciation for the conventional wisdom of their vocation. Thus, in-service education, to keep them up to date, to give them new ideas, to keep them in the fold. Most districts regularly set aside days for in-service education; some states even specify the number: 10 days per year is not unusual. Many districts, and some states, structure their pay scales in such a way as to give an incentive to continual course-taking, credit-seeking, and eventual degree-acquiring. And a course in ancient Greek doesn't necessarily qualify for the pay increase;

something in "Teaching Ancient Languages" might fill the bill, however (if elementary or secondary schools offered such things in enough abundance to justify the course). The direction away from content, toward method, toward the particular technology of the day, is always evident. If the teacher associations had control of continuing education, experimentalism could be advanced much faster.

Let us assume the profession got its way on all these points and became self-governing. The question might be raised: Is this local control? Obviously the public is not in control. It has already relinquished its rights, thereby enabling this scenario to get this far. Can anyone really believe, moreover, that this exercise of "professional self-governance" is the teachers of Montana deciding the direction of the teaching profession in Montana? Hardly. Will the ordinary, nonpolitical schoolteacher in any state have a real say about how his or her license is revoked or granted? Not bloody likely. The teacher organizers, the militants, yes; the progressives, the radicals, who follow the party line in order to climb the ladder of power, would gain the most if self-governance were granted, and would smother the meeker, more numerous members. That has already happened with the leadership of the NEA, and with the established channels for decisionmaking about professional matters; but at least now there is some access to public sentiment for teachers more in harmony with community desires. They can still be teachers, at least. No tyrant can be so merciless as a tyrant of one's own choosing, as the educators who today kick against the goad of public control might discover if they were subjected to "professional self-governance" tomorrow.

The scenario of self-governance as described above is not entirely theoretical. In 1973 Oregon enacted what has been called admiringly a "magna carta" of teacher rights. A state-wide Teacher Standards and Practices Commission was set up and given the authority, from the state board of education, to certify teachers, revoke certification, and regulate programs and teacher-training institutions leading to certification. The

Teacher Standards and Practices Commission, of course, is constituted of teachers exclusively.[48] Some citizens objected that enactment of such a measure would frustrate public control of education. The charge was anticipated:

> The fact that teachers want to govern their profession does not mean that they want to control education. Taxpaying citizens (including teachers) are the ones who should decide on the goals and financing of schools, but professionals should decide on how the goals can best be accomplished. . . .[49]

This is the defensive approach. A more patronizing note appeared in the popular press:

> It is entirely fitting that parents help set forth the end results of education—and then pick professionals whom they trust to tackle the nitty-gritty of everyday operations . . . professionals should "run the school"—not parents, nor citizen committees . . . most parents are not trained for decisionmaking in the operation of a school, nor for the task of teaching pupils in the classroom. . . .[50]

How generous of the author to grant parents the right to "pick professionals whom they trust." But what if parents can't find professionals worthy of their trust? Under self-governance, the profession would have picked its own before even allowing them to be considered for hiring. If parents could interview teachers or propose candidates for hiring, and decisions were made on the basis of individual merit, then it would be fine to say parents can pick professionals whom they trust. Given the situation as it is and as it may become, the statement is empty rhetoric, however.

And how generous to allow parents to "help set forth the end results of education." What ends are they to help set forth? How about the most basic one, literacy? How well have professionals respected that goal set by most parents? The rate of functional illiteracy is growing nationwide. Yet there is no hint of apology from the professionals who are responsible. Another end result of education that parents expect is preparation for college. This is commonly measured by SAT scores. Those scores have been declining for more than 12 years. Do the professionals ever acknowledge that they may have breached their trust? Hardly. Rather, they try to downplay the importance of literacy, the importance of objective information. They even have the nerve to turn around and lay the blame for the decline at the feet of parents.

What, then, is the good of being able to set goals if the goals can be comfortably ignored by those charged with meeting them? Some pedagogues even advocate limiting the role of boards of education:

> One legitimate responsibility of boards of education is the development of aims for the school district. . . . When they concern themselves with the determination of aims, they often confuse their responsibility and make institutional decisions, such as prescribing specific courses in economics, foreign language, or civics.[51]

This commentator would allow boards of education to set goals, but draw the line at determining how to attain the goals. That is like saying, you may eat anything you like, but don't go into the kitchen. The ends may not justify the means, but without control over the means there is no control over the ends, either. Rhetoric about allowing parents and the community to set goals or, more annoyingly, to help set goals is thoroughly hollow; sure, parents and the community should set goals, but they should also see to it that the goals are carried out.

Even with professional self-governance fully granted, however, the thinking militants recognize that there still is a public with which the profession must reckon. The public sometimes is uncooperative, and refuses to learn its proper place. In such cases, provision must be made to channel the public's desire for control. Neil Sullivan is recognized by the profession as a "brilliant administrator." He has played a significant role in desegregation from Virginia to California to Massachusetts. In 1972 he proposed a foreboding model for school governance that bears some scrutiny. Sullivan minced no words in criticizing the present system:

> Lay school boards cannot keep out of administration
> . . . school boards nearly everywhere make policy
> decisions in areas in which they are completely un-
> qualified . . . many board members use their
> positions to win higher political office. . . .[52]

He then proposed his alternative:

> Each community would elect its own local school
> board. A city the size of Boston, for example, might
> be divided into ten local school boards. Each local
> board would nominate some of its own members as
> candidates for a regional board of directors. The
> Boston metropolitan area—again, only for purposes
> of illustration—might be governed by three or four
> regional boards of directors, crossing political, eco-
> nomic, and racial lines. The state supreme court
> would choose members of the regional boards from
> candidates nominated by the local boards. The re-
> gional boards would set broad policy objectives for
> their areas and would hire a chief executive to carry
> them out.[53]

This is local control? Having the state supreme court name members of regional boards of directors for the public schools? Sullivan doesn't mention whether the local board would have any authority at all; if it is to be responsible to a regional board, its authority would be nominal at best. Perhaps he would like the local school boards to dissolve after the regional boards have been set up, with the appointment of future members a self-perpetuating process. Or maybe he would keep the local boards, giving them the sole function of choosing nominees to present to the state supreme court for further selection. It doesn't matter much; John Q. Taxpayer would have no control over his son's public school education either way. Under such a scheme as Sullivan's the taxpayer would have even less control than he does today. Unless taxpayers and parents start getting militant in defense of their oversight powers, schemes such as Sullivan's may become reality before anybody realizes what has happened.

3

Uncle Sam Steps In

Almost any history of American education that a casual reader is likely to pick up will repeat the standard version of the federal role in the education of American children: namely, that the federal government from 1787 was interested and active in education. Several things are cited as evidence of this always-presumed-rightful federal involvement. The Northwest Ordinance is usually the first.

The ordinance gave one section out of every 36 of public land on the frontier (changed in 1850 to two sections) for the support of education. This policy was couched in the famous language, "Religion, morality and knowledge being necessary to good government and the happiness of mankind, schools and the means of education shall forever be encouraged." Those who point to the Northwest Ordinance as a valuable precedent when federal aid is being discussed, however, usually fail to elevate the then assumed equation of religion, morality, and knowledge to similar significance.

Was the Northwest Ordinance really intended as an early form of federal aid to education? Some have pointed out that if the government had really been interested in education, it would have found a way to provide assistance for the north-

89

eastern states, where around 85 percent of the nation's youth lived at the time. More likely, the land grants for education just seemed like a good gimmick to get the local government set up, with a nest egg to boot. Independent-minded landowners had little time or inclination to set up a government, and almost certainly would not have bothered to raise "public money" for education. By giving the land Congress killed two birds with one stone. And ever since, education has been a governmental function directly, and a parental function only by delegation.

The next major federal move did not come until 1862, when President Lincoln signed the Morrill Act, which granted 30,000 acres per member of Congress for the establishment of colleges, to emphasize agricultural and industrial education. Another Morrill Act in 1890 established Negro colleges under federal benevolence (some years earlier the Freedmen's Bureau had taken upon itself many educational functions, which devolved upon the states when the bureau was abolished in 1870). The Agricultural and Mechanical Colleges of the Morrill Act developed the Extension Services, which by any standard were valuable resources in developing a productive national agriculture. In recent times, of course, they have become increasingly liberal-arts oriented, despite their express purpose, and are now, in most cases, typical state universities.

In 1917 Congress went along with one of the pet schemes of the progressive-education movement and stepped into the nation's high schools to promote vocational education. The entrée was provided by the Smith-Hughes Act. States were required to submit their plans to a federal Board of Vocational Education, which could refuse money until the plan had been modified according to the wishes of a federal agent. Further, the states were required to match the federal funds with their own. Thus, not only was disposition of a certain measure of a state's own budget prescribed by the federal government, but some very particular details of curriculum, schedule, teacher qualification, and the like were also dictated by federal fiat. Without a doubt, the federal demands ran contrary to many local customs and peculiarities of management, and by 1931 the program had created a certain amount of dissatisfaction.

The 1917 act was a departure from tradition in that it specified programs of education for particular groups of people. Prior aid had been general, handed out with the idea of fostering local initiative and self-government. Now that trend was reversing. Smith-Hughes was not quite the beginning of federal aid, and it certainly was not the end of it.

One of the last deeds of the Hoover administration was the report *Federal Relations to Education* of the National Advisory Committee on Education, chaired by Charles Riborg Mann. Already in 1931 that committee was noting the undesirable and debilitating effect of federal grants on educational programs: local control was weakened; the need for citizen approval was circumvented; interest groups, pressuring for their particular causes, were strengthened; certain aspects of education were favored over others; even temporary federal grants tended to become more permanent than temporary state grants for specific purposes.

The Advisory Committee made several recommendations for federal policy in education:

> Amend those existing laws which give or tend to give the Federal Government and its agencies power to interfere with the autonomy of the States in matters of education. These amendments should repeal all provisions that require the States and their local communities to match federal funds or that grant power to the federal agencies to approve or reject state educational plans, to prescribe the standards controlling instruction, or otherwise to supervise and direct educational or research activities within the States.

> Enact no additional laws that grant federal finan-

cial aid to the States in support of special types of education or that increase existing federal grants for such special purposes as are already aided.[1]

The Advisory Committee also recommended that "a Department of Education with a Secretary of Education at its head be established in the Federal Government"[2] in accordance with some very particular specifications. The gist of those specifications was that "no regulatory or executive responsibilities should be vested in the Department of Education."[3]

The federal Department of Education had been originally established in 1867 for the purpose of gathering facts, disseminating organizational-type information, and providing assistance for school systems—when asked. It had become, over time, the U. S. Office of Education, and in 1931 was located in the Department of the Interior. Representative James A. Garfield, who later became President, had introduced the legislation creating it and had received many thanks from the National Education Association for his action. Says one NEA biographer, "The Department, Bureau, and then the Office of Education was regarded as the virtual creation of the NEA. . . ."[4]

There was no other organization around to crusade for a federal Department of Education, of course. The titles of the office meant various things, and the department established in 1867 was never intended to be a cabinet-level post. It was not until 1919 that an NEA resolution specifically called for cabinet status for a secretary of education, a demand renewed annually until 1944, and then revived again recently. It is doubtful whether NEA would have been happy then with a cabinet-level office that possessed no enforcement or regulatory powers. Certainly, such a restriction would not be welcome today. Contemporary arguments for a cabinet-level Department of Education make no reference to that forgotten aspect of the history of the idea.

Nothing much became of the 1931 National Advisory

Committee report, however; the New Deal swept in a few months after it was issued, and doomed it to dusty library shelves as an historical curiosity.

As a curiosity, it is interesting to review the "Tentative List of Contemporary Activities" that the committee compiled. It was designed to be a complete list of educational activities of the federal government at the time. Unfortunately, no dollar figures were listed for any of the programs, so no comparisons with today's figures can be made. What can be compared, however, are the things that were considered educational activities: today, certain functions are regarded as managerial that in 1931 were deemed educational.

The legislative branch was then (and still is) responsible for the education of congressional pages, and for books and services to the blind through the Library of Congress. An apprentice school at the Government Printing Office was also listed.

The executive branch, then as ever since, was involved in many programs regarded as educational. Behold the following examples:

• Department of Agriculture: experiment and extension stations, cooperative and demonstration work.

• Department of State: Foreign Service School.

• Treasury Department: Coast Guard Academy, Internal Revenue training, Public Health training.

• War Department: National Guard training, Reserve Officer Training Corps, on-post education of enlisted personnel; Philippine, Puerto Rican, and Canal Zone schools; foreign military-school exchange.

• Department of Justice: education of federal prisoners; prohibition enforcement officers' training.

• Navy Department: Navy Reserve Officer Training Corps; nonmilitary education by correspondence and navy schools for enlisted men; Marine Corps Institute; Samoa and Guam schools; Naval Academy, Postgraduate School, and Naval War College.

• Post Office Department: free mailing privileges for land-grant colleges, for agricultural extension services and experimental stations, and for the blind.

• Department of Interior: agricultural and mechanical college subsidies; land grants; Indian education; Freedmen's Hospital Nursing School and Howard University; education services of the National Park Service; Office of Education research; Alaska and Hawaii schools, in part.

• Department of Labor: citizenship training textbooks distributed to the public schools, and naturalization requirements.

• Department of Commerce: itinerant teachers and correspondence courses for isolated stations under the Bureau of Lighthouses; mine research; standards for air and sea pilots; radio licenses; first-aid and mine-rescue courses.

There were also independent establishments, such as the Civil Service Commission, the Pan American Union, the Smithsonian Institution, the Federal Power Commission, and the still-extant National Screw Thread Commission, whose functions were less educational.

Despite the length of this list, the duties and functions it describes are pretty clear and simple, with readily apparent purpose. Probably most of the activities enumerated are still around today, though not included in any education budget and not of much interest to the education lobby. The Internal Revenue Service still trains its agents, and the Justice Department offers to educate federal prisoners, but neither is considered federal aid to education. For sure, two programs at least have been abolished: the training of prohibition officers, and free mailing privileges for the blind. Only the federal government itself is deemed worthy of the latter these days.

General Aid, 1938–65

The report of President Hoover's Commission on Education was doomed to obscurity. Franklin Roosevelt created his own Advisory Committee on Education in 1936, headed by Floyd Reeves. By then the federal government was construct-

94

ing educational facilities through the Public Works Administration, and was dabbling in adult education and nursery schools through the Federal Emergency Relief Administration. The Reeves committee came up with a report in 1938, which basically pointed out that there was a wide range of inequality in educational funding from state to state.

Mirabile dictu: "The report of this committee so nearly agreed with the policies of the NEA that the Legislative Commission devoted a great deal of time and effort to promoting the report as it was embodied in a succession of congressional bills."[5] These bills were the subject of extensive hearings, but no action. Briefly, they would have made federal aid available to states in proportion to need. These were the first general-aid-to-education bills, introduced in 1938. Some version of the general-aid idea was introduced into every single Congress from then until 1965. And since 1965 there has been a proliferation of proposals for categorical aid, general aid, and just about every other kind of education legislation imaginable.

In 1940 the Lanham Act passed. It established the principle of special federal aid to areas unable to raise sufficient revenue locally because of large federal landholdings or sudden influxes of federal employees' children. This impact-aid law was extended one year at a time until 1950, and turned into one of the biggest pork barrels ever. Impact aid remains to this day a major part of federal education involvement.

The years 1940 and 1942 saw no general education bill come out of Congress. The 1943 version, disguised partly as a war measure (to equalize the deleterious effects on the homefront of taking teachers away from their schools), came close to passage, but lost the support of southern senators at the end of the debate. Already the race issue was emerging, and a North Dakota senator's amendment to ensure that both races benefited equally from federal aid stuck in the craw of the Dixiecrats. Eleven years later the issue would come to a head.

In 1944, anticipating the end of the war, the Serviceman's

Readjustment Act was passed, known as the G.I. Bill. The boost this gave to higher education, in the name of benefiting the returning servicemen, needs no elaboration. Bill money could be applied to any private college as well as any public college, and even to a religious seminary. About the only thing G.I. Bill money would not pay for was a bartending or dancing course. It has since been noted that the G.I. Bill is in practice a large-scale national voucher system for higher education.

In 1945 a general education aid bill was again introduced, but it died in the Senate Labor and Public Welfare Committee, although the House Education and Labor Committee almost reported it out.

President Truman urged passage of a general-aid bill in 1946. Senator Robert Taft of Ohio, a leading conservative, reversed himself to support the idea, but the bill failed to reach the floor of either chamber. That same year the bill establishing the National Science Foundation passed the Senate, but died in the House Commerce Committee. The School Lunch Program was established in 1946, although federal milk programs did not begin until about 1954.

In 1947 the National Science Foundation legislation was cleared by both chambers and sent to the White House, where President Truman vetoed it because the foundation's proposed director would have been responsible only to an executive committee, which in turn would have been responsible only to 24 private foundations. The President thought this was too much independence for the NSF and reneged on his promise to support the bill, which came back for two more tries, winning enactment on the third, in 1950. Also in 1947 the general school aid bill was reported out of the Senate Labor and Public Welfare Committee for the first time, and was debated on the floor of the Senate. That year's version would have benefited even wealthy states, so nothing passed the Senate, because of objection to that characteristic.

A different version of general aid did pass the Senate in 1948, by 58 votes to 22, but did not reach the House floor.

The National Science Foundation bill also passed the Senate, but not the House. 1948 was an election year, and both party platforms endorsed the concept of federal aid to education.

General aid to education passed the Senate, 58–15, the next year, but set off a heated debate over the eligibility of religious schools for federally aided programs. Francis Cardinal Spellman and Eleanor Roosevelt began their famous series of disputes in the press over the prohibition of aid to private schools.

Religious controversy again caused the demise of the education bill in 1950, when the House Education and Labor Committee voted 12–13 not to report out the bill. Among those voting to kill the legislation were Congressmen John Kennedy and Richard Nixon. Impact aid was more or less made permanent that year with passage of PL-815, authorizing federal monies for construction, and PL-874, authorizing federal monies for teacher salaries in the impacted areas. Specific authorizations for appropriations were not made in the two laws; instead, criteria were established for deciding eligibility and the extent of the assistance to be received. In future years Presidents Eisenhower and Kennedy tried to reduce the program, unsuccessfully. The 1950 Housing Act authorized grants to colleges for the construction of dormitories, moving the federal government further into the field of higher education.

Proponents of general federal aid to education tried a different tack in 1951. Oil reserves in the tidelands, off the coastlines of several states, were being discussed, and the question of state or federal ownership and taxation rights was big. Educators wanted to see the federal government own the rights, and apply tax proceeds to educational causes. In 1952 and 1953 "oil for education" was again discussed and debated, but with nothing to show for the effort.

In 1954 the whole picture changed again, with the Supreme Court handing down *Brown v. Board of Education*, which outlawed racially segregated schools. Southern legislators quickly lost enthusiasm for federal aid to education: it might bring forced integration. Further, President Eisenhower had come out against general aid for the time being. Congressional friends of the educationist cause did try to get an aid bill, but to no avail.

The following year Eisenhower sent Congress a proposal to authorize $1.1 billion for federal aid to school construction, most of it to be repaid over time. It died in Senate committee, and Judge Smith's House Rules Committee sat on the version produced by the House Education and Labor Committee. In late November the White House Conference on Education convened, to the chorus of predictable accusations that it was stacked with opponents of federal aid. On December 1, however, the White House Conference endorsed the concept of federal aid.

By 1956 the race issue was coming into its own, and New York's Adam Clayton Powell was able to attach an amendment on the House floor that effectively killed the entire bill. An interesting situation developed in Congress: because they knew that amendments to bar aid to segregated schools would drive away needed southern votes, legislators who opposed *any* aid sometimes introduced such amendments, recognizing the net effect of their measures. Northern liberals who favored federal aid to education sometimes found themselves in the peculiar position of arguing against civil rights amendments whose intrinsic merits they favored. Withholding federal aid may or may not have speeded up integration in some areas, but the states that most needed financial assistance also tended to be states with a heritage of segregation.

By 1957, talk of cutting the federal budget was gaining some popularity, and that, combined with the segregation controversy, again killed the education bill on the floor. Hints of fiscal conservatism were abandoned in 1958, in a rush to enact the National Defense Education Act before the elections. Republican support for NDEA did not save congressional seats, however. The Democrats won big that year, so that in 1959 they were not inclined to compromise. Eisenhower proposed a bill to make federal payments over 30 or 35 years to local districts to help them pay the debt service on school-construction bonds, but his measure made no provision for increasing teachers' salaries. Liberals called this the "bankers' education bill" and scorned it. One bill did pass the House, but only after a floor vote forced it out of the Rules Committee.

In 1960, another election year, the general-aid-to-education bill came very close. It would have passed, but the House Rules Committee refused to authorize a House-Senate Conference Committee to reconcile differing versions of the bill. The next year, the scenario was repeated. The Rules Committee, packed so as to give the Kennedy administration a one-vote margin, helped kill the general-aid bill, much to the embarrassment of President Kennedy, who had made aid to education a big issue. On the campaign trail Kennedy had promised that although he was a Roman Catholic, if elected he would go out of his way to prevent his Catholic sentiments from influencing his decisions. In keeping with this, his education bill made no provision for private or parochial schools to benefit from the general aid. The racial and religious controversies, together with the opposition from conservative Republicans, were enough to defeat the proposal.

Kennedy made no effort to push for general aid in 1962, preferring to present Congress with a shopping list of programs: educational TV, subsidies for education of the handicapped, programs to combat adult illiteracy, support for medical and dental education, programs for migrant workers' education, a Federal Advisory Council on the Arts, and construction and salaries for elementary and secondary education. Congress gave him only the educational TV proposal. The House Rules Committee was still a major bottleneck; and Democrats complained that there were too many bills. Priorities were too vague.

In January 1963 Kennedy sent another omnibus education bill to Congress, containing 25 proposals. The bill was divided, and three major provisions were enacted: the medical and dental school assistance, assistance for adult basic education (as part of the Manpower Development and Training Act), and the Higher Education Facilities Act for college aid.

Lyndon Johnson had better control of Congress than Kennedy, and he was in a position to exploit the vast popular sympathy for the dreams of John F. Kennedy. Both factors enabled the Economic Opportunity Act to become law in 1964, as well as the Library Services Act, which had been around in proposal form for 14 years, and the expansion of the NDEA into subjects not so clearly connected to defense—history, geography, civics, and English. Impact aid was extended as usual. With the Economic Opportunity Act came Head Start and an adult education program; with the Higher Education Facilities Act the noose was prepared for today's federal strangulation of independent universities through dependence on federal subsidy; through the Library Services Act the groundwork was laid for today's heavy reliance on multimedia educational strategies and resources.

Johnson won the big plum in 1965: the Elementary and Secondary Education Act. Strongly geared toward the disadvantaged, it was not the general-aid-to-education bill that the professional lobby had advocated. But it was a breakthrough. The Higher Education Facilities Act became law in the same session of Congress, establishing federal scholarships, books for college libraries, and the idealistic Teacher Corps programs.

What had changed by 1965 to allow the comprehensive federal education bill to pass? The 1964 elections are probably the main part of the answer: Johnson had a two-to-one nominal majority in the House, 295 Democrats versus 140 Republicans. There were 69 freshmen Democrats, many of whom joined the new Democratic Study Group, which was strongly for general aid. A "21-day rule" was established in the House to bypass the bottleneck of the conservative House Rules Committee. It provided that 21 days after a standing committee requested a rule allowing debate on a given bill, the Speaker of the House could bring that bill to the floor without House Rules Committee compliance. This heavy-handed tactic was repealed in the 90th Congress—after it had immortalized the programs of Lyndon Johnson.

Compromises were very carefully worked out to satisfy the demands of the racial and religious interests, so that technicalities like the distribution formula and the poverty-level definition became the only major controversies. The Democrat leadership took pains to preclude the introduction of any substantive amendments from the House floor, for fear that these might disrupt the interest-group balances. Sure enough, no amendments passed. Eleven days after the House passed ESEA, the Senate did likewise. That is remarkable alacrity for so large and complicated a bill.

Also important: the lobby groups shifted to support of the Elementary and Secondary Education Act. The National Education Association had opposed any general aid that allowed nonpublic schools to receive assistance, but the American Federation of Teachers had been more flexible. NEA's continuing resistance had begun to annoy the U. S. Office of Education. When it became obvious by 1964 that ESEA was likely to pass, NEA feared—logically enough—that unless it patched up relations with USOE, its future input on policy matters might not be welcomed as warmly as the organization would like. Combined with the threat of competition from the AFT, this perception caused NEA to reconsider.

The National Council of Churches previously had opposed general aid that gave help to Roman Catholic schools; it too reconsidered. The National Catholic Welfare Conference, then in the process of becoming the U. S. Catholic Conference, had always wanted aid, but only if Catholic schools would benefit. The ESEA compromise seemed acceptable, so the Catholic bishops supported the measure. By this time the old Catholic–Republican–Southern Democrat coalition probably would have been unable to halt the bandwagon anyway.

The compromise that pleased the church-state group had been worked out by John Gardner, who promoted educational aid as an adjunct to the poverty program and was rewarded by being named secretary of the Department of

Health, Education, and Welfare. Gardner championed the "child-benefit concept," according to which the student, rather than the church that sponsors his school, is deemed to be aided by a particular program. This, of course, has become increasingly plausible since ESEA went into effect, as established religious education more and more fails to imbue its pupils with religious principles. But in 1965 it was more theoretical, though satisfactory to a Supreme Court headed by Earl Warren.

By 1965 President Johnson had amply demonstrated his commitment to the cause of civil rights, so that it was simple enough to tack onto ESEA a provision that denied aid to any school that violated the Civil Rights Act of 1964. Who could object? Congress merely wanted to enforce the law of the land. In subsequent years, the act was amended and amended —to prohibit sex discrimination, for example. As a result, schools today are bound by regulations and laws that did not exist when they began receiving federal aid.

The ESEA Route to Tyranny

Was ESEA necessary? Are America's schools in danger of succumbing to federal control as a consequence of ESEA? These two questions have been asked in all the debates over federal aid.

Educationists, of course, claimed there was an urgent need for the federal government to "do something." In the 1950s, public school enrollment had climbed 45 percent.[6] The supposedly overburdened local school systems could not pay enough to compete with other industries for decent teachers. President Kennedy noted in his 1961 Education Message to Congress that some 90,000 teachers fell short of full certification standards, and that 600,000 new classrooms were needed in the next decade to meet the projected demand.[7] To him, it seemed simple enough to solve the problem with federal money, and he thought his program "modest . . . with ambitious goals."[8] He saw no need to worry about federal encroachment: "Education must remain a matter of state and local control, and higher education a matter of individual choice,"[9] he said. That settled the matter. Kennedy was confident that the investment of $866 million over three years would "pay rich dividends in the years ahead, in increased economic growth, in enlightened citizens, in national excellence."[10]

The National Education Association generated some of the statistical ammunition in the debate and agreed that professional standards must be raised:

> Very soon we must begin to think very seriously about making the master's degree the basic requirement for elementary as well as secondary school teachers. If it took four years of college education to teach the children of the 1930s, it is certainly logical to say that it should take five years of preparation to teach the children of the 1960s.[11]

A more farfetched disguise of self-interest would be hard to imagine: after all, the babies of the 1960s were not born knowing nuclear physics. Their elementary school teachers did not have to know any more than their parents' elementary teachers in order for them to learn. The way things have turned out, one might wish that the teachers of the children of the sixties had known as much as the teachers of the previous generation.

Proponents of ESEA harped on another theme: property taxes are already too high; there is no new state and local base to be tapped for more money for education; therefore, it must come from federal sources. That theme is still being sounded today. Educators don't mention that if federal taxes were lowered, local taxes might be raised without inciting a revolution. The patronizing education experts assumed, or pretended to assume, that local communities would not want to fund education at higher levels, and that if they had the option of voting against higher taxes locally, citizens certainly would do so. But why would local communities vote against more money for schools if their children were the ones on split-day schedules in overcrowded classrooms with unqualified teachers? The question wasn't faced.

Economist Roger Freeman pointed out that it was unnecessary to dismiss the competence of local authorities to raise revenue. From 1944 to 1961 federal revenues grew by 68 percent, while state and local revenues grew by 259 percent, evidence that state and local governments succeeded in increasing taxes. In the decade of the 1960s, enrollment was projected to expand only about 22 percent, about half the rate of the 1950s. National income during the same period was expected to grow by 40 or 50 percent. "Why should states and communities not be able to keep raising their school appropriations sufficiently in the decade of the 60s?" Freeman asked.[12] He was not answered. Another critic of federal aid pointed out that the American people were generous in support of their schools: from $215 million nationally for schools in 1899–1900, expenditures had gone to $14 billion in 1959–60, and from 1950 to 1961 alone, had risen by over 100 percent.[13] But no one wanted to hear about the sufficiency of local and state revenues. America was discovering the perverse joys of self-criticism and guilt. It did not want to hear how well it had done in the past, but preferred to flagellate itself for failing to meet the ideals of liberalism.

Roger Freeman found some errors or discrepancies in the statistics circulated by the education lobby. For example, NEA reported early in 1960 that enrollment would rise that year by 1,447,525, but teachers on payroll by only 60,422. The next year's edition of "Estimates of School Statistics" revealed that enrollment had risen, in fact, by only 1,085,660, while teachers had increased by 70,017: 10,000 more teachers and almost 362,000 fewer pupils than predicted.[14] The miscue was not publicized. The secretary of HEW reported in early 1960 that classroom construction had dropped from 70,000 per year in

1958–59 to 62,700 in 1959–60. But a January 1961 summary, discovered by Freeman, showed 69,400 classrooms under construction in 1959–60, and about as many for 1960–61.[15] The presence of 7,000 more classrooms than were originally counted was not publicized either. Freeman also predicted a teacher surplus by the end of the 1960s.[16] How ironic that today's teacher surplus is the pretext the profession uses for demanding more federal aid, when that surplus was in part caused by federal aid a decade earlier.

A more serious consequence of federal involvement than even the waste of money is the shift of educational policymaking to Washington. By 1976 just about everybody on the educationist spectrum, and all segments of the public, were complaining regularly about growing federal control and the inconvenience, injustice, and problems it causes. In 1961 predictions of heavy-handed bureaucratic control were regarded as ultrarightist nonsense. After all, President Kennedy had promised that control would remain with states and localities. Wrote one supporter of federal aid:

> It seems that the argument against government control is an argument designed to knock down a straw man. Control in this sense implies that the Congress or the discretionary administrative body would prepare formulas or rules which would determine the conduct of state and local school authorities. This kind of control has never been proposed and is not worthy of consideration. . . . The payment of three-quarters of a billion dollars a year . . . to elementary and secondary school budgets . . . will increase vastly in the immediate future [but] does not provide a handy control to federal administrators, regardless of how devious they might be.[17]

Republican Senator John Sherman Cooper, who should have known better, ridiculed one objection to federal handouts, that "teachers would come to depend on a federal aid program—that they would lose their close relationship with the local community."[18]

And Sidney Sufrin, an economics professor and consultant to the New York State School Boards Association, specifically outlined the mechanisms for federal control as it came to be practiced, and still professed to believe that the mere invocation of American "tradition and custom" would be sufficient to stem the tide of federal dictate:

> Clearly the Congress could not write into law all the administrative provisions necessary to run the national school system. Congress would . . . have to delegate authority to an executive agency. . . . The agency which received the delegation of power would then be in a position, theoretically at least, to prepare rules, policies, and guides to the school system of the entire United States.
>
> But this in itself is not sensible, since in the American scene education is historically, by tradition and by operating custom, a local and state matter. . . .[19]

Not everyone was so naive. There were a few observers who saw that federal control would follow federal aid, and said so, and welcomed both with open arms. Perhaps there were more of that persuasion who kept their happiness to themselves.

The perennially leftist *New Republic* espoused this position, on the Orwellian ground that federal control brought more "freedom" to local schools. The editors of the *New Republic* doubtless found themselves more in sympathy with federal bureaucrats than with middle Americans:

> Once Federal responsibility is an established principle (it is already an established fact), will Congress not feel compelled to remedy what it sees as the

more glaring defects of the schools? And won't these remedies mean changing the way local schools operate? . . . But if congressional appropriations lead sooner or later to congressional control, does it follow, as everyone seems to assume, that this is undesirable, much less disastrous? Americans are still shackled by the Jeffersonian untruth that the best government governs least, and that central government is worst of all.[20]

Myron Lieberman, then a staff member of the Educational Research Council of Greater Cleveland and an AFT activist, and now on the Board of Directors of Phi Delta Kappa, the professional education fraternity, was even more emphatic:

Public education in the United States has been strangled for more than a century by the myth that local control is a good thing. . . . As a practical matter . . . our present system results in the same kind of intellectual protectionism that characterizes schools in totalitarian countries. . . .
Intellectually, local control of education is already a corpse. The only question is how long these and other myths can prolong its zombie-like existence in a highly interdependent society. . . . The indications are, however, that the practical sense of the American people will be forced to assert itself, and that they will develop a centralized school system while simultaneously reaffirming their faith that any such system is un-American.[21]

Lieberman's cynicism seems to have proven prophetic in the last dozen years or so, but at the price of great harm to American schoolchildren. The leftists of the early 1960s have seen their wishes come true; the American public has been relieved of control of its public schools. One cannot help wondering what else they want.

NDEA and ESEA

At the end of calendar year 1965, then, where did the federal government stand on education?

The last pre-ESEA year for which data on federal expenditures by agency are available is 1958–59. In that year $618,-394,064 was spent on education through 18 agencies.[22] By 1965 a few agencies had been added: both the Office of Economic Opportunity and the Manpower Development and Training Administration had started up educational programs. In 1958 the National Defense Education Act became law, to the tune of about $1 billion, but without establishing a new agency.

President Eisenhower got the NDEA into law, and when it expired in 1962, President Kennedy tried to make some major amendments, modifying or eliminating some programs, as well extending other programs. What he got was a two-year extension with no substantive amendments, costing $500,-200,000. In the space of four years a strong enough constituency had been created to ensure not only the survival but the health and growth of education handouts.

The provisions of NDEA, according to title, were as follows:

Title I. Statement of purpose, with customary disclaimer of federal control of education.

Title II. Money to university and college student-loan funds. Eisenhower wanted federal scholarships, but instead loan funds were established. Federal funds could provide a maximum of 90 percent of any college's student loan program; undergraduates could borrow $1,000 a year up to five years; if the borrower became a teacher, 50 percent of the loan could be canceled at 10 percent per year of teaching; if the borrower became a teacher in a low-income area, an additional 50 percent of the loan could be canceled at 15 percent per year. Here is one cause of the much lamented teacher surplus of the 1970s.

Title III. Matching federal grants to states for public

schools, and 10-year loans to private schools, for purchase of equipment for science, math, or foreign-language instruction.

Title IV. This was the bone to the graduate school lobby. It established 5,500 three-year graduate fellowships, to be used only in new or expanded graduate programs.

Title V. The pork barrel for the state education agencies, this title authorized grants to assist them in establishing and maintaining testing, guidance, and counseling services in secondary schools. With the security this brought to counseling, the subprofession of the semiprofession of education, revised and expanded guidance programs became an established feature of public school life.

Title VI. Grants to establish advanced institutes for modern foreign languages.

Title VII. Grants for research into modern teaching aids—another gift to the educationist-technocrat group.

Title VIII. Added a new section to the 1946 Vocational Education Act, and authorized grants to states to assist in training highly skilled technicians.

Title IX. Authorized the National Science Foundation to establish a Science Information Service.

Title X. Authorized assistance to state education agencies to improve their statistics gathering, mentioned a few administrative details, and required a loyalty oath for receipt of money under this act. One amendment did succeed in the 1962 extension of NDEA: the elimination of the loyalty-oath requirement.

The National Defense Education Act was passed in the heat of the national furor over Sputnik. Of a sudden, Americans—or at least their media people and opinionmakers—realized that American children were not learning as much as European or Soviet youngsters. The cold war was still cold enough to make that thought uncomfortable. The response was typically Yankee: spend more money; our youth must have the best education money can buy, the assumption being that money was the significant, perhaps the only, variable in education. That attitude grew stronger throughout the 1960s, as

109

money was viewed as the solution for all social problems until such time as hyperfunded education could get around to correcting them. Because the rationale behind NDEA was more defense than education, however, for a while only languages and scientific or technical subjects qualified for assistance. By 1968 education was more popular than defense, and the program was opened up to the liberal arts generally, making it just another education handout.

ESEA, of course, never wore the guise of anything but a cash subsidy to education, although it was presented as assistance to the education of deprived children in particular. Technically, the Elementary and Secondary Education Act of 1965 was tacked onto one of the innumerable impact-aid bills as a long amendment; but its status has always been that of a separate law. In 1965 ESEA had eight titles:

Title I. This returned tax money to local districts, via state education agencies, for serving the "special educational needs of educationally deprived children" in whatever way the locality felt best. A formula for deciding how much Title I money a district could receive was: multiply the number of children in the district who are from low-income homes by one-half the state's average per-pupil expenditure. This was broadened in 1966 so that any state could use the national average rather than the state average to determine its allotment. In states with low per-pupil expenditures this could mean a very significant increase in federal money. Notice the great emphasis on statistics as the basis of governmental decisionmaking. The element of human judgement was eliminated with almost surgical completeness from the money-dispensing end of the business. At the opposite end, however, sort of the reverse occurred, as medical care, guidance, food service, and various kinds of counseling suddenly became the appropriate duties of the school, an overpersonalization that teachers who would rather not be social workers have much cause to regret. This shift in the concept of education, from a primarily intellectual pursuit to a process of social amelioration, was not debated in Congress. Maybe it was not recognized for what it was.

110

The debate over ESEA in the year of passage centered almost exclusively on the above-mentioned formula, and whether or not it was fair to the poor states and their citizens. That such an insubstantial issue was the center of attention shows how completely Lyndon Johnson controlled Congress. The attitude seemed to be: substantive issues have been debated for more than 20 years, now let's have the legislation, never mind that the substantive debate is unresolved—and to pacify your argumentative impulse, here's a formula to fight over.

Title II. This was popular with the library lobby, for it granted money to states for library resources, textbooks, and other printed material. Both public and private schools could procure such materials with Title II funds; however, title and control of all material had to stay with the public agency administering the request, and before any materials could be bought for private schools, they had to be approved for use in public schools. Because most districts already were budgeted for textbooks, Title II tended to give the most benefit to libraries.

Title III. This was the title whose purpose and practice have been to seek out and foster educational innovation. Grants were made for developmental educational centers, which could serve as models for, or supplements to, regular curricula and programs. In the initial law the U. S. commissioner of education made grants directly to agencies requesting them; but in 1966 Congress transferred most of the control to state education agencies, which, naturally, had to draw up state plans to suit the commissioner.

What has come out of Title III? It has been a boon to the educationist-technocrats and their gadgetry, funding things like special equipment for science and foreign languages, or educational radio and TV production. Title III has funded development of many curriculum "packages," some in standard academic subjects, some in "special" courses like "Political and Legal Education" and "Environmental Education." Under its aegis have been experiments with year-round school sessions, with credit for student service to the local community, with lavish Pupil Personnel Services Demonstration Projects. Art and music courses, and special rural education programs, were authorized as well as the guidance and the gimmicks.

Title IV. This was the only title that actually did not use up all the money appropriated for it: federal construction assistance to new educational research facilities. In later years authorizations for this title were omitted. Evidently, the public schools were found to be fine research facilities just as they were.

Title V. Here was the direct aid to the state education bureaucracies: federal grants to state departments of education for statewide planning, "improving the competence of employees" and of teacher-training efforts; and more and better data gathering. There was the inevitable allotment for experimental programs, initially 15 percent of the authorization for the title, to be made directly by the U.S. commissioner. In 1965 this special allotment was reduced to five percent. The impact of this title is hard to estimate, since no one can say whether the "professionalization" of educational bureaucrats would have occurred as rapidly without the assistance. Certainly, every state department of education has done things because of its federal subservience that it might not have done otherwise.

Title VI. Not part of the 1965 act, this was added in 1966 to provide special assistance for the handicapped. Aid under this title went not to local agencies, but only to states. In 1967 the provision was broadened further, to include recruitment of personnel and regional resource centers.

Title VII. An addition from 1967, this purposed to improve the education of children from non-English-speaking families. Although projects have been proposed for teaching children in at least 17 different languages, the intended and practiced emphasis has been upon Chicano and Puerto Rican children.

Title VIII. Also from 1967, this was the antidropout section, which funded local demonstration programs for the ben-

112

efit of other localities. At one point a small project of technical assistance to rural schools, to assist them in applying for federal aid, was found in this title; that has been eliminated. Added were a nutrition program in 1971 and an Indian education plan in 1973.

The act contained some miscellany too. There was the usual repudiation of federal control over curriculum, selection of books, and personnel, and of payment for religious worship or instruction. In 1966 Congress tacked on language prohibiting the federal government from requiring assignment or transportation of students or teachers to overcome segregation—in short, an antibusing amendment. Of course, school districts were allowed to use federal funds for busing if it was a local decision to do so—to help in the education of the deprived children in the district. When the federal courts started ordering busing, however, this amendment became a dead letter.

In 1966 Congress also transferred the adult education programs of the Office of Economic Opportunity to the U.S. commissioner of education, as part of the ESEA programs, with the reservation of 20 percent for the commissioner to expend directly on experimental programs.

By 1967 the dependence of local districts on federal support was so great that Congress decided to make a standard procedure of approving appropriations one year in advance of the time the funds are to be given. This has been the custom since, and is dearly cherished by educational planners who must arrange their budgets a year in advance. Yet the typical fraction of a local-education budget that comes from the federal government is less than 10 percent. Imagine how desperately American education would depend on Washington if the 33 percent federal funding demanded by NEA were to become standard.

Also by 1967 the problems with categorical, or specific, aid were again becoming apparent, as they had been to the 1931 Advisory Committee. Republican Albert Quie introduced a hotly debated amendment to substitute block grants for categorical aid: instead of earmarking a dozen different checks for special purposes, a block grant, or one check, would be given to the state education agency, to divvy up according to priorities and standards determined by the state. Had this amendment been adopted, much more power would have gone to state education bureaucracies, and the proliferation of HEW staff might not have been so great. But the proposal ran into considerable opposition, including opposition from church groups, which feared they would lose their federal money if the states administered it: many states have laws forbidding aid to religious schools. As it was, the Quie amendment was defeated.

Since 1965: Expansion and Reorganization

The block-grant scheme was an idea whose time was just arriving. It became a major point in President Nixon's education program during his first term, under the catch phrase of revenue sharing. Other points in Nixon's program during the first term included a national institute to direct educational research; this became the National Institute of Education, set up in 1972. A similar proposal for a national foundation to encourage innovation in postsecondary education was rejected. A college-student assistance plan and "emergency school aid" to meet desegregation costs were the other major points of his program. Both were enacted, in modified form, by a spendthrift Congress that passed four federal aid-to-education bills that Nixon felt compelled to veto. The 1972 version of the Higher Education Facilities Act, with $19 billion in authorization, was finally signed. But the first of Walter Mondale's seemingly endless succession of child-development bills was vetoed in December 1971. Along with haggling over spending, desegregation and equality of education consumed inordinate portions of time and attention during that first Nixon administration. Constitutional amendments concerning

114

prayer and busing came as close as they are likely to come to consideration or enactment.

In his second term, when ESEA was up for extension, President Nixon proposed as an alternative the education revenue-sharing plan. This would have consolidated some 32 categorical grants into five main block grants: aid to the disadvantaged, impact aid, aid to the handicapped, vocational education aid, aid for supporting services. There were hearings in the House Education and Labor Committee, but the education interest groups were definite in their opposition. During 1973 Nixon was besieged on many fronts. Aside from the Watergate troubles, he faced multiple lawsuits arising out of his attempt to close down the Office of Economic Opportunity and to impound other funds. By June 1973 Nixon had to abandon any hope of getting education revenue sharing enacted.

In 1974 the ranking Republican member of the House Education Committee, Albert Quie, did succeed in consolidating four programs under Title II of ESEA: strengthening of state departments of education, supplementary services, nutrition and health, and dropout prevention. ESEA was revised and extended in 1974, becoming Public Law 94–94.

Gerald Ford took up where Nixon and Quie left off, and in 1976 proposed a major consolidation of 24 elementary and secondary programs into a single block grant. He did stipulate that certain portions of the money would be earmarked, in order to maintain what were by then explicit federal priorities: assistance to the handicapped, to the disadvantaged, and for vocational education. Beyond those limits, the discretion of the local district would have prevailed.

President Ford geared the appeal of his proposal to the economic fact that administrative costs in categorical grant programs were running around 10 percent of the entire cost, whereas the administration of other general revenue-sharing programs was about one-twelfth of one percent.[23] The education lobby, never particularly interested in fiscal caution, was predictably cool to Ford's proposal, but no great outcry was

115

raised against it. Probably this was because Ford's proposal was never a threat. Congressman Quie introduced the measure reluctantly, and not one senator would endorse it. A spokesman for the National Association of Secondary School Principals, at whose convention Ford made the proposal, stated, significantly, that "the grassroots are more interested [in consolidation] than the national representatives," indicating "a general trend in the country toward greater local control."[24] The grassroots may indeed want local control, but the Washington pressure groups still want Washington control. There need be no suspense regarding the outcome, at least for the foreseeable future.

The education revenue-sharing proposal was a lukewarm gesture, anyway: a compromise in principle between the fact of dependence on federal aid and the ideal of local control. Theorizing about political possibilities is not our purpose here, but it may well be that such a gesture, being neither fish nor fowl, will never win much support. It lacks any intrinsic appeal. Some philosophically consistent proposals have been advanced, but they have never gotten much action because they represented the conservative view. At least, however, their integrity deserves respect. The proposals also have intrinsic merit.

During the 93rd Congress, when ESEA was up for extension, Representative Earl Landgrebe (R–Ind.) introduced H.R. 10639, technically an extension of ESEA, but with a novel provision that would have reduced the funding level each year: Title I was to be extended four years, with funding levels reduced by 25 percent each year. During the phaseout, only programs that promoted cognitive skills, particularly reading and math, were to be funded. Title III, the innovation funder, was to be similarly restricted, with social-development and behavior-modification programs specifically excluded. Landgrebe's bill would have added a statement of moral and legal parental rights, required parental permission before children could participate in experimental programs, prohibited

116

psychotherapy techniques, and guaranteed the right to work for teachers.

Admittedly, the Landgrebe bill was something of a "shopping list" of parents' rights principles. It was introduced for the purpose of broadening the spectrum of debate to matters of principle, away from the interminably fascinating (to Congress) technicalities and formulas. Landgrebe offered a rallying point for education-minded conservatives. They were now able to say to the educationists, "This is our position, our substitute proposal. Why don't you consider adopting some of our demands, since we're not going to vote for yours?" At least that strategy brought criticism of ESEA into the forum of public debate.

Congressmen Dave Treen (R–La.) and Bill Armstrong (R–Colo.) came up with a further idea. Along with the major provisions of the Landgrebe bill, Treen and Armstrong proposed to phase out the federal excise tax on tobacco. More money is presently paid in federal tobacco taxes than is given to the states through ESEA. The plan was to decrease the federal tobacco tax, allowing states to increase their share of the tax, while not raising the consumer's cost of tobacco. States could then apply their revenues from the tobacco tax to education, and the net result would more than compensate for the ESEA money they would lose, not to mention the added benefit of giving the states the responsibility for administration and decisionmaking. That the Treen-Armstrong proposal got nowhere confirms the suspicion of many parents that it is not the money so much as the control that the educational planners want.

It is not surprising that the Treen-Armstrong and the Landgrebe proposals never reached the floor of Congress. Earl Landgrebe was defeated for reelection in 1974, and so was unable to carry on his leadership of the parents' rights cause. ESEA was extended in 1974 for five years, so that 1978 will be the next year for major action on it. That will be the second session of the 95th Congress, a disconcertingly large number of whose members were elected with NEAPAC assistance.

After the revisions of 1973 and 1974, ESEA emerged hardly recognizable. Eleven titles had been created, under which grants were made and programs operated, as follows. This information can be helpful if one is trying to trace the history of a grant: for instance, to know that a certain program was Title III in 1970 and Title VI in 1975 is of little use unless one knows what those titles signify.

1. Grants for disadvantaged education
2. Support and innovation for
    a. costs of consolidating the programs
    b. strengthening state departments of education
    c. Supplementary Services (innovative programs)
    d. nutrition and health
    e. dropout prevention
3. Bilingual education
4. Right to read
5. Follow-through
6. Educational broadcasting facilities
7. Civil rights advisory services (technical assistance in planning and implementing desegregation plans)
8. Libraries and instructional resources (funded through a separate appropriation for library resources)
9. Educational television programming ("Sesame Street" et al.)
10. Drug-abuse education
11. Environmental education

When ESEA comes up for renewal it will probably be reorganized again. Although supplemental appropriations can be made anytime, major policy changes are usually decided when the whole act is up for renewal. And each time it is redesigned, the people who knew it before redesigning become a little more valuable to the beneficiaries of the aid, and their jobs are a little more secure. This factor should not be overlooked. More and more the livelihood of school boards, state departments of education, and institutions of higher education depends on federal handouts. Such handouts are not given without asking, but knowing what to ask for and how to ask for it is a highly specialized line of work, sometimes called "grantsmanship." When President Nixon was trying to phase out the Office of Economic Opportunity, he appointed Howard Phillips acting director. Since there was still money at OEO's disposal, Phillips and his staff thought it would make sense to try to direct some of that money into worthwhile projects. One or two such projects did get funded, but many more did not, and part of the reason was the ineptitude of the Phillips staff, most of them nonbureaucrats, at managing the grant process. While the task is hardly noble, it can be quite difficult.

Consider for a moment the monumental task of keeping abreast of the educational programs administered by one division, the Office of Education, for fiscal year 1977. That year OE had responsibility for the following programs:[25]

- ESEA, at about $2,211,888,000
- Indian Education, at a budget authority of $42,055,000 (four categories of grants)
- Impact Aid, with $325,000,000 (construction, operation, and maintenance grants)
- Emergency School Aid, with $249,700,000 (to meet problems incident to desegregation)
- Education for the Handicapped, with $236,375,000 (six programs, including an early-childhood one)
- Occupational, Vocational, and Adult Education, with $606,849,000 (six categories of state vocational education grants; five categories of other grants)
- Higher Education, with $1,994,251,000 (seventeen categories of grant)
- Library Resources, with $137,330,000 (five categories)
- Special Projects and Training, with $67,350,000 (ten projects, including metric education, career education, education of the gifted, women's educational equity, "packaging and dissemination," and Teacher Corps)

119

• Student Loan Insurance Fund and Higher Education Facilities Loan and Insurance Fund (financial affairs of which are so tangled as to render impossible a simple statement of budget authority for fiscal year 1977)
• Educational Activities Overseas, with $2,000,000

To carry out all these programs, the Office of Education was budgeted, for salaries and expenses, about $115,434,000 for fiscal year 1977.

Nor are Office of Education programs the sum of federal education programs. Established in 1972 was the National Institute of Education, primarily a research and development think tank. Recent programs here include development of means to acquire basic skills; search for improvement of understanding of the relationship between education and work; and an educational equity project to develop means "to help the educational community meet its responsibilities to provide high-quality education for those with limited educational opportunities" (translation: find and eradicate racial, cultural, language, sex, and socioeconomic distinctions). NIE had for fiscal year 1977 a budget authority of $90,000,000.

The Office of the Assistant Secretary for Education has its own budget authority of the relatively meager amount of $32,946,000. This office handles the Fund for the Improvement of Postsecondary Education; the National Center for Education Statistics; surveys and special studies; and the National Assessment of Educational Progress (NAEP). Information-gathering, and that alone, remember, was the initial purpose of an Office of Education, back in 1857.

Other time-honored federal commitments still remain, as follows:
• Printing House for the Blind: $2,762,000
• Technical Institute for the Deaf: $12,675,000
• Gallaudet College: $40,840,000
• Howard University: $81,909,000

Many of the social reform programs that have provoked controversy because of their debilitating effect on the American family are funded under the Assistant Secretary of HEW for Human Development, rather than under any education authority at all. Included here are such things as federal child development, which includes Head Start ($434,300,000); research and demonstration ($10,700,000); child-abuse prevention ($18,928,000); federal youth development, including the runaway youth program ($5,000,000); research and demonstration ($1,000,000); and youth services system (unfunded in fiscal year 1977), as well as special programs for native Americans ($32,000,000). Other activities of the Human Development office are programs for the aging, some rehabilitation services, and grants for "developmentally disabled" persons, as well as the White House Conference on Handicapped Individuals. The attack on the American family comes not only from educationist and welfarist quarters; the National Academy of Sciences in early 1977 produced a report on the plight of the American family, and made numerous recommendations for federal child and family policies. This report, it was expected, would furnish the pretext for a gaggle of new legislative proposals, just as the 1970 Report of the White House Conference on Children and Youth was the pretext for Walter Mondale's child-development bills.

Cited above are only the chief budget items for education. Experts have estimated that as many as 40 federal agencies have a finger in the educational pie.[26] Keeping track of them is no mean task: nobody in the country could really draw an adequate organizational chart, except perhaps a latter-day Rube Goldberg.

Has ESEA Accomplished Anything?

By fiscal year 1973 ESEA had been responsible for spending over $13 billion, and quite a few people were interested in finding out what ESEA had accomplished. That turned out to be a difficult demand.

Perhaps the best critical study of ESEA's record was compiled by the House Republican Study Committee. Granted, the RSC, as it is called, is a partisan organization. However, the information it provides to the members of Congress who support it is known to be carefully researched and reliable. The committee prepared a detailed fact sheet on ESEA in March 1974 and reached the following conclusion:

> The preponderance of evidence has shown that the Act has achieved little and, in some cases, has caused irreparable harm to American education. Through ESEA and its programs, the faith and trust necessary for any institution to function effectively in this country has been undermined, and the current legislation shows no indication of addressing itself to these very real problems.[27]

This conclusion was reached after a title-by-title analysis of the programs.

Title I, which was funded at $1.8 billion in 1973, represented 81 percent of the total ESEA appropriation. By equating educational failure with poverty, Title I is automatically turned into a poverty program, rather than an education program. No less liberal a source than the *Harvard Educational Review* has called Title I "among the biggest and most expensive losing battles of the War on Poverty."[28]

It is practically impossible to evaluate a program without first determining how the moneys in question have been spent; yet that initial hurdle has been insurmountable for most researchers. What research has been done has been limited to specific "Title I Programs," which represent only a small portion of programs benefiting from Title I money. Yet of these specific programs not much good can be said:

> Nearly all empirical analyses of survey data on educational inputs and outputs such as Project Talent, Equal Educational Opportunity Survey, and ESEA

> Title I evaluations show little or no relationship
> between variations in educational expenditures and
> educational outputs.[29]

This is the same study that found that the ten least successful programs had a slightly higher average cost than the ten most successful programs.[30] A General Accounting Office study found that the reading achievement of 50 percent of students in seven selected districts was higher before they enrolled in Title I programs, and most students either were falling further below national norm or, at best, were failing to close the gap.[31]

It was even more difficult to evaluate how students benefited from Title II, the title that authorized acquisition of library and other published materials. About all that was known was that the program had stimulated support for libraries from other sources.[32]

Title III, the innovative "Supplemental Educational Centers and Services" section, was and always will be impossible to evaluate because there is no one target group. Parents whose children may have suffered through some of the more egregious Title III–funded programs would have a more definite statement of their worth. Not only has a monumental amount of time been wasted under a variety of guises, but in some cases the mental stability of children and their whole moral foundation have been shaken by the "affective education" programs developed under these auspices.[33]

Title V provided grants to state education agencies. No formal evaluation of Title V has ever been made; Congress did not demand to know whether its money was being wasted or put to good use.

Title VI, aimed at the handicapped, was superseded by the Education for the Handicapped Act of 1976, but evaluation of Title VI was not available anyway in the short amount of time, bureaucratically speaking, between 1967 and 1973.

Title VII, bilingual education, was also deemed impossible

to evaluate because the source of data was reports submitted by the individual projects, which, to nobody's surprise, are their own best public relations agents.

Title VIII: Evaluation of dropout-prevention programs was difficult if not meaningless, since only ten school systems received grants during the period 1969–71, without enough lead time before 1973 to do proper evaluations. Of course, there had been no time either to evaluate the nutrition programs or the Indian education programs.

So much for the sound basis of congressional decisionmaking. It should be noted in fairness that the only evaluation stipulated in the original legislation was of Title I programs. But Congress has not bothered to ask for further evaluations since then. Many legislators, it seems, would rather keep pouring billions of the taxpayers' dollars down a rathole than face the organized wrath of the teaching profession.

ESEA appears to have made few tangible achievements. One cannot point proudly to the various programs to demonstrate how America's children have become more literate or more proficient in computational skills. They may have learned how to operate a filmstrip,[34] but how much good will that do for their future? A case can probably be made, although this is not the place to do it, that many Title I children have learned counterproductive things from their Title I experience. Attitudes, for example: toward themselves as deserving of partial treatment and special consideration; toward the government as a source of every blessing; toward middle-class society as stingy and "against" them. Probably no empirical research on this point will ever be attempted, because the "professional" critics could always find fault with it. But common sense and a familiarity with human foibles suggest that such a phenomenon exists.

It has been documented that, for high school students at least, some federal assistance programs create negative incentives: kids *try* to do poor work in high school because "they have special programs for deprived kids with averages 79 and below but not for those 90 and above." The Educational

124

Opportunity Program (EOP) provides more money for indifferent students than other federal scholarships do for students with high grades.[35] Youngsters are not so dumb that they cannot figure out the loopholes and find the inanities in federal programs offered to them. One wonders, though, what respect they have for a system that cynically rewards them for doing poorly. What respect does such a program deserve?

Unquestionably, the massive inundations of federal moneys for educational purposes, broadly defined, have created a whole new socioeconomic class in America. Former Congresswoman Edith Green, a founder of the liberal Democratic Study Group (DSG) at the start of her congressional career, gradually came to be more moderate as she watched the results of liberal schemes unfolding:

> For several years now I have been particularly interested in what I have come to call the "education-poverty-industrial complex"—people and companies devoted to reaping profit from the nation's legitimate interest in education and welfare. . . . What I have learned has not been encouraging. Studies made at my request by my staff and by the General Accounting Office have revealed serious irregularities in numerous areas. Over and over again we have found educators enriching themselves at public expense through sizable consulting fees, often for work of which there is no record at all. Over and over again we have found educational organizations taking money for work not done, for studies not performed, for analyses not prepared, for results not produced. Over and over again we have found educators using public funds for research projects that have turned out to be esoteric, irrelevant, and often not even research.[36]

In the article from which this passage is quoted, the congresswoman goes on to complain specifically about the duplication of research, the abysmal internal organization of the U.S. Office of Education, the unethical practices of USOE and of contractors and grantees, and the uncontrolled commercialism, in the worst sense of that term, threatening to dominate education. Mrs. Green noted that prearrangement of contracts was common, that USOE often disregarded the intent of Congress in making grants, that specifications of contracts were often vague, that solid budget information on grants was unavailable, that evaluation was slipshod or nonexistent, that USOE seemed determined to spend every dime it had regardless of whether there was a worthy proposal offered. The public has no reason to believe the weaknesses pointed out by Mrs. Green have been corrected. In fact, a familiarity with patterns of bureaucratic behavior would suggest the contrary. Yet between calendar years 1972 and 1976 an additional $1,420,671,000[37] was transferred from the pockets of the taxpayers into the hands of this same education-poverty-industrial complex.

Government bureaucracy nowadays has become so pervasive, so demanding that a two-year Federal Paperwork Commission was established in 1975 to study the problem. (A classic bureaucratic maneuver!) Congressman Frank Horton (R–N.Y.), chairman of the commission, stated in late 1976 that federal paperwork requirements were costing the country $40 billion a year. The cost is probably considerably more than that, but Congressman Horton was at least in the ballpark. Still, the head of the International Society of Professional Bureaucrats was unperturbed. Of the Federal Paperwork Commission he said: "We are no longer concerned since we realize that we can produce more paper faster than they are able to implement their nondirective projection for paper residuation."[38] Tongue in cheek? It is hard to say.

One thing is certain: Congress cannot control the education-poverty-industrial complex it created in the 1960s. Parents must not expect salvation to come from Washington. Whether grassroots resistance can paralyze the educationist juggernaut remains to be seen.

126

4

Federal Tyranny

The preceding lengthy description of federal education programs is not, of course, a complete catalog. But the average citizen or parent is only vaguely aware of even those programs. What galvanize him into action are the three "hot" issues that touch parents and children immediately and personally: prayer, busing, and textbooks.

The three "hot" issues have this in common: they are all foisted on American parents by legislation that is not educational in intent or description, or by courts acting in total disregard of the public will, or, worst of all, by bureaucrats acting on their own whim. Busing time and again has been prohibited by Congress in various appropriations bills—but busing continues apace because courts order it. The Supreme Court ordered the desacralizing of the public schools and Congress has not acted to override that decision. The most widely known federal curriculum, *Man: A Course of Study* (MACOS), comes from the National Science Foundation, which is supervised not by any of the congressional education committees, but by the Science and Technology Committee. The outrageous "sex-discrimination guidelines" were promulgated by HEW bureaucrats (acting, it is true, under gen-

127

eral authority of an amendment to the Civil Rights Act). Child-care centers are included under antipoverty legislative authority. From the federal government's point of view, at least, education certainly encompasses all of life.

Roll, Buses, Roll

Busing as a means of transporting students to distant public schools, or to private schools, is nothing new. Most people don't object to it in itself, and about 43 percent of the nation's schoolchildren are transported to school in buses.[1] In 1973–74 that meant about 21.2 million children.[2] The National Institute of Education estimates that about seven percent of those children are bused exclusively to provide racial balance in the public schools,[3] but some suspect that NIE's estimate is low. In any case, busing for racial balance is not busing for education, and therein lies the rub.

Americans are not opposed to integration of public facilities, including schools. The Gallup poll organization asked a series of identical questions in 1963, 1970, and 1975, and the results indicate that neither northern nor southern white parents object to integration as strongly as they once did. Asked whether they would object to sending their children to a school that had a few black children, only 10 percent of northern white parents said yes in 1963, and only three percent in 1975. Southern white parents objected in proportions of 61 percent in 1963, but only 15 percent in 1975. Asked about sending their children to schools where more than half the students are black, however, both northern and southern parents have greater reservations: 53 percent of northern parents and 86 percent of southern parents objected to that in 1963; 47 percent of northern parents and 61 percent of southern parents objected in 1975.[4] Participating in racial integration is not what parents want to spare their children; being outnumbered in a potentially dangerous and probably hostile environment is.

128

Busing was not much of a problem until the end of the 1960s because it scarcely existed prior to that time. The revolutionary Civil Rights Act of 1964 contains the reassuring language: "Nothing herein shall empower any officer or court of the United States to issue any order seeking to achieve a racial balance in any school by requiring the transportation of pupils . . . from one school to another school or one district to another."

It was a classic political gesture. Title IV of the same Civil Rights Act empowered the Justice Department to bring suit for violation of students' civil rights, and Title VI stipulated that no federal funds under any program were to be allowed to school districts that practiced segregation. This was the big stick; the carrot came the following year, in 1965, with the enactment of the Elementary and Secondary Education Act. President Johnson's appointees to the Civil Rights Office at HEW were criticized for their lack of zeal in cutting off federal aid, as were President Nixon's. (Nixon's policy was to seek Justice Department lawsuits in cases of violation.) But the NAACP and other civil rights activists groups did not wait for the wheels of bureaucracy to turn; they filed cases directly with the federal courts. From these courts, then, came the flurry of busing orders.

In 1896 the Supreme Court had heard a case, *Plessy v. Ferguson* (163 U.S. 537), on the subject of racially segregated schools, and had decided that "separate but equal" school systems were quite acceptable. In 1927 a similar case, *Gong Lum v. Rice* (275 U.S. 78), reached the Court, which ruled that segregated schools were a state matter of no concern to the federal government. In the 1930s, the increasingly militant NAACP won several favorable decisions against segregation in higher education.

The year 1954 was memorable for the decision outlawing segregated schools, *Brown v. Board of Education* of Topeka, Kansas (347 U.S. 483). As in some of its other decisions, the Warren Court had only the thinnest of legal precedent for its conclusion and relied heavily on sociological evidence. Sociol-

129

ogy and psychology and demographics continue as the bases for desegregation decisions and busing orders to this day. By the mid-1970s judicial restraint had been thrown to the winds; in Detroit, a federal court of appeals judge, George Edwards, shortly before he was to hand down a supposedly "impartial" decision on a new busing order for the city, appeared before the American Issues Forum to raise the specter of domestic violence unless massive cross-district busing was introduced to purge America of its "strange and dangerous kind of apartheid."[5] If statues outside courthouses show Justice with a blindfold, it does not necessarily mean that her servants are unbiased. They may simply prefer to ignore the facts.

The *Brown* decision ordered the South to desegregate its schools with "all deliberate speed." In most places this meant very little. Some districts adopted "freedom of choice" plans under which students were technically free to choose any school in the district but in practice stayed where they were; some states enacted laws giving local districts the authority to assign pupils to schools on any basis deemed appropriate. Because this kind of law was not passed explicitly to maintain segregation, but to facilitate management and the like, for several years it withstood legal challenges. Eventually, however, the Supreme Court saw through the ruse, and this measure went the way of its predecessors.

In 1966 sociologist James Coleman issued a report of some findings about the achievement of black children in school. The main finding of Coleman's report was that class and family background were of absolutely huge importance in perpetuating inequalities in education. At the time the report was released, however, HEW was busy trying to force desegregation of southern schools, and seized upon the Coleman Report as a new sociological dogma; black children score better on standardized tests when they sit in classrooms with middle-class white children. Therefore, HEW pronounced, black children should sit in classrooms with middle-class white children. Integration is synonymous with quality education, which is synonymous with justice, which in this instance is translated as busing.

Hardly ten years later even James Coleman had reversed his endorsement of busing. He had done another study, which showed that busing and other racial desegregation measures increased racial isolation, encouraged resegregation in the suburbs, and resulted in worse schools than before. Citizens with common sense could have predicted this second finding, just as they could have told any court willing to listen that home environment is more important to a child's achievement than schooling. Coleman, however, discreetly takes no stand on how to remedy the harm done in the name of his original research.

Actually, very little is known about any *good* effects from busing. When Daniel P. Moynihan, then ambassador to the United Nations, asked the National Institute of Education to provide him with some conclusions about busing, he was sent 60 pounds of substantiating documents and a whole list of inconclusive non sequiturs.[6]

It was 1971 before the U.S. Supreme Court decided that "all deliberate speed" was not speedy enough, and sanctioned the first large-scale busing campaign. The case was *Swann v. Charlotte-Mecklenburg Board of Education* (402 U.S. 1, 16). Part of the Court's reasoning was that busing was deserved because the North Carolina city and county in question had deliberately and knowingly taken steps in the past to frustrate the integration of their public schools. It was not necessary to state bluntly, "This is punishment for your past sins." North Carolinians got the idea.

Only a few years earlier HEW had received evidence of intentional segregation in the Chicago public schools and had withheld $32 million from the city's educational handout. Mayor Daley put his machine into action, though, in Congress, in the Democratic Party, and even in the Johnson White House, and next thing you knew, HEW handed over the $32 million. The sins of the South might be visited upon her children, but in the North it was a different matter. There was more than a hint of self-righteousness in the northern senators and congressmen who orated about the need for racial justice in the South.

It was not without a wry feeling of vindication, then, that the South saw the North receive belated equal treatment. The place: Denver, Colorado. The case: *Keyes v. School District No. 1* (40 USLW 3335 [1972]). In 1968 the Denver school board had decided—on its own—to start busing. The goal was to give each school a 20 percent minority, 80 percent white ratio. In 1969 two board members who favored the busing program were defeated at the polls and replaced by two antibusers. Following this rather clear evidence of the public will, the board reverted to the *status quo ante,* occasioning an injunction by the federal court. The judge found that the board's decision to revert to neglecting its duty to integrate not only had a chilling effect upon the constitutional rights of minorities, "it had a freezing effect."[7] The district judge admitted that there was no state policy of segregation, but because the "minority" schools were inferior to the "white" schools in Denver—by virtue of their being minority schools—it was necessary to redress the inequality. The Supreme Court eventually upheld this confused logic in an equally confused opinion. Scholars are still unsure how to interpret *Keyes.*

The next landmark was 1974, *Milliken v. Bradley* (418 U.S. 717), in which the Supreme Court refused to uphold a district court ruling that required busing between Detroit's black schools and the suburban white schools. The basis for that respite was that the suburban districts were not engaging in *de jure* segregation, so no interdistrict remedy was necessary. A year later the Supreme Court ruled just the opposite in Delaware, and mandated mingling of Wilmington's black schools with New Castle County's predominately white schools—having found that New Castle County had encouraged segregation at some time and by some means in the past. It is interesting that the Court, in its efforts to assign the blame

132

for segregation, never bothered to look back to the policies of the Federal Housing Authority and the Veterans' Administration, which used to encourage strictly segregated housing patterns, the ancestors of today's unacceptable segregated neighborhood schools.

Effects of Busing

It would seem superfluous to state that busing does not accomplish what it is supposed to. It does not bring about a joyous mingling of the youth of many races in harmony and delighted self-discovery, culminating in striking academic and social progress. Yet that is the so-called model that the courts seek to realize. Some useful statistics:

Washington, D.C. in 1951 had two separate but equal public school systems, with overall populations of 52 percent black and 48 percent white. By 1957, only three years after the *Brown* decision, the proportion was 71 percent black and 29 percent white in an integrated system. In 1961, when the New Frontier came to town, the public schools were 81 percent black, 19 percent white; by 1967 that was 92 percent black, 8 percent white; and by 1970, 95 percent black, 5 percent white.[8] Washington, D.C., is often cited as an example of "successful busing" because there was no violence. Violence was hardly necessary; retreat to the suburbs was easy in the 1950s and 60s. But, pray tell, what has been accomplished for integration in the public schools of Washington, D.C.?

One of Washington's suburban areas is Prince George's County, Maryland. Prince George's is not one of the affluent suburbs; it has always had a minority population. Before the county was ordered to bus to achieve racial balance there was a districtwide black enrollment of 19 percent. Three years later this was 34 percent. Why? Because of the black flight to the suburbs? Although that phenomenon exists, during the first six months of busing 8,000 students disappeared from the public school system.[9] Who can blame parents for resorting to

133

extreme measures to spare their children the misery and hazards of a cross-county bus ride at 7:10 A.M., to be repeated at 4:30 P.M.?

Another injustice has been perpetrated in Prince George's County. In order to inflate the scores of black students on achievement tests, the Maryland State Board of Education ordered schools to assign preset handicaps to students before the tests were given. These handicaps were calculated on the basis of father's income, mother's education, and place of residence.[10] The more the income and education, the greater the handicap. A policy like this, in the name of racial tranquility, or in the name of anything else for that matter, is an abomination. A black parent will be told his son is doing well. But when the boy scores dismally on his College Board exams no one will be around to explain that these tests are not adjusted for socioeconomic variables (up to now, at least, the College Boards have been straightforward; one never knows what the various committees studying the score declines might recommend). And if he doesn't go to college, but gets a job instead, the Prince George's County graduate is likely to discover that he doesn't get promoted. Rather than realizing this is because he doesn't know as much as he should, he is likely to ascribe the blame for his slow progress to racial discrimination by his supervisors. What has been accomplished by busing students in Prince George's County, and by rigging the test scores so as to boost the feelings of minority groups? Yet Prince George's County is regarded as another highly successful example of integration in action.

Nobody will claim that Louisville and Boston set an example for the nation in their reaction to busing, although the national media duly noted the absence of riots at the start of the 1977–78 school year. Two years of forced busing cost Boston about $56.6 million—Boston residents saw a $53 a year tax increase per $1,000 evaluation of their property.[11] In five months Detroit spent $11 million on busing, excluding police costs. And on top of that, a judge ordered new school construction estimated at $41 million.[12] What about the time-

134

honored American tradition of the citizens, through their school boards, deciding when to build a new school and how much to spend? Or, once a court has decided that a school district committed the sin of segregation sometime in the distant past, does the district forfeit its rights of self-government?

Students at South Boston High School, which was put under federal receivership because local residents did not welcome busing, pass through weapon detectors as they enter school.[13] Parents in Boston did not take kindly to busing: in 1973–74 the Boston public school system had 93,000 students; by the spring semester of 1976, there were only 55,000 and the figure was going down.[14] True, there is a national decline in birthrate. But it is not *that* precipitous.

Inglewood, California had what many citizens, probably most, would consider busing with a happy ending. In 1970 the Inglewood schools were 72 percent white. In 1976, after forced busing, they were 19 percent white, 71 percent black, and 10 percent Chicano. It was obvious to everyone that this was not desirable; the latest news is that a judge in the area has ruled in favor of a return to neighborhood schools.[15] Whether this radical innovation will withstand the legal attacks of busing-happy activists is a big question.

Portland, Oregon transferred 3,000 black students to white neighborhood schools, but because white children were not forced to attend black schools as well, no large-scale exodus took place. Here again is evidence of the willingness of middle-class white parents to be a part of integration, while refusing to imperil their children's safety and future to satisfy a busing requirement. Voluntary transfer plans have also been tried in cities like Racine, Wisconsin; Dayton, Ohio; and Omaha, Nebraska.[16]

Christopher Jencks, an educator and sociologist of impeccable liberal credentials, favors busing as a tool of economic equalization, regardless of its educational merits. Even he, however, recognizes that *forced* busing serves no legitimate purpose:

135

If the 14th Amendment means anything, it means we must guarantee black children the right to attend desegregated schools if they want to do so. We must guarantee this right even when it involves busing blacks to schools in white neighborhoods where whites do not want them. Busing whites to schools in black neighborhoods is another story. This is not a clear legal or moral issue. . . .[17]

Today, it is actually reactionary to be in favor of busing. Progressive blacks are most offended when a do-gooder liberal tells them their children must sit next to a white child in order to learn. Many black parents, particularly in the center cities, have struggled long and hard to gain control over the schools their children attend. Now these parents are told that their kids must be sent miles and miles away, to some school they've never seen and over which they have not the least control or influence, while some white kids take their place. Black parents don't want this and neither do the white parents who have also worked long and hard to get some control over their own children's schools. For years, everyone has listened to appeals for federal aid to poor (that is, minority) schools because they were substandard. No matter how much aid was forthcoming, more was always needed. Are middle-class parents now to believe that overnight these minority schools have become just as good as affluent suburban ones? The mere fact that a federal judge says middle-class children have to go there does not mean the school is good, or ever will be. And poor parents don't want their children to go without a suitable education any more than middle-class parents do. Without close parental supervision of curriculum and teaching, however, no public school is likely to provide good education. How much less likely if the school in question is across town or in another county.

Then who does want busing? Liberals like George Meany and the AFL-CIO, for one.[18] Meany's reasoning is unclear, and since few of his members are similarly inclined, one sus-

136

pects that Meany's support of busing is more political than philosophical. The NAACP Legal Defense Fund is an active supporter of busing, having initiated and pursued most of the controversial busing suits.

To men of reason it is increasingly obvious that "quality education," the supposed goal and purpose of school desegregation, simply does not result from forced busing. Why the supporters of forced busing continue to defend their position with sonorous rhetoric about "quality education" is a mystery. Perhaps they can find no other grounds of defense, and figure that this, at least, sounds good.

It is a source of never failing interest how the most vocal supporters of busing nonetheless find some way to rationalize their own children out of it. Senator George McGovern (D–S.D.), for example, lives in the District of Columbia, but pays a fistful to send his children to public schools over the line in Maryland. Eugene McCarthy's children have always gone to exclusive private schools. So have the children of liberal Senators Birch Bayh, Tom Eagleton, Edward Kennedy (and before him, Robert Kennedy), Charles Percy, Edmund Muskie, Claiborne Pell, Jacob Javits, and Abraham Ribicoff, and of former liberal Senator John Tunney. It goes without saying that a Rockefeller child has never darkened the door of an integrated public school. Nor have Sargent Shriver's children, although their father was the first head of the Office of Economic Opportunity and has never retreated from his liberal sentiments.

Thurgood Marshall, the attorney who pleaded the NAACP's case in *Brown v. Board of Education* and later was appointed to the Supreme Court, saw to it that his children were not educated in Washington, D.C.'s public schools: they attended private schools. The mayor of Washington himself sends his daughter to an exclusive private school. So does Washington's delegate to Congress, Walter Fauntroy. So does militant black columnist Carl Rowan.

Leading opinionmakers write and publish about the advantages and necessity of busing, few more energetically than the

137

Washington Post. Yet the executive editor and the editorial-page editor of that great liberal organ both send their children to private schools, although they live in the city of Washington.

A few prominent probusers have taken their own medicine —and spit it out. They have not, however, changed their opinion that it is good for other people's children. Walter Mondale, while still a senator, put his son in an integrated public school for a time, until the lad got "roughed up." Congressman Donald Fraser (D–Minn.) tried it too, but when it became clear that his children were learning nothing, he and his wife decided not to sacrifice their children's futures on the altar of ideology[19]—a conclusion the congressman's more hypocritical colleagues had arrived at intuitively.

Of course, not all politicians give lipservice to busing. Nor do all intellectuals. More and more of the psychologists and educators whose theories did so much to cause the whole mess are retreating from their former optimism. A particularly good case in point is the Miller and Gerard study of busing in Riverside, California.

Riverside was a pioneer in busing, voluntarily launching a program in 1965 to distribute its 11 percent Chicano and 6 percent black student population among the 11 schools in its district. Right at the beginning two psychologists were on hand to set up a careful study, which they expected to confirm the standard "model"—namely, that the personalities of the children would change with integration, and thus their academic achievement would improve also (how many behavior-modification programs in the schools are based on similar assumptions?). The team chose 900 minority children and parents, and 900 white children and parents, ranging from kindergarten through sixth grade in 1965, and followed them for nine years.

What happened? Well, personalities did not change, except that anxiety among the minority children increased. Motivation did not improve, nor did achievement, relative to national norms or in absolute terms. All three groups performed at the same level they had previously, as measured by standardized achievement tests, but the grades of the minority students declined after desegregation. And socially not much was accomplished either; rather than mingling with other ethnic groups, "the children in each group became more and more cliquish over the years and less accepting of those outside their own group."[20] The psychologists had to conclude: "In retrospect, the whole model we were using—the idea that academic achievement would change as personality changed—embodied an arrogant, white middle-class ideology that was and probably still is useless as a means of improving minority education."[21]

Most middle-class parents will agree that busing is useless as a means of upgrading anybody's education; they will object, however, to labeling the whole idea of busing a "middle-class ideology." It was from the start an ivory-tower abstraction, quite removed from sensible middle-class existence.

Other researchers besides Miller and Gerard are finding that the liberal panaceas are dismal failures. Wrote one:

> I am intrigued by how the current educational research parallels a contemporary conservative swing politically. It suggests fundamental processes are occurring. But I guarantee that none of this research is sponsored by some conservative group.[22]

A Harris survey, which found in April 1972 that 73 percent of the public was opposed to busing while only 20 percent favored it,[23] might also be construed as lending evidence to a "conservative shift" among the public. And those who hunt for conservatives under every bed were no doubt terrified by a Roper poll in mid-1976 that asked people: "Suppose a candidate took stands that you agreed with on all but one of these issues. Which one issue on the list would be most likely to turn you away from him if you disagreed with his stand on the issue?" Roper found that more than any other, busing was such a deeply felt issue: 22 percent of those polled said school busing for racial integration would be crucial for them; only 20 percent perceived inflation as so vital an issue, and only 13 percent rated abortion as so decisive an issue.[24] No wonder that candidates for election in 1976 weaseled on the subject of busing.

Congress and Busing

Foreigners are amazed at the American system of self-government. America brags to the rest of the world that here the people rule. Meanwhile the international mass media point to the widespread conflict over busing. It is only natural that an outsider would wonder, "Well, if they govern themselves, why can't they get rid of something they obviously don't want?" It would seem to be a fair question.

All along, busing has been the result of decisions by the two branches of government least responsible to the people: federal judges and bureaucrats. And no matter who is President, the bureaucrats mostly stay in place (only 142 HEW positions are appointed)[25] and the Supreme Court is bound by decisions of earlier years.

Popular pressure has moved Congress to attach "riders" to various education bills, attempting to limit busing. For instance, in 1974 Congressman Esch of Michigan succeeded in attaching an amendment stipulating that busing could be ordered only as a last resort, and then only to the closest or next-closest school. The following year Congress approved an amendment saying that HEW funds would be available only for busing to the closest school, not even the next closest. This was the Labor-HEW Appropriations bill, which was vetoed because of its other inflationary provisions, so that particular amendment never had a chance to go into effect. Its impact would have been slight, anyhow: if federal funds will not pay for the busing, the local tax assessments must go up, as they did in Boston. Money, when it comes to busing, is no obstacle.

Neither is shortage of fuel to run the buses, despite the widely proclaimed energy crisis.

There is fundamental question whether Congress can do anything to restrict or stipulate the means of enforcing Supreme Court decisions. Some years ago North Carolina passed a law saying:

> No student shall be assigned or compelled to attend any school on account of race . . . or for the purpose of creating a balance or ratio of race. . . . Involuntary busing of students in contravention of this article is prohibited, and public funds shall not be used for any such busing.

The U.S. Supreme Court declared this law unconstitutional, because it would have hindered enforcement of constitutional guarantees.[26] Can Congress do what the state of North Carolina may not? Theoreticians may debate the point, but the *modus operandi* seems to be that Congress is just as subject to the dictates of the High Court as are the states, particularly when the Court has declared that busing is the "only and essential" remedy for an unacceptable situation.

Article III, Section 1 of the Constitution gives Congress power to establish (and presumably, to abolish) the "inferior Courts," but not the Supreme Court. Section II of the same article states that the Supreme Court shall have jurisdiction "with such exceptions, and under such regulations as Congress shall make." While this might be taken to mean that the Supreme Court operates in some areas at the pleasure of Congress, precedents are so few, and so limited, that no relief should be expected from that direction.

It has been suggested that Congress simply pass a law limiting the jurisdiction of the Supreme Court on matters of school desegregation. Right-to-life legal advisers sometimes recommend doing the same on the matter of abortion. But for such a measure there is little precedent, and precedent is the central feature of Anglo-American jurisprudence. In 1869 a case was appealed to the Supreme Court that involved a habeas corpus proceeding under one of the Reconstruction Acts. Frightened that the Court might find all the Reconstruction Acts unconstitutional if it pursued this one case, Congress quickly passed a bill removing habeas corpus proceedings of that type from the jurisdiction of the Supreme Court. *Ex parte McCardle,* as this case is known, is the only known precedent, and it is shaky at best.

Given the assumption, then, that busing is and will be, strategies have been devised to work around it, to limit it. In June 1976 President Ford sent to Congress a draft of legislation devised by Attorney General Edward Levi to restrict the outrages of busing.

The objectives of the School Desegregation Standards and Assistance Act were four:

1. Prevent courts from imposing busing orders on entire school districts when they were seeking to remedy only isolated instances of segregation.

2. Limit the courts to cases where school boards had deliberately brought about the segregation, not where housing patterns and other independent factors made it accidental;

3. Establish a national council to study the problem and propose integration plans for areas in need of them—before seeking relief from the judiciary.

4. Limit all busing orders to periods of five years.
The bills (S. 3618 and H.R. 14553) received no action in the 94th Congress, predictably enough; but they do have merit. Congress *can* curb forced busing if it really wants to.

Another proposal redefines integration so that a school system will be considered integrated whenever students are allowed to make voluntary transfers between schools, provided these transfers improve the racial balance. As the word is now understood, it means that each school in the system must maintain a certain set proportion of blacks to whites. The idea behind defining integration as free movement is that blacks who wanted to get the education offered in predominately

142

"white" schools would be free to do so, and would even be bused there at public expense, but those minorities who preferred their own schools would also be free to exercise that choice. Likewise, whites who wanted to go to an inner-city school would be welcome to do so, but they would not be compelled to attend predominantly black schools in black neighborhoods. Recall it is the involuntary busing of white students, that has precipitated the most violent confrontations.

The true believers of the busing cause will fight such a redefinition of integration because they suspect few whites, given the choice, will want to go to a mostly black school, just as not very many blacks will choose to go to a mostly white school. The proposal is logical, however. Supposedly, busing is a remedy for ancient wrongs against black people. If so, the wrong is righted by giving black students free access to any school they like. But to perpetrate a wrong on white students in the name of remedying one against black students is no kind of justice, and assigning white students to schools on the basis of their color is as wrong as assigning black students on the basis of theirs, which *Brown v. Board of Education* specifically declared unconstitutional.

Alas, the discussion is academic, because to be effective on a national scale, Congress would have to write the redefinition into law. That is not likely to happen. It did not happen in the 94th Congress of 1975–76, and it is even less likely to happen in the 95th Congress of Jimmy Carter.

Enough heartache and torment have been caused by busing to bring many people to support what is usually deemed a remedy of last resort—a constitutional amendment. The House Republican Policy Committee endorsed an amendment in 1975, but the majority-party Democratic Caucus killed the measure for the duration of the 94th Congress. Finding appropriate words for such an amendment is a great difficulty: to be effective, the amendment would somehow have to limit the 14th Amendment (the "due process" amendment), which applies to state action and thus, the courts reason, furnishes the basis for federal involvement in desegregat-

143

ing local schools. Limiting one constitutional amendment with another is a delicate operation, and no constitutional scholar of reputation, no congressman or senator, really wants to try it. Expert testimony before a congressional committee on any constitutional amendment, whether to ban busing or to ban abortions, always emphasizes the dangers of such action, so much so that two-thirds of the legislators of both chambers seldom want any part of it—even if, miraculously, a majority of the committee in question is willing to support it.

But where there is a will there is a way, the saying goes, and politically speaking, that is very true. When the pressure grows unbearable, the legislators will suddenly find suitable language for the amendment. Heretofore, there has not been consistent, organized, steady pressure on Congress for a constitutional amendment to ban busing. In 1976 a national parents' organization was formed for the specific purpose of working for a constitutional amendment against busing. The National Association for Neighborhood Schools (NANS)[27] says its goal is "to stop forced busing, as well as federal intervention in schools, either by a constitutional amendment or by such other means as may be necessary to accomplish this objective." The leadership of NANS is politically experienced and has practical, specific plans for advancing its viewpoint in the public eye and the congressional consciousness. Parents to whom busing is a high-priority issue would be well advised to contact NANS.

One last word on the subject of busing. There could be worse tyrannies imposed by the courts, and there could be worse tyrannies legislated by Congress. The mayor of beleaguered Louisville declined to support a constitutional amendment on the grounds that if successful, it would merely divert court action into other avenues of compulsion: racial quotas in housing sales, for instance, or assigning students to schools on the basis of family income.[28]

A college professor, writing in a little-known scholarly journal of education, has enunciated one ultimate solution. It is easy to avoid the hassle of forced busing, says Johannes Gaertner, if all schools are of equally good quality.[29] Let's just get all the schools up to one standard, and there will be no need of busing. How to get all schools up to one standard? Easy. Federal standards of achievement should be drafted, vigorously enforced, and impartially administered. Schools that don't meet the federal standards should be closed. Local boards won't have to waste so much time deciding how to spend local money, because they will be amply occupied trying to meet the federal standards. Everybody in education will know exactly what is expected of everybody else. Life will be free of hassles.

Johannes Gaertner might well be of Prussian ancestry. Prussia was one of the first nations to establish compulsory attendance at government-controlled schools, so at least the man might be said to be in touch with his roots. Which is more than can be said of the Americans who are likely to get behind such a scheme when it works its way through the academic percolator and onto the floor of Congress.

Restoring Prayer

The options available to parents who are concerned about the banning of prayer from the public schools are basically the same as those available to parents faced with busing orders. They can move to some place where forced busing is not an issue and the community is homogeneous enough tacitly to preserve respect for religion in the public schools. Saint Jo, Texas, population 500, comes to mind as such a community.

But who can pick up and move to the hinterlands? If the jobs are in the city, so are the employees. Parents can try private schools—if there are good ones around, and if they can afford them. If there aren't, or they can't, parents can defy state laws and educate their children in the basement or the attic. Or they can band together with other parents and start their own schools.

Political action can be pursued simultaneously, by working

145

for a constitutional amendment to ban busing or to restore prayer. Political action, defined as raising cain and attracting TV cameras, might still have some impact where busing is concerned. But it is absolutely futile to try to restore prayer in the schools. Striving for a constitutional amendment to restore prayer is unproductive in itself, even though almost everyone agrees that a constitutional amendment is the only possibly effective remedy. The question is whether the remedy is worth anything.

In 1962, when the Supreme Court outlawed prayer in the public schools, public outrage ran high. Fifteen years later, however, there is so much more in the public schools, and the laws affecting them, to provoke outrage that restoring a one-minute prayer ranks very low on the list of promising remedies. Even if, miraculously, a prayer amendment were to pass the House and the Senate by two-thirds vote of each, and were ratified by 38 states, what would it accomplish? Suppose school boards or principals had the option of preparing prayers for recital over the public address system in the morning. How many would bother? And how many students would pay attention? And how much good would it do, anyway?

The reverential mention of God is gone from the public schools; but that is only half the problem. In the intervening decade and a half since the Regents' Prayer decision, God has been not only removed from the public curriculum, but replaced by a vigorously pursued antitheism. The antitheistic agenda is called secular humanism. While saying a prayer in the morning does have immense symbolic value, and real personal value to some students, it cannot compete for effect with antitheistic course content. From the divine perspective, of course, prayer can accomplish anything; and nothing can prevent a person from saying a prayer at any time. Among the problems that plague the public schools, however, antitheism is a more dangerous trend than nontheism (although, of course, the former could not have gotten a foothold until the latter was commonly accepted.)

146

From Protection to Attack

The Supreme Court had looked at explicit religious instruction in the public schools as far back as 1940 and found it unacceptable. "Release-time" programs, in which religious instruction took place on public school property, were ruled unconstitutional in 1940; "dismissed-time" programs of off-campus religious instruction during school hours were found acceptable in 1952.

In 1961 a case not pertaining specifically to education established an important principle. The case was *Torcaso v. Watkins* (367 U.S. 488). Roy Torcaso wanted to be a notary public, but Maryland required notaries public to swear or affirm that they believed in God. Torcaso, being a secular humanist, would not do this. The Supreme Court ordered that Torcaso be made a notary, on the ground that secular humanism was a religion, even though a nontheistic one. The Court declared that the law cannot aid religions founded on belief in God over against those based on something else.

The following year came the New York State Regents' Prayer decision, *Engel v. Vitale* (370 U.S. 421), which ruled that an optional, 22-word, nondenominational acknowledgement of Almighty God was unconstitutional. This was followed in 1963 by *Abington Township School District v. Schempp* (374 U.S. 203), which ruled that reading from the Bible in the public schools was also an unconstitutional government-sanctioned religious exercise. Several years later some states tried a "moment of silent meditation" as a sop to parents, and the Court has found nothing objectionable in that. Of course, neither is there any substance to it.

Noted legal commentator Charles Rice has observed that in the Regents' Prayer case, as in *Brown v. Board of Education,* the opinion of the Court does not cite a single precedent to support its conclusion, but relies instead on abstract logic and historical documents.

147

The absence of legal citations in *Engel v. Vitale* has been hailed as evidence of the pristine purity of the principles there avowed, the lofty eminence of which precludes their dependence upon mere court decisions. On the other hand, it can fairly be said that the Court cited no precedent because it could find none beyond its own gratuitous dicta in prior cases since 1947.[30]

Dicta refers to *obiter dicta,* sort of an extension of remarks, or marginal comments, often made by justices in rendering a decision, but not part of the decision itself, and thus not truly part of judicial precedent.

One justice, Potter Stewart, noted that the prayer decisions were inconsistent with what otherwise appeared to be the spirit of the age. In 1954 the words "under God" had been added to the Pledge of Allegiance; in 1956 "In God We Trust" had officially been made the national motto. Since 1952 Congress had asked the President, who in turn had always complied, to declare a National Day of Prayer. Justice Stewart asked: "Is the Court suggesting that the Constitution permits judges and congressmen and presidents to join in prayer, but prohibits schoolchildren from doing so?"[31] The only Catholic on the Court, Justice Brennan, managed to excuse the national motto on the ground that it had no religious meaning, but Justice William O. Douglas intimated that it also was unconstitutional. Brennan enunciated a secular point of view regarding the duty of the public schools: namely, to provide "an atmosphere in which children may assimilate a heritage common to all American groups. . . . This is a heritage neither theistic nor atheistic, but simply civic and patriotic."[32] Educators might prefer the word *humanistic* as descriptive of the values to be inculcated in public school students.

Paul Freund, a law professor at Harvard University, delivered the prestigious Burton Lecture at Harvard a few years after the prayer decisions. After discoursing at some length on the legal aspects of prayer in the schools, Freund found cause for optimism:

> The school prayer decisions are more important for the doors they leave open than for those they shut. The study of religious traditions, training in moral analysis, and the cultivation of sensibilities beyond the intellectual are all left open and beckoning. . . . Education of this kind . . . calls for the collaboration, among others, of philosophers to clarify the objectives, psychologists to advise on the techniques of learning. . . .
>
> Today the need is not to reform the First Amendment, but to examine and reform our ideas and practices of moral education in the schools.[33]

Here indeed was a clarion call to be answered by the theorists who had been working for years to develop programs of "moral education," "values instruction," and "values clarification." What better opportunity to begin to put these notions into practice than an invitation from the Supreme Court? If parents complained that without prayer the public schools could give their children no moral formation, educators could now respond by pointing to programs geared specifically to moral training.

The Supreme Court had all but declared that morality was separate from religion. It had to be, because state support for religion was held unconstitutional, whereas support for morality was not criticized. Separation of religion and morality had been dear to the hearts of progressive educators for a long time, but had never caught on with most American parents. Parents also tended to feel that public education was lacking unless it taught students about the religious heritage of the country, and helped to maintain that heritage. Well, the Court said it was all right to "teach about" religion; therefore, a senior elective on "comparative religions" could be created while history-book pictures of George Washington kneeling to pray in the snow at Valley Forge could be eliminated. Parents also had the idea that without religion, education failed to develop a proper sense of man's place in the universe, as a dependent creature under a sovereign God, a creature of inherent weakness and fallibility. Such a view of man tended to make educators uncomfortable, and in the process of "reforming" moral education that archaic, authoritarian concept could be eased out and replaced with more reassuring, humanistic notions.

And that is what happened. In Kanawha County it became obvious that parents who opposed the immoral textbooks were demanding freedom *for* religion. The Supreme Court had charged public schools with guaranteeing freedom *from* religion, but so far to the extreme had that been carried that religion was under open attack by the schools. Since the Court had prohibited the teaching of religious beliefs, parents fought to prohibit the questioning of religious beliefs in the textbooks and in some innovative courses and programs. In almost all 50 states, the battle has shifted comparably. The "eccentric deference paid to the inflated scruples of a small minority"[34] in banning prayer has fueled an active campaign against the sincere beliefs of the vast majority. Traditional religion is under attack in the public schools.

Secular Humanism

Religion is being replaced by the platitudes of secular humanism, passed off as a harmless, consensus-based universal morality to which religious people should not object, because it really makes no difference what somebody believes—he can still subscribe to the universal humanism. Well, belief in any dogma is antithetical to secular humanism, but children not trained as apologists for their religion cannot be expected to

150

recognize the poison and cannot be expected to defend themselves against it.

The U.S. Supreme Court has recognized that secular humanism is a religion, in the strict sense of the word. The Court said in *Torcaso v. Watkins:*

> Among religions in this country which do not teach what would generally be considered a belief in the existence of God are Buddhism, Taoism, Ethical Culture, Secular Humanism and others.[35]

What are the tenets of this religion? They are easily enough established, and changed from time to time as circumstances may require. In 1933 Humanist Manifesto I was issued, signed by prominent intellectuals of the day, one of whom was John Dewey. In 1973 Humanist Manifesto II, also signed by prominent intellectuals and educators, appeared. A few details changed in the 40 intervening years (the earlier version endorsed socialism; the later endorses euthanasia and suicide), but the highlights were the same:

> We believe that traditional dogmatic or authoritarian religions that place revelation, God, ritual or creed above human needs and experience do a disservice to the human species.
>
> Promises of immortal salvation or fear of eternal damnation are both illusory and harmful. They distract humans from present concerns, from self-actualization and from rectifying social injustices.
>
> We affirm that moral values derive their source from human experience. Ethics is autonomous and situational. . . . Ethics stems from human need and interest. . . .
>
> We strive for the good life, here and now.

In the area of sexuality, we believe that intolerant attitudes, often cultivated by orthodox religions and puritanical cultures, unduly repress sexual conduct. . . .

We must extend participatory democracy in its true sense to the economy, the school, the family, the workplace and voluntary associations.[36]

What is the goal of life according to the secular humanists? "Self-actualization," "the good life, here and now." Nothing could be more antithetical to the desire dearest to a Christian heart, to find eternal happiness with God in Heaven. "Self-actualization" is jargon; "doing your own thing" is the popular translation.

If this sounds like the younger generation, it is because public schools are the most effective inculcators of secular humanistic values. Speculation about whether humanist values have been incorporated into the curriculum intentionally or accidentally is not in order here; for our present purposes it is sufficient to indicate the pervasiveness of secular humanism. Secular humanism is propagated in the public schools. Usually it is not called by such an obvious name, but instead is coated with sugary rhetoric about developing desirable social attitudes: what reasonable person can object to a teacher's efforts to help a youngster "make decisions," "improve his perception," "get to know himself," and so on?

A parent who understands what is meant by these glib expressions must object to them. They all come down to situational ethics sooner or later. In practice, the steps used to teach such things to a schoolchild overstep the bounds of family life and personal privacy; it is possible that a constitutional right to family privacy is also being violated.[37]

Some common names under which situation ethics and other secular humanistic principles are taught include "values education," "moral education," and "values clarification." The psychologists most responsible for the theory and practice are Sidney Simon and Lawrence Kohlberg and their disciples. To them, a value is not an unchanging belief; rather, a value is the result of a process. Since the process occurs many times over, in different circumstances, it can have different results as situations dictate, and thus values can change constantly. The process has seven steps:

1. Cherishing
2. Publicly affirming
3. Choosing from alternatives
4. Choosing after considering alternatives
5. Choosing freely
6. Acting on one's beliefs
7. Acting according to a pattern

The person who adheres to theistic religion follows a somewhat similar pattern in the process of maturing, which suggests that there is some psychological validity to the Simon-Kohlberg technique. Its effectiveness, of course, makes it all the more iniquitous. Theistic religions all propose some absolute values that exist independently of the person holding them. For Simon and Kohlberg, there are no such extrinsic absolutes, and no "value" is larger than the valuer (except, perhaps, the recognition that all values are relative).

Following these seven steps, the values educator puts the students' home- and religion-taught values through a relentless meat grinder. Because personal life is the most revealing source of values, it is the most closely examined by the values educator and the peer group who engage in the "process" of changing, clarifying, and creating values. Rarely are there special courses in the curriculum called values education (though some progressive Catholic schools have reportedly watered down religious instruction to such a level). Values clarification has the distinct advantage (in its practitioners' eyes) of being easily incorporated into just about every course in the curriculum. Most susceptible, as might be expected, are courses in the humanities: literature fairly invites discussion of personal feelings, and hence of values. Social studies, taught in "relevant" modes that encourage the forming of opinions rather than the imparting of information, is similarly susceptible. Other obvious occasions are family life or sex education courses, sociology courses, and psychology (as it is sometimes offered to advanced students). But mathematics, biology, and environmental education are also suitable vehicles.[38]

Man: A Course of Study

An entire social studies curriculum has been organized around the principles of secular humanism, designed, written, and promoted with federal funds. *Man: A Course of Study* (MACOS) ostensibly proposes in one year to teach fifth graders the principles of anthropology. It studies in great detail the life cycles of salmon, the social behavior of baboons, and, as the example of humankind, the nearly extinct Netsilik Eskimos of Pelly Bay, Canada. At the end of the year students are supposed to have some idea of "what makes human beings human." In the course of answering this question, MACOS teaches 11-year olds various practices of primitive Eskimo life and encourages them to discuss the merits of infanticide, wifeswapping, and euthanasia, under the circumstances of Eskimo life, of course. And of course, the conclusions they are to reach are "open-ended." Accompanying the course, to make it more realistic to the children, are numerous graphic movies of Eskimo life, including hunts and slaughters.[39]

MACOS is only one of the curriculum programs developed by the National Science Foundation. NSF is the group which gave the nation the $17 million gift of "modern math," which NSF evaluations continue to find successful although few teachers, and hardly any parents, would still defend it.[40] A sequel to MACOS, *Exploring Human Nature,* is being tried out in several states, as are *Biological Sciences Curriculum Study* (BSCS) and *Individualized Science Instructional System* (ISIS). In all of these programs family values and loyalty to America's social and economic traditions are undermined.[41]

154

MACOS is the most widely used curriculum program, however, and it has met with vigorous resistance all over the country. Psychological damage to children exposed to the course has been documented for the Science and Technology Committee of the House of Representatives, the body responsible for supervising the National Science Foundation. MACOS is currently cited in several lawsuits, including one in Albany, New York that contends it constitutes the teaching of the religion of secular humanism.[42] Other parents' groups have tried to point out the incompatibility of certain public school programs with the two positions of the Supreme Court: (a) that public education cannot aid one or all religions, and (b) that secular humanism is a religion.[43] The obvious difficulty, of course, is trying to prove precisely how those broad platitudes of the Humanist Manifesto apply to MACOS.

Another case of apparent violation of the First Amendment is the teaching of Transcendental Meditation in public school classrooms. Though TMers like to claim that their technique is just that, and not a religion, the connection between TM and Hinduism is quite clear. The federal government has supported Transcendental Meditation with funds from the National Institute of Mental Health and with a grant from HEW to four New Jersey school districts to study whether TM can improve grades and discourage antisocial behavior (wasn't busing supposed to do that too?). Even if TM is not specifically Hinduism—and probably the version that finally reaches the high schools is so diluted that the Maharishi wouldn't recognize it—the fact remains that children are being taught a "spiritual" technique in TM, which can interfere with or undermine the practice of their prior religion. The Supreme Court may have worked itself into a corner, so that it will have to rule on whether mental or psychological techniques constitute a religion—if belief in God or lack thereof provides no definition of religion, is the presence or absence of certain techniques any more reliable an index?

Former Congressman John Conlan, perhaps the most active

leader in the House of Representatives for parents' rights during his tenure, introduced an amendment to the Higher Education Act Amendments of 1976 (H.R. 12851):

> No grant, contract, or support is authorized under the Foreign Studies and Language Development portions of Title II of the bill for any educational program, curriculum research and development, administrator-teacher orientation, or any project involving one or more students or teacher-administrators involving any aspect of the religion of secular humanism.

As Conlan explained it to his colleagues, "This amendment is designed to cope with . . . the fundamental threat to individual freedom when government participates in and supports the imposition of any type of religious belief—the attempt thereby 'to control the mental operations of persons.' . . ."[44]

Thanks to the organized efforts of parent groups all over the country, the House of Representatives was persuaded to adopt the amendment—by a 222–174 vote. Since the Senate did not pass a similar provision, it did not become law in 1976. Even if it had, the language would have been more a demonstration of the intent of Congress than an effective protection of religious privacy. The intent of Congress is not to be scorned, but one must remember that the wording of the amendment affected only the legislation to which it was attached, and would have restricted only those funds under Title II of the Higher Education Act—which is not a primary source of funds for values education in elementary and secondary schools. However, regardless of strict legal significance, the Conlan amendment would have sent a message to the values educators.

The previous year another Conlan amendment had been approved, barring the National Science Foundation from implementing in fiscal year 1976 any courses that focus on political or moral values. With Conlan absent from Congress in

156

1977 (he was defeated in a primary race for the Senate in 1976), his amendment was not renewed, and without a bloodhound on the Science and Technology Committee to track down the activities of NSF, the effect of the amendment would be slight—unless, of course, another defender of parents' rights should emerge in the U.S. Congress. To reduce the effect of the ban further, NSF saw the amendment coming and awarded grants for two-year periods, thus ensuring that certain pet projects could go on uninterrupted by congressional scrutiny. This is how a determined bureaucracy circumvents Congress.

If it seems that tacking on amendments to legislation in Congress does not accomplish much, take comfort in this observation: debate over seemingly trivial amendments about who could and could not receive federal money, and for what purpose or not for what purpose, kept federal aid-to-education legislation stalled for many, many years. If there were more than one or two parents' rights members of Congress, and if there were a larger, stronger coalition of grassroots support throughout the country, then more amendments, more strongly worded, to more pieces of legislation, could be introduced with better chances of passing and better prospects for monitoring and enforcement. The tactic of amendment adopting can work wonders when practiced fully. And parents have only begun to fight!

5

Fighting
Within the System

So your children cannot pray in public school. You have very little say where they go to school anyway. If there are bullies or hoodlums in the school, the authorities are powerless to enforce discipline. A computer makes up your child's class schedule. An unseen but intimidating guidance counselor selects the classes. And who decides what subjects shall be taught? Who decides what books are to be used? Who decides who teaches what? Who decides how the material should be handled? Not you, the parent.

Is it any wonder, then, that the younger generation is so different from the parent generation? But that complaint has been made for decades, educators will say. Yes, and for decades American public education has been controlled more and more by professionals and less and less by parents. As long as local communities were close-knit and education was truly centered in the community, local values could prevail, and usually did—much to the annoyance of educators and liberals who scorned those values as narrow-minded "Babbittry," "Protestant ethics," or worse. But today's world is more mobile, more urban and more suburban, more sophisticated, and the education profession is more homogeneous. The political significance of vanishing local control has already been discussed. It has a personal aspect too: a parent feels left out of his child's schooling.

Many parents are convinced that educators want it that way. Undoubtedly there are some teachers and administrators with such a superiority complex that they look on parents as objects of scorn. It would not be fair, however, to cast all educators in this mould; many teachers are anxious to be on good terms with parents, and many administrators are quite concerned when they hear of parental dissatisfaction. Educators generally do act surprised if a parent displays a keen interest in his child's education. Few parents used to, or if they did, their interest was safely diverted into PTA and playground monitoring. Educators—particularly administrators but also teachers to some extent—are as much bureaucrats as pedagogues. They are not accustomed to working with real things like maternal anger; they prefer paperwork, and impersonal concerns like budgets. They enjoy the challenges of a computer printout. Of such things cozy nests are made; and when disturbed, educators resent the interruption.

So they tell parents that their concern is unique, that no other parents in the district share it, that they are really blowing things out of proportion, and that they are overanxious. The bureaucrat hopes the parents will be embarrassed or intimidated, and will quietly retreat, so he can go back to his routine. And, sure enough, the parents must be genuinely concerned to keep pursuing the matter.

So what, the frustrated parent must reply, if other children are wandering down a federally funded primrose path? I'm not going to let my children do it. If other parents are satisfied to be told merely that their children are "reading up to their ability," fine for them, but if my son's supposed "ability" is two years behind grade level, I want to know, because I'm going to do something about it. And so what if my concern is unique? That doesn't make it any the less valid or any the less worthy of your attention, Mr. Bureaucrat. My child is unique too. My concern may decide the direction of my child's

159

whole life, and I'm not going to ignore that awesome responsibility. I'm sorry for the inconvenience I may cause you, but I promise I will continue to disrupt your routine until you do what is necessary to let my conscience relax.

Senator Jacob Javits is very concerned about educating America's children for the benefit of the nation.[1] As a parent, you are concerned about educating your children to be decent, competent adults who will be a credit to you in your old age. Chances are, you are concerned about such things as their immortal souls too. These interests are not at odds with the national well-being. If more children were educated in the old-fashioned virtues, the nation wouldn't face so many problems. But if education is designed solely with the "public good" in mind—as it is now, for the most part—then, naturally, the private good of your individual children will be brushed aside, and your private concerns as their parent will merit very little interest from the public schools.

Messianic Roots of American Education

It is true that the public good is the sum of millions of private goods, properly sought. But in an age of collectivism, the principle of private good is not well understood. The laws (particularly the federal laws) tend to regard children as tools for social reform. And so do many educators. Title I of ESEA is interested much less in helping deprived children learn to read so that their lives will be fuller or more virtuous, than in making the national spending pattern more "equitable" by pouring money into education. (Individual teachers, of course, may not share this attitude.) Historically, although one hesitates to admit it, such collectivist motives have always been lurking about the roots of America's "common" or public education.

Everyone has heard the self-congratulatory interpretation of American history taught by the defenders of the public schools —namely, that the public schools are the bulwark of democ-

160

racy, perhaps the very source of our democracy; the guardians of freedom, the keepers of the American tradition, and so on. Perhaps the rise of compulsory public education is historically related to the rise of American democracy. But a republic is what the Founding Fathers intended.

And today, how can one speak of freedom, when the public schools are both the victims and perpetrators of as much compulsion as the notorious Internal Revenue Service? Democracy does not remain democracy forever—history shows that it turns into one kind of tyranny or another. One can only hope that the American experience will disprove the truism. Given the present state of the public school system, however, indications are that public education is in the forefront of the drive toward an all-too-predictable totalitarian future.

The theoretical foundations of public education in this country are unquestionably messianic, to use Rousas J. Rushdoony's term.[2] Horace Mann is dubbed the father of American public education; he it was who made state-run schools a going concern. With Rousseau he romantically believed that children were innately good, corrupted only by ignorant parents. Through education, Mann thought, the commonwealth could create a perfect society on earth:

> The Common School is the greatest discovery ever made by man. . . . Other social organizations are curative and remedial; this is a preventive and an antidote. . . . Let the Common School be expanded to its capabilities, let it be worked with the efficiency of which it is susceptible, and nine-tenths of the crimes in the penal code would become obsolete; the long catalogue of human ills would be abridged . . . all rational hopes respecting the future brightened.[3]

James G. Carter, a colleague of Mann, played a significant role in establishing state control in Massachusetts. He also founded one of the first normal schools. Carter saw quite

161

clearly the symbiosis between government and education, and he endorsed it:

> As the first object in the formation of every government is to provide for its own preservation; and as the general diffusion of knowledge and virtue is the most effectual, if not the only means of insuring stability to republican institutions, the policy of the liberal appropriations made by Congress for education . . . is undoubtedly an enlightened policy, and worthy of an enlightened and free government.[4]

The implications of this kind of theory were seized upon by the NEA, meeting in 1895. Francis W. Parker, a leading progressive educator, advocated the deification of the state and the subjection of children to its will:

> The child is not in school for knowledge. He is there to live, and to put his life, nurtured in the school, into the community.

> The day will come when ministers will preach the gospel of common education from the pulpit; yea, when it will be the grandest part of the great gospel of Jesus Christ.[5]

Somehow it is difficult to imagine America's public schools as "the grandest part" of the gospel of Jesus Christ. But such is the intellectual ancestry of public education, try as educationists will to sugarcoat or disguise it. Deep down, the education establishment really believes it has a right to appropriate a child's private thoughts and receptive mind. It should therefore come as no surprise that the system refuses to be responsible to mere parents. Parents must stop trusting public education—on general principles.

Knowing the past, one is *not* doomed to repeat it. Parents who know about the messianic background of American education have a further incentive to become militant in their children's behalf, and in behalf of the next generation of children, whose parents may be less able to act. Clearly, if parents do not look out for their own children's well-being in the public schools, nobody will. The children will be categorized and handled like so many eggs in a carton, according to their usefulness for broader social purposes.

To be sure, in some communities the situation may seem wholly unobjectionable. There are still about four thousand one-teacher schools in the country, and whoever teaches in a one-room school is probably old-fashioned enough to be trustworthy. A district like that would not be rich enough to innovate anyway. But most parents who sense that all is not well with their children's education are likely to live in some "progressive" suburban district where austerity means keeping the band uniforms for another year; where economizing on fancy equipment or special new programs is not necessary. This kind of district is receptive to the worst kind of innovation, provided it comes with the proper establishment imprimatur.[6] Parents do not carry such an endorsement. Parents who try to do something about the public schools are pioneers, and might as well expect the hardships of striking into new territory.

Parent Awakening: Scenario One

What provokes parental concern? It could come gradually, with a vague but growing sense that all is not well. Or it could come with the sudden realization that nine-year-old Johnny can't read Dr. Seuss.

What happens then? Probably Johnny's mother, Mrs. Adams, goes to Johnny's teacher, Miss Johnson. Miss Johnson seems a little surprised that Mommy is worried, because Johnny is a good student. Mommy is a little surprised to find that Miss Johnson means only that he doesn't disrupt the class and generally does what he's told. She asks for samples of Johnny's classwork and is unhappy to find an arithmetic exer-

163

cise—with mistakes—posted on the bulletin board and marked "Very Good." She asks to see Johnny's achievement-test scores. Miss Johnson launches into a lecture about the irrelevancy and meaninglessness of standardized achievement tests. Mommy insists. Finally, Miss Johnson says Mommy will have to talk to the principal.

So Mommy makes the appointment and comes back next week to see Mr. Doe. If she is very sophisticated, Mrs. Adams while there asks to see Johnny's comprehensive file, but chances are she doesn't know she has that right, or even that such a thing exists. Mr. Doe is reluctant enough to give her the reading scores, but suppose she finally wangles them out of him. Mr. Doe then defends Johnny's being two years behind grade level. Mommy is not happy. She asks how she can find a tutor for Johnny.

A tutor? Oh, that might upset Johnny, the principal says; it might make him anxious and competitive. Mommy bites her tongue, but keeps trying. Maybe she can help Johnny at home? Oh, no; oh, dear no, that won't do at all; reading is taught so differently these days than when you learned, it will only confuse Johnny. Well, says Mommy, I'm sure I can learn the school's method too. What is it?

A fatal question. There is no turning back. Mommy can only get deeper and deeper into the quagmire now. The school may or may not let her see the books Johnny uses to learn how to read; chances are, if she sees them they will mystify her. And soon she will be going to PTA meetings in search of other parents with similar dissatisfactions. If she finds the PTA unreceptive, she will stop wasting her time there. Then she will go to libraries to look for books on education. She may volunteer as a teacher's aide to try to find out what goes on inside the school. She may venture to a nearby teachers' college to find out why the teachers are so hard to understand when they talk to her. And sooner or later she will encounter other mothers who have done all the same things on their own, and together they will try to prove the axiom, "In unity there is strength."

Parent Awakening: Scenario Two

Other parents don't have so much time. Their awakening may be dramatic. Fifteen-year-old Nathaniel starts hating school. He used to like particularly his advanced English class, but now Dad finds out he has been cutting it. Inquiry after inquiry finally yields the information that "all we do is sit around with the guidance counselor and talk about what's wrong with each other, and then we had to write this essay about what it feels like to be dead." Mr. Bowditch is furious —what sort of nonsense is going on? He tells his wife to go talk to that teacher. It might be better if he went: fathers are still a rare enough sight in schools to merit more respect than mothers.

But Mrs. Bowditch goes. The teacher, Miss Reilly, is surprised she's there, and even more surprised to learn why. She acts almost as if Nathaniel were not supposed to tell his parents what goes on in English class, and pooh-poohs his description. "He was exaggerating. Here, you see, we're already on page 201 of the literature book . . ." Mom persists. Does this guidance counselor come often? Oh, that was just a little sensitivity session. What's that? Oh, it helps the kids develop a sensitivity to other people's feelings, that's all, so students can realize why some people act the way they do. What about the essay? Well, you know, this is an advanced class, and we try to develop, y'know, creative writing skills, and, y'know, using the imagination is such an important aspect of creative writing, you know.

Mom asks to see some other essays. They happen to be unavailable. Well, then, how about Nathaniel's last test? Here it is, with a B. Mom looks it over, and sees four spelling mistakes not even noted by Miss Reilly. But spelling doesn't matter, says Miss Reilly; what matters is that he has a feel for what the poem is saying. What is the poem? A contemporary one, from the *New Yorker* of March 15. Oh. Mom knows what she'll hear if she ventures the observation that last month's *New Yorker* does not constitute great literature, in her opinion.

165

So she leaves, feeling that she has accomplished nothing.

Then a little while later Nathaniel comes home and says, "Mom, you really got that English teacher scared. Today she spent half the period explaining to us why we aren't supposed to tell our parents about the weird things we do 'cause they can't understand the new methods. Chuck Carroll's mom had talked to the principal about the poem we were s'posed to write making believe we had killed somebody, and I guess ol' Miss Reilly really caught it from him."

Nathaniel's mom just happens to know Chuck Carroll's. All through dinner she wonders whether she should call Mrs. Carroll. She doesn't want to seem like an alarmist . . . or an interfering parent . . . but Nathaniel said Chuck wasn't happy either . . . maybe there are other kids who aren't getting anything out of the course . . . maybe if their parents knew what was going on they'd care too . . .

So finally Mrs. Bowditch calls Mrs. Carroll. Mrs. Carroll is very pleased to hear from her and confides that Chuck has been having bad nightmares ever since that essay about what it feels like to be dead. She wishes something could be done. . . . And so a concerned parents' group is conceived.

A Parents' Group Is Born

Are these scenarios farfetched? Not at all. Consider the shock of the pious fundamentalist parents of West Virginia who suddenly hear about textbooks that feature cursing and gross immorality. Consider the Columbia, Maryland parents who suddenly discover that they cannot exempt their children from taking part in a federally funded survey that asks them —without giving any assurance of anonymity—their reactions to such statements as: "My parents don't like me to disagree with them . . .," "I sometimes feel I have no control over my life," "Give the first and last name of the child who fools around in class."[7] Consider the many, many parents in inner cities who work like dogs so their kids can graduate from high school and get skilled jobs, only to discover too late that the diploma awarded to Enrique or Foster doesn't mean anything because Enrique and Foster can't read, but the school never bothered to tell that to their mothers.[8] Consider the parents in a middle-class suburb of a thriving southwestern city who go to their local superintendent to find out more about the values-education program in the high school, only to be told, "We're going to teach my values, and if you don't like it, you can get out of the public schools."[9]

No, these scenarios are not farfetched. They are not alarmist. And the reaction of Johnny's mom and Nathaniel's mom is not out of proportion to the provocation. Their reaction is absolutely normal, understandable, and, in fact, commendable. Nathaniel's mom was correct in a very fundamental observation: most parents do not know what is going on. If they did know, many of them would react and might be willing to work to correct the situation. After all, their children are getting shortchanged too. Also, most parents, like Nathaniel's mom, lack self-assurance, but as they talk to other parents with similar concerns, they realize their complaints have merit.

This is the first and immediate goal of parent action: to spread information. The parents' group must try to find out as much as it can, and then distribute that information to other parents, to the public, to the press, to the school board, to the city council, to the precinct chairmen—to anyone who has any public visibility or public responsibility at all.

As the newborn parent group is struggling along, it must beware of false optimism. Nothing can be so disappointing as to expect a warm welcome and some success, and to meet with just the opposite. Your family may admire your efforts, but when they realize it means hanging up their own clothes and learning how to serve their own dinners, be prepared for their enthusiasm to dampen. This problem is usually self-correcting, however: they soon get accustomed to helping around the house in significant ways, and the young ones may even brag to their playmates about their important role in running the home. Encouraging responsibility, after all, is part of your purpose.

Don't expect husbands to get deeply involved in your parents' group, although one lawyer husband went so far as to write briefs for his wife's fight with the school board. Few husbands will really mean it when they complain that all you ever talk about is education; but they may ask you occasionally to pursue other subjects of conversation—say, at the boss's Christmas party. At heart husbands are usually very pleased that their wives are so attentive to the children's education.

The people who will be unhappy to see you get started, and who will become more unhappy as you keep going, are—guess who?—the education establishment. The principal will be the first to sit on the hot seat, most likely. Then on up the line, through the staff to the superintendent and finally to the board. The local PTA, which is likely to be a "kept" parents' club, will bristle at the competition and maybe even pass resolutions against you. In a few localities the PTA is what its title says, thanks to persistent effort and good politicking by some local activists. If you can wangle control of the PTA, it is certainly worth the effort: mailing lists, instant credibility, a modest budget, and the ear of education officials are frequently among the assets. But the job is not easy. The average PTA member (here again, we must generalize) usually accepts as gospel what the professionals tell him. He is not inclined to question their judgement.

Educators tend to think that parents have one supremely proper place in the system of public education. They can vote yea on bond issues. If they are truly concerned about the schools, that should be their first interest, and the less beyond it the better. In the mid-1960s there was a great hubbub from parents who for the most part didn't even pay taxes, but were nonetheless concerned about their children's education. This was the community-control movement.

Liberal establishment-type educators were in a bit of a predicament: they couldn't willingly surrender control of the

168

schools to parents, but neither could they afford to seem racist by declining to do so. After an outpouring of journal articles, a rash of conferences, and a maze of compromises, Congress defused the issue by attaching amendments to federal poverty and education programs saying that parents had to be included on planning boards and the like.

New York City was a major battlefield in the community-control struggle. The Ford Foundation studied the situation and proclaimed as if it were some new discovery that "staff professionalization . . . especially had brought increasing rigidity, in-breeding, and reluctance to any kind of structural change."[10] Militant New York City teachers had long fretted about this rigidity, and initially welcomed the community-control advocates as allies against "downtown." Soon enough, however, the parents realized that the teachers' union was as rigid, as uninterested in children, and as uncooperative as the superintendent and his minions. The union wanted guaranteed jobs for its teachers—the parents wanted the right to dismiss teachers. Who won? Between 1962 and 1967, only 12 tenured teachers out of a staff of over 55,000 were fired. During the same period only 170 regular untenured teachers were evaluated as "unsatisfactory," which does not mean they were not reemployed, because a New York City teacher is dropped only after a number of "unsatisfactory" ratings.[11] Even militant, organized parents could not prevail against the United Federation of Teachers.

Advocates of community control in Detroit succeeded by 1969 in reorganizing the school system into eight subdistricts, each with an elected community school board. The chairmen of the local boards, along with five at-large representatives, constituted a central board of education. Five years later one observer noted: "The change has not generated a strong supporting movement, nor has there been any reported impact on student achievement."[12] Community control didn't bring much relief to the hard-pressed taxpayer either: in 1976 Detroit, the nation's fifth-largest school system, faced an $11 million deficit. The voters refused a $5.00 per thousand increase in the tax rate and the district went on an austerity program, cutting first-grade classes to half a day, phasing out instrumental music teaching, eliminating interscholastic sports, and reducing the allowable number of high school credit hours from 25 to 20.[13] (When one considers the range of electives available in a large school system like Detroit, it is hard to cry over the loss of courses in oriental religions, minority psychology, filmmaking, and so on. But other losses might present a serious academic hindrance.)

Quite evidently, the taxpaying citizens of Detroit felt that the community-control enthusiasts did not represent *their* communities. To exchange one set of tyrants for another set is no advance. So the taxpayers exercised their only remaining option: the pocketbook veto. For sure, it was not easy, because the professional educators and their retinue could also be counted on to vote. And, alas, even this last-ditch effort at the polls might not help middle-class citizens if the state of Michigan decides to bail out the Detroit school system.

Chicago has more to show as a result of the community-control drive: local school councils, composed 60 percent of parents, hold monthly meetings. The principal reports to the parent-dominated school council. The council cannot fire a principal, but when a vacancy occurs, the council can name a successor, albeit from an official list of eligibles. Parent involvement has been channeled so as not to disturb collective-bargaining agreements.[14]

Militant community control, with its racial connotations, is not what middle-class parents want. Much can be learned from the community-control fight, however, and in some places middle-class parents might even go for a little ride on its coattails. It would be splendid indeed for parents to have some say in the selection of principals, even more so in the selection of teachers, but those goals are a long way off. More important to middle-class parents than control of the schools is control of their children. Insofar as children are trapped in the public system by compulsory-attendance laws, it is necessary to know how to work within the system.

170

From Shyness to Militance

Many parents are shy about interfering in their children's schooling. Generations of indoctrination about the supremacy of teachers over parents have left their mark. Of course, it is lovely (if you can) to send your children off to school and not have to worry about much more than their grades and other achievements. In the halcyon days of public education parents could do that. More recently, parents did it and came to regret it. Today, parents may try to believe all is well, but if they are even moderately curious, they cannot be at peace.

It is difficult for an ordinary middle-class citizen to become an activist. Precinct chairmen have long lamented the difficulty of getting people interested in political activities. Nevertheless, young, idealistic aspirants to political office, whether on the left or the right side of the spectrum, have found of late that they can raise a phalanx of volunteers and stimulate grass-roots enthusiasm for their campaigns if they personally approach citizens and convince them to join their cause. A man or woman on fire because he believes in a cause is entirely different from one who just ambles routinely through life.

What motivates parents' rights activity around the country? One of the most fundamental impulses of human nature: an awareness of the significance of parenthood, prompted by a sudden awareness that professional educators are undermining that vocation. It is a self-consciousness of the rights of parenthood. Children are not taken lightly; for these parents, children are a personal experience and an inescapable responsibility in time and eternity. In vivid contradistinction to the prevailing trends of society in general, these parents welcome their responsibilities, seek them out, exercise them, and defend them. The NEA may still believe that it, in conjunction with teachers and government, is responsible for the future of the nation through the education of young children, but parents are rising to resist such progressive nonsense.

Parents are the primary and most important educators of their children. That principle is grounded in natural law and is as ancient as civilization. Without it, civilization would not be. For purposes of argument, the principle of parent sovereignty can be assumed *a priori*. To be sure, parents may delegate some of their responsibility: they may share it with teachers. But the parent is the senior partner in any such power sharing and must not lose sight of that fact. The parent must not—cannot in conscience—abandon his responsibility to oversee the education of his child, no matter how tempting it might be to do so.

When parents get into a confrontation with the school system, it is only natural for them to feel embarrassed about making "such a fuss" over their children. After all, many reason, there are hundreds of other kids in the school and they're probably all as wonderful to their own parents as mine are to me, but the other parents aren't making a fuss. True enough. But a parent opposing use of a sordid film is not trumpeting the merits of her Johnny. The personal element is all but gone from a public conflict over policy. The objective merits of that film are at issue: the harm it could cause to the children who view it, the inappropriateness of spending tax money to show it. Those are the terms of the public debate. Personal elements need not and should not enter the public arena, except as necessary on rare occasions to verify a history of bad-faith dealings by teachers or administrators. Personal factors provide the motivation, but not the rhetoric, not the topic, of debate.

Parents who stick with the fight to improve the public schools often find their concerns broaden out to reach other children besides their own. Her own child's well-being might have initially prompted a mother to action; but as she goes along she sees so many other children at the mercy of the system that her interest ceases to be merely protective. Also, it takes so long for an issue to be resolved that by the time a question of reading method in first grade is settled, the child may be already in fourth or fifth. Chances are, the mother has been following up the question of the reading method, even after it ceased to be related to her child's own needs.

172

Jil Wilson, a mother-activist in Wisconsin, wrote that her concern gradually shifted from her own children to the future of society:

> As my children got into the 3rd and 4th grades I was convinced that either I was a failure as a parent or something else was wrong. . . . One day I saw my children's reading books, and I was filled with mixed emotions. I was relieved to find the problem, to know it was not me, and stunned that the schools and teachers I trusted with my children would even consider exposing my children to such material. . . .
>
> I felt the need to warn other parents because I wish someone had warned me. . . . I would love to stop. I spend money on stamps and phone calls which could go to my family's desires but it is like being a witness to someone planning a murder: if you didn't warn the potential victim you could not live with yourself. . . . I used to paint, go to plays, read books instead of the *Congressional Record,* etc. My whole life has changed. It has become a struggle, but I can't quit, not even if everyone else does. When I want desperately to quit (and I do sometimes) I know I am exhausted, and I sleep as much as possible and wake up ready to try harder. There is no ego involved in this. It embarrasses me to see my name in print, because it seems to take away from the issue, and that is what is important to me.[15]

If there is still residual embarrassment about bringing your personal motivation into the fight for better schools, remember: not only are you a parent, you are also a citizen and, most probably, a taxpayer as well. You are a voter and a member of the public. Therefore, these are *your* schools. Even if you have no children in school, your sense of civic responsibility should prompt an interest in what is happening to the children who will run America in the next generation. To be sure, that is a political interest. Your means are bound to be political, one way or another. And politics, particularly at the local level, makes individual educators personally uncomfortable: the bureaucratic instinct for self-preservation feels threatened. Teachers' unions are politically aware and active, but individuals still have the same old dislike of politics. Classroom bureaucrats tend to teach that "government . . . is a sorry business and politics unclean."[16] This is despite lipservice to "citizenship development" and rhetoric about "political awareness." Parents actively working within the political system give more positive (and more vivid) lesson in American politics than all the civics lectures in high school. In fact, parent activism is a rare example of the "textbook" American political system in action. It is a grassroots popular movement that seeks political change by working under the traditional ground rules, using the traditional channels for redress of grievances.

Education bureaucrats would breathe easier if education were sacrosanct and removed from politics. Private education is—provided it abstains from taking public money, something few administrators nowadays can or will do. As long as education is public, however, and tax-supported, and admits all comers, it is a political, governmental concern like highways or sewers and should not receive special treatment. What makes public schools different from public roads? Citizens deserve equal power over both. If a parents' group stands on its right to be concerned about the schools as part of the democratic process, educators are hard put to quarrel with the assumption. Remember how John Dewey nearly deified democracy.

The Goals of the Educationists

So not only do you, as a parent, have a natural right to be concerned about your children's education. You have a political right to be concerned about theirs and other youngsters' education, and about the future of the commonwealth in general.

Backed with those interests, what do you look for in the public schools? In 1918, an NEA Commission on Reorganization of Secondary Education listed what it thought should be the goals of public secondary education,[17] goals that were soon applied to education in general:

1. Health
2. Command of fundamental processes
3. Worthy home membership
4. Vocational efficiency
5. Civic participation
6. Worthy use of leisure time
7. Ethical character

The scope, even then, was broad, indeed revolutionary. Education as "preparation for life" was launched and given respectability by this commission, and its "Seven Cardinal Principles" were shortly adopted by the National Congress of Parents and Teachers as acceptable standards for all education. In 1918, however, few schools were likely, in the name of fostering worthy home membership, to ask students to analyze their love-hate relationships with other members of their families. Drug education was not considered important for students to make worthy use of their leisure time. On the other hand, command of fundamental processes such as reading and arithmetic has steadily lost prestige since 1918, and the goal of vocational efficiency is perpetuated mostly in the testimonies before Congress requesting money for vocational education.

In 1976 NEA's Bicentennial Committee studied these principles and found them adequate statements of the prevailing educational interests sixty years later.[18] Naturally, the Bicentennial Committee broadened the meaning of several principles.

In 1976 "health" means mental and emotional health too, and includes environmental awareness and "healthful family living." Fundamental processes still include the three Rs, but a few more have been discovered: skills in "humanistic processes" (interpersonal relations and the like), neo-academic skills (for instance, computer languages), and anticipatory skills (for example, understanding how political power is exercised at various levels from neighborhoods to international capitals). Worthy home membership should recognize that "in addition to the home cluster, there are many affinity groups of value in which children and youth might find family experiences." And the best vocational education in 1976, predictably, is a general education, since it is more likely to facilitate the self-realization necessary for meaningful personal satisfaction in vocation, if you will pardon the NEA jargon!

Citizenship today means world citizenship, according to NEA. To make worthy use of his leisure time, the student must first learn to show concern for the millions who are obliged to work a second job. Ethical character comes from self-direction, rather than "acceptance of the dictates . . . of authorities" like parents and pastors. Such, says the NEA panel, are the goals of public education as the nation enters its third century. Significantly, the panel included such profound thinkers as Norman Lear (TV producer of "All in the Family" and "Mary Hartman"), McGeorge Bundy (of the Ford Foundation, former adviser to JFK), David Rockefeller (of the Chase Manhattan Bank), and John Johnson (of *Ebony* magazine), along with a number of academicians in NEA's stable.

This statement of purpose exemplifies perfectly what parents object to in the pronouncements and practices of professional educators today. Middle-class parents (and lower-class ones, and upper-class ones too) believe it is *their* job to supervise the mental and emotional health of their children and to teach family living. A third-generation welfare recipient, it is true, might not sense as strongly her authority over her child, but that is partly because three generations of welfare workers have acted as if children were their responsibility instead.

For the school to undertake identification and diagnosis and in many cases even treatment of mental-health problems is

176

neither necessary nor desirable—especially when public education is failing at its essential duties. Unemployment is high; working-class parents expect their children to be employable after finishing school. If the school fails to teach a young mechanic how to install an electronic ignition, all the self-realization in the world won't get him a job. Patriotism, though deplored by NEA, is not dead, and all classes of parents justifiably resent textbooks that teach their children that the Soviet Union is just as fine a country as America, if only America would be more friendly. Ethical character is the province of home and church. Bureaucrats or professional behavior modifiers, whether they are called teachers or school psychiatrists, have no business interfering with a child's moral code—especially if their ultimate purpose is to instill hostility toward legitimate authority, as this statement implies.

The goals and values of the 1976 NEA Bicentennial Committee are at variance with the goals and values of average American parents. But the 1976 statement is only a recent example. For two or three decades the discrepancy has been growing. Yet educators have won out—so far—because they carried an aura of infallibility. The fallibility of the professional educators is now being exposed, as well it should be.

Parents must object strenuously when the schools trespass on their domain. The life of a child is not a statistic. Whether a child knows right from wrong is not unconnected with whether he is happy or miserable. But the social engineers don't care about that. Only parents and family care. That is why the burden of education must rest on parents.

Parents should make clear what they expect the schools to do, as well as what they expect them not to do. As the Council for Basic Education points out, the job of the schools is much simpler than educators like to admit (remember the bureaucratic tactic: confuse the issue, make it seem dense and arcane to outsiders). Mortimer Smith, former chairman of the Council for Basic Education, suggests a four-fold primary purpose for education:[19]

    1. to teach children to read, write, and figure;

2. to transmit facts about the heritage and culture of their race;

3. in the process of (1) and (2), to train the intelligence and stimulate the pleasures of thought;

4. to provide an atmosphere of moral affirmation.

So simple and yet, it seems, so difficult. Because the schools have lost interest in these four bedrock principles, Americans today are spending more on public education, and getting less for their dollar in tangible results, than ever before. The newest tendency is to blame home and society, or even genetic mutation,[20] for declining test scores. True, standardized tests are not the final word; but they are some kind of objective evaluation of the tangible accomplishments of students. College entrance standards can be lowered; youth unemployment may rise for any number of reasons; but standardized tests do indicate, even if indirectly, what the young are learning in school. The Hudson Institute has said it well: "The evidence tends to lead one to consider the hypothesis that the problems of education are more likely to originate from forces within the schools than from outside factors."[21]

To begin with, parents can look for Mortimer Smith's four basic goals, and they can work toward establishing those goals in their own schools. But many parents are likely to have more immediate, more dangerous problems that require prompt resolution:

- Unacceptable textbooks
- Unacceptable "special programs" of the guidance or psychiatrist's office
- Sex education
- Unproductive or harmful programs for "gifted" children
- Harmful classification of students
- Behavior and attitude modification
- "Parenthood" classes
- Drug education
- Busing
- Incompetently taught modern math

178

- Improper or worthless reading methods at elementary levels
- Vandalism and physical safety problems
- Drugs available at school
- Unsatisfactory teachers on the faculty

Problems such as these are urgent because for each day that an impressionable youngster is exposed to them irreversible harm can be done. The harm may not always be dramatic— the youngster may not come home and shoot his father because he was told in school it's O.K. to "let his frustrations all hang out." But the lad may gradually develop a preference for sensational books, or may become excessively introspective, or feel that studies are a waste of time, or become preoccupied with sex, or feel unloved and unwanted, or feel condemned to failure, or develop slovenly habits, or turn to drugs for kicks. These things do happen, but they would happen less if certain other things were not taught, implicitly or explicitly, in the public schools.

Step One: The Teacher

How does a parent begin to try to exert some influence on the public school? Like Mrs. Adams and Mrs. Bowditch of the earlier scenarios, most start by discussing their complaint with their child's teacher. That is the best place to begin. An individual teacher most likely cannot solve a problem that she did not start, but it is absolutely vital not to give your child's teacher the idea that you have gone over her head by not talking to her. Your child, do not forget, is at that teacher's mercy six hours a day. You do not want the teacher thinking you are some kind of a nut, or an agent of some right-wing cabal.

Approach the teacher on a person-to-person basis: discuss your child's schoolwork and the class in general, and be sure you manage to express the depth of your concern over whatever is bothering you. It is not so terrible if the teacher thinks

179

you are nervous or tend to worry—it probably is an accurate assessment. You *are* worried about your child's education. Don't act hostile; avoid letting the teacher think you feel she's just a pawn in the hands of a monolithic NEA conspiracy; never slur her intelligence or competence. If she proves uncooperative or hostile, turn the other cheek as much as you can. Remember, you must shield your child from her personal animus. If she cannot or will not give you the information you are seeking, such as test scores, ask her where you can get it, and politely let her know you will be pursuing the matter. And thank her for the time she took to meet with you.

Above all, protect the privacy of your talks with your child's teacher. Don't go around saying, "Miss Johnson herself said she thought the principal was a little uptight on the subject." Any remark like that is bound to get back to either or both the individuals mentioned, and pity Miss Johnson if she hears it from the principal. You can be sure she won't like you at all —and unless she has a saintly disposition, she will be hard put to treat your child impartially thereafter. Sometimes classroom teachers are blessed with good instincts and good sense, despite their training, and are inclined to be sympathetic to you. If you find such a teacher, don't encourage her to rock the boat. Don't try to milk her for information. Don't pass her name around to your friends either, unless they ask you a year later who taught your child in fourth grade and was she any good. Do let the principal know you think she is a fine teacher. A good custom is to write a personal letter to the principal at the end of the year, if you have something good to say about the school. Chances are, the principal will know when something displeases you: work strenuously to avoid being known as an excusively negative, disagreeable malcontent.

If you don't have good rapport with your child's teacher, be very careful not to give her any ammunition against you. If it's your turn to be playground monitor, make sure nothing interferes with your being there. If the class mothers are expected to bake cookies for the Christmas party, send some cookies.

A very important point: don't unburden on your elementary schoolchild your disagreement with his teacher. If action on the child's part is unavoidable, tell him: "It's not Miss Johnson's fault. But she knows I want you to go to the library when the green books are used. So be sure you say, 'Excuse me, Miss Johnson,' and be sure you remember to leave the class and not return until she sends for you." The last thing you or your youngster needs is for your son to be overheard telling his classmates that you think Miss Johnson is a crypto-pinko. As your children grow older, you will know how tactful they are, and can judge as you go along how much to discuss with them. Even at the youngest age, you should always try to make them understand, according to their ability, that mother and father have serious reasons for doing what they're doing, and what those reasons are.

Schools and individual teachers vary greatly in their attitudes toward parental involvement. Few actually welcome it with open arms. Some strenuously discourage it.[22] In New York City a teacher is supposed to "maintain good relations with other teachers," but must only *"make an effort* to establish and maintain good relationships with parents" (emphasis added).[23]

Recently, as criticism of their performance has heated up, schools have more and more been allowing or encouraging parents to serve in a variety of volunteer programs. If parents make themselves useful to teachers and advance the purposes of the school, NEA endorses their participation since "school volunteer programs can do much to stimulate community interest, understanding, and support for education. This in turn can help pass bond issues. . . ."[24]

The most militant activists regard volunteer programs as a means of co-opting parents. That aspect is not to be overlooked. If a more or less innocent parent hears only the school's version of things, any criticism he may voice will naturally be muted. Particularly in inner-city areas, mothers who make their presence felt are often invited into the establishment in some nominal capacity, to lessen the likelihood of their complaining over the head of the principal. But once she gets her foot in the door, a mother can personally keep track of who teaches her child, what bullies are in the class, and other matters essential to survival in a high-danger area.

Parents can learn a great deal by volunteering inside a school, if they find the time to do it. Substitute teaching on a regular basis is also a good way to gather intelligence. If something seems wrong, don't be lulled by the glib explanations and the "we've always done it this way" copouts; instead, find out where the decisionmaking power really lies. If you want to stay on as a volunteer, keep your criticisms mostly to yourself; if you want to remain a parent activist, do not let your critical faculties be put to sleep. This is not to say you should be a malcontent, looking for NEA iniquity under every desk, because you will not find it. You will find many sincere teachers who are doing the best they can.

If in the course of volunteering you come across something really good, a filmstrip or textbook, or a sensible logistical plan, let the person responsible know that you think it's a good idea. But guard against the temptation to shift your loyalties. Don't start looking at things from an educationist's point of view or from a bureaucratic angle. Explanations and excuses come easily if your assumptions are collectivist and your values are those of the school and your goals are theirs, namely, full funding, innovation, professional status, job security, docile subjects, and no boat rocking. As a parent you care about the moral and intellectual growth of your individual youngster and want the same for other youngsters. When those goals conflict with the professionals' love of innovation or love of status quo—and it could be either way—you must recognize the conflict.

Step Two: The Bureaucracy

Having made a strong effort to mend fences with the teacher, your next likely stop is the school's administration office. If you want your child switched to another class, the principal is the one to see. If you object to a film or a book, the odds are that responsibility has been delegated to someone else in middle management. Find out who is the proper person to see, even if it means working your way up the ladder, as it probably will.

For example, in high schools department chairmen sometimes exercise considerable discretion over textbook choice, and sometimes none. In some new schools an "instructional materials specialist" may know where ultimate authority rests, if not with himself. In some areas, decisions on materials are made for the whole district; in that case you must go to the district administration office. Should that happen, do not skip over your school's administration officials. It may not be necessary to spend much time with them (which will probably please them), but at least the requirements of protocol will be met.

The principal may try to get you to meet with an assistant. Resist that brushoff unless you know from experience that the assistant is in a policymaking position. Very likely he is not. He may be a charming individual whose job description includes defusing irate parents, and who is neither interested in nor capable of helping you, although he will give you the impression that all will be taken care of in due time if you leave it to him. If you run into this type of character, and he makes vague promises of action about your complaint, write down his exact words while you're sitting there in his office. This will unnerve him, because he probably wasn't expecting to find you so serious, but it is vital to you. Read back his remarks and ask him to correct them. After your meeting, write him a letter setting forth your understanding of his promises, quoting him as he told you to, and saying that unless you hear to the contrary you will regard his statements as school policy on the matter. Watch carefully to see if anything happens that he said would. If nothing does, your copy of the letter will then serve as documentation of your case when you take further action.

Of course, this little tactic is not limited to dealings with no-bodies in administration; it works just as well with somebod-ies. Use it!

Never go alone to a meeting with the administration when policy is to be discussed. If your meeting is about your child, try to get your husband there too, so you will have at least one witness even for a private matter. But for policy meetings you should have at least two other parents; more than five people, however, is usually a crowd.

If Nathaniel's mom can talk Chuck's mom into going to see the principal about Miss Reilly's sensitivity training in English class, that is a good beginning. Chuck's mom may know an-other anxious parent. Failing that, ask Nathaniel and Chuck if there is another lad in the class who has reservations, and talk to his parents.

If the meeting is set up by an already organized parents' group, it should not be hard to find the requisite number of parents. However—and this principle applies to all meetings and hearings you will ever attend, and statements you will ever make—if the topic under discussion is fifth-grade social studies, be absolutely sure that the parents who open their mouths have children in the fifth-grade social studies program, or at least had them in the same program last year. The mother whose youngest is a high school junior will not be a credible witness, not to the principal, not to the school board, not to the press, and not to other parents either. Make sure your spokesmen are credible.

The advantages of going in groups to visit the administrator are several. First is morale: one mother may feel very timid, and it will show. Even a bold mother may be thrown off balance when the principal asks someone else to "sit in with us"—for instance, the guidance counselor whose activities are being questioned—and later she will have her word against both of theirs as the only record of the meeting.

If there is an extra person along, that one can be assigned to take notes. Don't be shy about note-taking: this is a meeting on the public record. If the principal (or whoever) retaliates by calling his secretary in to take notes for him, fine. Don't object. You are getting a response.

Of course, it is not polite to show up with four people when you had made an appointment for two. To satisfy etiquette, call the principal's secretary the morning of the meeting and tell her you will be bringing along two more people. If the principal doesn't get your message, it is not your fault. About timing, by the way: do not settle for an appointment at 2:00 P.M. on the day of a big football game. You can be sure something will be happening around 2:30 that will urgently need the principal's attention. Also avoid lunch periods. You have gone to some trouble to set up this appointment; make sure you get every minute of it.

How to act in the meeting? Well, how not to act is probably more important. From time to time NEA advises readers of its journal how to deal with angry parents. Examining those guidelines may help you to design a counterattack.

For example, in a December 1975 article, NEA writer Walter St. John reminds his readers that "imagined grievances are as serious to the person who feels them as real ones," "that people are *primarily* emotional, not rational" (emphasis in original), and that "even those who have no justifiable beef are entitled to a diplomatic explanation of why they are in error."[25] The educator's assumptions, then, are these: most parents' complaints are likely to be imaginary, irrational, and unfounded. Nonetheless—oh, generosity!—the complainers deserve to be treated politely.

Six specific guidelines are given, including two of special note:

1. "Do not interrupt . . . let the person talk as much as . . . she needs to talk. The experience may act as a cathar-sis. . . ."

2. "Assure the person of your genuine concern. Usually, if you have . . . displayed understanding of the complaining person's perception of the problem, the battle is half won. The climate should be such that you can now begin to explain things as you perceive them."

What does this say about how NEA thinks irate parents typically act? Since the administrator-educator is cautioned not to interrupt, it suggests the parent is expected to monopolize the conversation, babbling on in a torrent of words, which the administrator can let flow over him as long as he catches the general idea. After the parent has exhausted himself, the administrator starts to gear his answer to what he deduces the parent expects to hear. In all likelihood, this sketch conforms to reality. Undoubtedly, angry mothers, having finally gotten the ear of somebody in the bureaucratic maze, are determined to give a piece of their mind—and out it all comes. Suddenly it's the end of the meeting, mommy has gotten everything off her chest, but the administrator has said hardly anything and has not been questioned, and nothing has been achieved.

Lesson: do not go on a verbal rampage. In fact, try to avoid voicing your opinions first. Appoint one spokesman for your little group, and let that one speak for you all. After the usual pleasantries, the spokesman might ask the principal directly, "What do you see as the purpose of the sensitivity training sessions in Miss Reilly's honors English class?" If the principal doesn't seem familiar with Miss Reilly's class at all, show your surprise that he doesn't know what is being done to some of the brightest kids in the school. If he does know something about it, he will give you his feelings on sensitivity training in very general terms, full of platitudes and jargon. *But at least it is jargon volunteered by him.* On the other hand, if you the parents had spoken first and talked about the iniquities of sensitivity training and the offense against parental values and so on, the administrator could couch his answers in your kind of language. So, for general purposes, let the other side speak first. The other side will be cautious, and so must you be. Don't explode with your frustrations and opinions until the principal has had a chance to commit himself to something. Then, if all four of your group have some contribution to make, each one should identify himself, come right to the point, and state his evidence. No more.

Above all, *do not become emotional.* Emotional parents, particularly mothers, seldom get anywhere with a bureaucrat. If you are all worked up, steel yourself and let your anger make you forceful. Do not allow yourself be handled like a frenzied feline—by being mentally put into a cage. If the administrator dismisses you, in his own mind, as an emotional female of no significance, almost automatically he will dismiss your case as trivial. That is easy for him: you have showed yourself incapable of speaking in cold, hard facts. Can you expect to be regarded as a serious threat? Remember, if you are not a serious threat to the complacency of bureaucratic routine, you will accomplish nothing. Collapsing in tears or in rhetoric is the most ineffective thing you can do.

In sum, then, plan your meeting carefully. Bring with you people who have something pertinent to add, and are credible sources. Prime them to say their one piece, and no more. Let your spokesman speak for all of you. Stay on the subject; do not lecture on the evils of internationalism; talk only about the fifth-grade social studies program. Have one of your group take notes. Ask the administrator to make his statement before you let him know your opinion. Follow up his remarks with questions and facts. Have plenty of facts at the ready (but remember to preserve the anonymity of your sources, unless you are talking about matters of general information). Do not be satisfied with vague promises of "looking into it." Have suggestions ready on how you think the situation can be improved. Do not promise you will be satisfied if such and such is done; indicate only that you think it might be the beginning of a solution. Let the administrator know you will be closely following the problem to see the solution. And then, by George, do closely follow it. If three weeks pass and nothing has changed, make sure the principal hears from you.

If your parent group is small and spread too thin, as most parent groups are, that is no excuse. It damages your group to start something you cannot finish—to say nothing of the harm it does to the prospects for a happy resolution of future parent grievances. Bureaucrats generalize. If one parent delegation comes in to talk about sensitivity training, and is emotional and disorganized, and talks about an NEA conspiracy to undermine American morals, and then is never heard from again after all that, the next time a parent delegation tries to get in to see the administrator, on whatever topic, he is likely to push them off on an assistant and ignore them. You do not want to poison the well for all parents by making a bad impression with your own group.

Accuracy!

The parent activist's watchword is *accuracy*. If your neighbor has a baby and the woman in the next hospital bed tells her she heard that the federal government is requiring all school districts to introduce a psychological test for students in Title III programs, that is no reason to run to the principal and ask him if it is true. It is not enough evidence to merit mention at your public meeting. Don't even put it into your newsletter. If that is all you know about the matter, forget it. Hearsay like that is fraught with hazards. Remember the old table game, where one person whispered something to the person next to him, and it went around the table, and by the time it got back to the originator it was totally unrecognizable? Well, the same thing can happen on the concerned-parent circuit. Baseless rumors can only harm your cause.

The case for parents' rights can be made with facts and figures, and a basic principle or two. If you rely on fantasy, you unwittingly support the contention that parents are not reliable. This book has many footnotes. They are intended to be used. The newsletter your group puts out should also have many footnotes. The position paper you present to the board of education should have many footnotes too. And they should not be to the same two sources. After all, Max Rafferty is expected to be against affective education. To quote black militant William Raspberry in favor of basic education is more effective. You want to be taken seriously; you want to be treated as responsible, reliable, reasonable people who are part of the real world. You want, most of all, to avoid being stereotyped as the "little old lady in tennis shoes" or the "teased-hair trio" or the "pantsuit brigade." To avoid this you must keep the opposition guessing—not about your next lunacy, but about how well you can handle them on their terms. What if their terms are liberal-biased and ungodly? That, unfortunately, is the condition of the world today. If you are going to fight the world, you have got to make yourself understood and you have got to gain the only respect the world knows how to give. So be as wise as serpents.

In 1971 both chambers of Congress passed a Comprehensive Child Development Bill. It was headed for the President's desk and was expected to be signed. There had been no outcry against it. Then, in November, parents around the country started hearing what was in this bill and what it would do to the American family. The Washington, D.C.-based Emergency Committee for Children prepared solid information and distributed it around the country to various parents' groups, which in turn copied the information and distributed it further. The Emergency Committee quoted the bill in question, with line and paragraph number; when it quoted senators in debate, it provided the page number and date of the *Congressional Record;* when it quoted testimony before congressional committees, it provided the name of the committee, name of witness, date of hearing, and page number of transcript. The response was excellent. Thousands of letters were sent to the White House. President Nixon vetoed the bill. In the meantime, thousands of letters were also mailed to senators and congressmen, letters citing page number, date, and name so that the congressional offices could check the sources and find out that the letter writers were not kooks. Realizing that their constituents felt so strongly, and for good reason, dozens of senators and congressmen reconsidered their position. The veto was upheld.

Compare this with what happened five years later, in 1976. A similar bill was before Congress. This time somebody, operating on his own, prepared a flyer, full of sensational statements, quoting from an unidentified "declaration of children's rights," appealing to citizens to write Washington to stop the bill. No sources were given for any of the statements, and the author did not say where he had found the declaration of children's rights (it turned out to be a left-wing British document, but the impression conveyed was that it was a U. S. government statement). But the flyer was circulated far and wide among churches and parents, and 2,000 to 6,000 letters a day came into the office of Senator Walter Mondale, the bill's chief sponsor.[26] The letter writers took the flyer at face value and quoted it, basing their outrage upon the "facts" in the flyer. Mondale could afford to laugh at this deluge of mail; he compared it to hoof-and-mouth disease, and in a sense it was a memorable example of foot-in-mouth disease.

To this day nobody knows who originated that flyer. Very few of its claims were correct. Sure, the author had the correct idea of the general direction of family-undermining legislation. But he did not have *facts* to support his perception. Those who quoted him did not have facts. Therefore, it was easy for Senator Mondale to say, "These people are objecting to something that doesn't exist. My bill doesn't say this; these letters don't represent opposition to my bill." If the child-development lobby had wanted to undermine the effectiveness of the parent lobby, it could hardly have found a better way to ruin the credibility of parental objections to the Child and Family Services bill.

Furthermore, the author of the flyer did not realize how foolish it was to have parents send letters of protest to the sponsor of the bill. Of course he was not going to change his mind! Those hundreds of letters should have been sent instead to uncommitted and unaware congressmen from the districts in which the letter writers resided, and to the senators from the states in which they resided. Then at least those elected officials would have learned that their constituencies were concerned about parents' rights. As it was, Mondale got a good laugh, and the nation got closer to a child-development

190

bill. The saddest aspect is that many parents may not try again for a long time to flex their political muscle.

This is an example of the great harm that can be done at a national level by simple inaccuracy. Without a doubt, the same story has been repeated on a smaller scale in every school district in America. A parents' group is careless about a fact: perhaps it takes somebody's word that so-and-so said such and such, that the proposal before the board would do this or that, that the department head had agreed to do a or b. Somebody's word is not enough. If it is a newspaper article, and you cite it, you're a bit safer, because then the newspaper reporter gets blamed if he is careless with his facts. Which is why newspaper reporters try to be accurate in reporting events.

If you mean to circulate a rumor, don't do it on your official stationery or in the name of your group. If you are going to present a statement to the board of education, be sure there is nothing in the statement that an unfriendly board member can point to as evidence that you don't know what you're talking about. Not one single error of fact. Yes, of course, if you were the NEA representative, you might be able to get away with it. But you are on the minority side, so you will be subjected to merciless scrutiny, and you must be prepared to cope with that if you intend to accomplish your purpose.

Step Three: Boards and More Bureaucrats

You have exhausted your personal contacts; you have explained yourself to your child's teacher. You have informed the principal of your concerns and your intention to get satisfaction. In all likelihood the classroom teacher was powerless to help you, and the principal almost the same, plus maybe unwilling. Now you must start finding out who runs the schools.

One state, Hawaii, has what is called a single-echelon school system, that is, the state education agency controls everything everywhere. If you live in Hawaii, therefore, you need not bother with local politicking at all, but can concentrate on statewide decisions. Of course, if you live on one of the remote islands this may be difficult to do. Perhaps that built-in handicap is why Hawaii does not have an active parents' movement.

A number of states have two-echelon systems, in which the local education agency deals directly with the state education agency. Thus, if your local board tells you it has to teach drug-abuse education because it is "state policy," you at least know that some bureaucrat in the state capital is probably to blame. States with two-echelon systems are: Alabama, Alaska, Connecticut, Delaware, Florida, Georgia, Idaho, Kentucky, Louisiana, Maryland, Nevada, New Mexico, North Carolina, Tennessee, Utah, Virginia, and West Virginia.

The most up-to-date thing to do is to confuse the picture with a three-echelon system: the state education agency, an intermediate body, and then the local education agency. These intermediaries vary in responsibility and function from state to state. Finding out who does what can be a near-impossible task. And responsibilities can change overnight, since only executive decisions, and no public knowledge or input, are required to make a change. Thirty-two states have the three-echelon system, including New York, where the middleman is called Boards of Cooperative Educational Services (BOCES), Texas (Regional Education Service Centers), Wisconsin (Cooperative Educational Service Agency), and Colorado (Boards of Cooperative Service). The large states, which have consolidated numerous small districts into fewer larger ones, often feature the three-echelon system.

So the picture rapidly becomes confused. Add to this the fact that the bureaucrats in the state capital most likely hold their jobs under some kind of a state civil-service system, which means they will probably never leave (although they may switch from division to division and title to title with infuriating frequency). The policy-level people are appointed by the state commissioner of education, often on the recommendation of the state NEA affiliate. In 29 states, the commissioner's office is not even elected, but filled by appointment of the governor or the state board of education, which itself is elected in only 15 states. State legislatures, of course, can write laws affecting education, so the education lobby devotes a good part of its resources to the care and feeding of friendly legislators. Getting into that game is just about the only direct means of influencing state-level decisions, however. It is difficult, it is expensive, it is time consuming, and it is very sophisticated. But to be effective, parent action must eventually zero in on the state legislatures, as well as the Congress of the United States.

That is not to suggest that local boards should be ignored. Far from it. When a local board gets itself into trouble with parents, the higher level is usually quite happy to leave it to its own devices. In many states, though, local school districts operate under Dillon's rule, according to which a local governing body has only those powers specifically granted to it by a superior governing body—sort of a reversal of the Tenth Amendment. Far better, from a parents' rights standpoint, is the principle of subsidiarity: let the local body do whatever it can, let all problems be solved at the lowest level of bureaucracy. Home rule, in short. Local boards, for obvious reasons, prefer this principle. To include it in state education codes would be a good project for a friendly legislator to undertake in a state where Dillon's law prevails.[27]

The "organized profession" dislikes local school boards. They are the traditional roadblock to progressive education:

> It must be recognized, too, that our time-honored system of local control has not been an unmixed blessing. Local school boards have been responsible for much that is mean, petty and repressive in American education. It has been local boards of education, for the most part, which have banned and burned books, fired non-conforming teachers, and restricted educational opportunity for reasons of race or social class. Small school districts have

often served as havens for hoarded wealth, privilege, and race quite contrary to our democratic
principles.[28]

With enemies saying things like that, local school boards
need friends. The only place they are likely to find them is
among the local citizenry. The teachers' union, of course,
resents the board because of its stinginess at contract-negotia-
tion time. The professional staff tries to keep the board on its
good side, so that the members will be receptive to the staff's
programs, but the professionals seldom have much respect for
mere laymen.

So, if as a citizens' group you can befriend the board, you
will be appreciated. How much good it does you is another
matter. Boards are not like city councils; they are not legally
responsible to those who elect them. Rather, a school board
"is purely a creature of the state. Its power may be enlarged,
diminished, modified, or revoked by the legislature."[29] The
popular mythology is that parents delegate to the board the
power of educating their children; in fact, the state has already
snatched that right away from parents and in turn has delegated it to the board. Such, at least, is what courts have held.
But the myth of local control persists.

Of course, a local board of education can do a number of
things, often simply because they are too monotonous for a
higher body to care about them. Education textbooks enumerate the general areas of local responsibility as—

1. development and improvement of the educational program;

2. selection of chief administrative officer and provision of
professional staff;

3. provision of funds and facilities;

4. maintenance of good relations with the community.[30]

Thus, it is within the competence of the local board to
mandate some aspects of the curriculum, to require certain
courses or to prohibit certain courses. The local board can
require that phonics be taught. It can prescribe courses in

194

free-enterprise economics for the high schools under its control. In about half the states, local boards have sole responsibility for selection of textbook and materials. Slightly less than half have state textbook commission lists from which the local districts may choose materials. Local boards can establish "alternative" public schools if they are convinced the community wants them, and if logistics permit. The board has authority to fire the superintendent. It has the authority to put up a new school building. If parents want junk-food vending machines banned, the board can do it; some boards already have.[31] If parents are unhappy about some aspect of school management, the board can set up a committee to investigate and study the matter. However, such citizen advisory committees are usually created to divert parental energies into unproductive outlets, and too often they succeed.

Concerned parents must not ignore the activities of the local board. But as the focus of parent activity shifts to the state and federal levels, it is easy to understand how local goings-on become less compelling. Even so, local concerns must not be ignored. Perhaps one member of a parents' group can be assigned to monitoring local affairs exclusively. Board meetings are held regularly, about once a month, and generally are open to the public. It may be possible to make a presentation to the board if the matter is sufficiently grave and if a member of the board is sufficiently interested to put you on the agenda. If you should have the chance to appear before the board, do not use your appearance as the springboard for a new campaign. Consider the board as a last resort, if principal and superintendent fail to satisfy you on a particular problem. The board is busy and is not well disposed to take up a new issue before all other channels have been exhausted.

Many boards publish newsletters, or reports of their meetings. Sometimes they have other publications as well. An activist parent should read all such things and read them carefully, between the lines. The same exhortation would apply to public relations items and anything else put out by the administration or the individual schools. All that reading is a good-sized

195

job, but it can be made easier by dividing the labor among members of a parents' group.

Since the board most often is elected by the public, its members can also be defeated by the public. To some extent, therefore, board members are interested in public reaction to them and their deeds. Let the board know your opinion on matters of importance, but do not make yourself a nuisance on every little item. You want your remarks to be taken seriously; space out your complaints. Don't be the boy who cried wolf at every board meeting. Local boards, more than almost any other political institution, can be swayed by a stack of petitions submitted before a major vote. But it does no good to get 10,000 signatures from nonregistered voters if you are working toward long-range goals. It is possible to replace an undesirable board member, but not with nonregistered voters as your ammunition.

The school district administration also has a large load of responsibility. Again a textbook enumeration:

1. Administration of the education program
2. Administration of finance and facilities
3. Personnel administration
4. Administration of school-community relations[32]

Here lies considerable effective power. The board may prescribe a general policy, but even in that it usually acts on recommendations from the administration, and by logistical necessity leaves the execution of its policies up to the administration. Thus, the administration actually revises the curriculum, if the board mandates a revision, and recommends renewal of teacher contracts, supervises student behavior, evaluates school programs, and sets criteria for admission and graduation and promotion above the basic state standards, to name areas of frequent parent concern.

The superintendent is subject to firing if public pressure against him becomes strong enough, but the professional staff under him is not generally bound by similar limitations. Just as a senator relies on his aides to tell him how to vote, a superintendent takes the word of his staff about what to do,

196

but himself bears the brunt of responsibility for that decision. Even if the superintendent departs, the problem is not solved, because the bureaucrats are likely still to be there, administering the school district during the vacancy and making recommendations to the successor.

The local school administration is not a very good place for parents to start applying pressure for school reform, because it consists of bureaucrats, who have no real authority to make changes. Bureaucrats nestle in paper and love to be limited by regulations from the local board and the state and federal governments. They need a buffer to insulate them from the public. Even if the regulations do not preclude what you may be demanding, a true bureaucrat will believe they do, and act accordingly.

A rule of thumb might be to deal with the administration only on specific matters that directly touch you and your child. If a school program is adversely affecting your child, and the principal cannot or will not exempt your child, then go to the superintendent before you go to the board. If you want to see your child's test scores and cannot get them from the principal, talk to the superintendent of schools (more likely his administrative assistant, unless you're very insistent), and visit the appropriate suboffice that handles such a request. You may end up taking the matter to the board after all, but you will be better treated there if you have tried the established channels first. Naturally, if you get the feeling that you are just spinning your wheels, you will not spend too much of your time going through established channels.

In any event, much of what local boards and administration can do is prescribed already by the state commissioner (or superintendent) of education and his bureaucracy, under more or less vague direction from the state board of education or the state legislature. These bureaucrats in the state capital are the main regulators of both private and public schools: they draft state plans for this or that, they distribute state and federal moneys, they interpret the state laws pertaining to education, they present budget requests to the legislature, they inaugurate pilot programs, they resolve local conflicts, and so on.

Examples: a local board cannot allow parents to keep their little boys home until the more appropriate age of seven because state law says they must go to school at five or six. A local board might want to allow students to graduate after receiving a certain score on achievement tests, but most states have either laws or policies that stipulate 18 hours or no diploma. A local board may want to allow credit for correspondence courses, but the state education agency forbids it.

In Texas, in 1973, the legislature passed a bill requiring free-enterprise instruction in the high schools. Representative Kaster, who wrote the bill, intended the course to be a graduation prerequisite for all students. But the language of the law was not indisputably clear, so the Texas education agency was able to interpret the law so that public schools in Texas merely had to offer the course.

Many reforms desired by parents probably could, technically, originate with the state education agencies (depending, of course, on the state), which would save everyone the difficulty and effort of taking the legislative route. But in most places state-level education agencies are staffed by ambitious professional educators, who by definition are a bit more progressive than their peers and simply are not sympathetic to "conservative" or "backward" parental concerns.

However, remember this: the bureaucrats in the state education agency do not always have the last word. Advisory commissions are often set up to assist the state commissioner or board. In practice, these special commissions usually take the suggestions of the state education agency because nobody else knows they exist. But that can be changed. A board of examiners, for instance, might set teacher training and licensing standards, and may be appointed by the state board. The law establishing this board of examiners might be decades old and forgotten, but it just might stipulate public hearings before teacher-licensing standards can be changed. Similar public committees may have jurisdiction over vocational-educa-

198

tion programs, or over state college policies, or over early-childhood education in the state. Parent activists should explore all avenues for opportunities to organize and state their views, buttonhole members of the commission, call the attention of the press to the issues, and thus budge the governmental system. It may be discovered that the state education agency is recommending nine college credit hours in behavioral psychology as a prerequisite to a teaching license. A knowledgeable parent could go to the hearing on that proposal, armed with textbooks from college behavioral psych courses and documented quotations from leaders in the field, to make the case that this is not the kind of thing teachers in our state should be forced to study. A substantive presentation may provoke a reaction from the commission, whose members may be ordinary citizens who usually get stuck with very dull and repetitive business. They may be happy to have something interesting to talk about for a change, and to get some publicity for themselves as well.

Keeping informed about such hidden opportunities is another big job. It will vary from state to state. In some cases, a close reading of the state education code will reveal the existence and function of many forgotten commissions. In other cases, the state board of education itself will have created the commission, making it harder to find out about. Some state boards of education issue policy summaries; others do not. Once you find your opportunity, however, and spark some forgotten commission to take an interest in your topics, be prepared to find that commission very soon unforgotten by the rest of the education establishment in your state.

Whatever you do, do not approach the commission with the martyr complex that is all too common among parents new to the fight. Don't be paranoid. Don't assume that the commission members are all evil schemers who have signed the Humanist Manifesto. Officials appointed to part-time commissions frequently know nothing about the subject matter and are at the mercy of their advisers. You cannot expect them to be knowledgeable: assume they are innocent of nefarious intentions until they prove the contrary. Approach them as you would an uncommitted, uninformed legislator. Give them a brief orientation course. Explain the issue. Then tell them what they should do about it.

Step Four: The State Legislative Route

A few states in the nation hold short, sweet legislative sessions. The Texas legislature, for example, meets only in odd-numbered years, and then for only a few months. No doubt the brevity and infrequency of legislative sessions helps explain why Texas is one of the five states without an income tax.

The tendency, of course, is to go in the opposite direction: long sessions, lasting almost all year, every year. Under such conditions a given piece of legislation may have more than one chance to pass in a single session. There will also be more opportunities to introduce legislation. However, the education interest groups know these advantages too, and often find it worth their while to maintain full-time lobbyists during the year. The net effect is that measures favored by the education establishment tend to be enacted into law, while measures favored by parents are not, because parents have other things to do for most of the year than to dog the heels of lawmakers.

Success in politics, whether it is a matter of getting yourself elected or a bill passed, requires, first and foremost, *organization of effort*. And, alas, the typical concerned parent is politically inexperienced and disorganized. One should not say naive: he has transcended naivete once he realizes that public schools are not really controlled by the public, and that decisions of school boards and legislatures are not really made according to textbook descriptions. But inexperience is harder to remedy, because parents lack free time and usually lack teachers as well as leaders. State Senators Joan Gubbins of Indiana and Jim Skelly of Arizona are exceptional in their commitment to parents' rights, their willingness to work with parent groups, and their skill at coaching inexperienced but

200

sincere parents in the tactics of legislative influence. If only there were at least one such person in each of the other 48 state legislatures, the parents' rights cause would have come much further by now.

As time passes and parent issues become more widely recognized, similar leaders may emerge in other states. At present, however, the job of developing leaders belongs largely to parents who need a spokesman for their cause. The American Legislative Exchange Council, a national alliance of state legislators, is available to offer assistance along these lines. ALEC is also working to develop leadership potential for a wide range of comparable issues.[33]

Human nature sometimes hampers organization of parent efforts. Parents naturally put the needs of their families first. If a son or daughter gets the measles at the precise time that lobbying for a bill will make the crucial difference, a hired persuader will go right ahead and lobby, but a parent will stay home to nurse the child. This is the Achilles heel of parent groups. But could a concerned parent put in a better performance without neglecting family duties? Probably not, as long as the children are young and the extended family is uncommon. As the children grow up, parents have more freedom to operate—but alas, by that time many have gotten over their anxiety about education. For the present, though, knowing that you are not as efficient as an NEA lobbyist should be no reason not to try your hardest all the same, in hopes that your fervor might win for you something that his comfort cannot win for him.

How do you identify a potential parents' rights leader in the state legislature?

Suppose a group of parents is lobbying against a proposal that would mandate kindergarten attendance. Going door-to-door in the state house, the parents meet a legislator who agrees with them. He also indicates in conversation that he resents being pressured by the educrats and wishes his colleagues could hear more of the parents' point of view. He assures the parents that he will vote against this new measure,

201

and thanks them for the information they have given him in their brief presentation today.

What do you, the parents, do to make maximum use of this individual's cooperative spirit? First, tell him you appreciate his vote. Then ask him what else might he be willing to do. Offer to help him every step of the way. Would you give a speech against the bill on the floor? We'll draft one for you. Would you issue a press release against it? We'll come to stuff envelopes for you and will mail copies around the state to our own press lists too. Would you be willing to come to Our Town to speak on the subject? We'll see that you're invited and guarantee 60 people in the audience. Would you introduce a substitute bill to raise the compulsory attendance age to eight? We'll provide you with research documenting the merits of keeping youngsters at home until that age, and we'll write speeches for you.

The legislator will be impressed—not only that you have ideas for further action, which is rare enough, but that you are prepared to help him carry them out. You just might have put a bee in his bonnet. If he does ask you to write a speech for him, make it good. Err on the side of being too precise, too correct, and horribly meticulous in everything from grammar to typing, but especially in content. Cite a source for every quote you use. Do not make a statement that you do not back up. Do not misrepresent the bill under discussion. Remember, you do not want to give the opposition an excuse to jump all over your friend.

In other words, turn out a better performance than he expects. That gets you started toward becoming indispensable to him. Never, never disappoint him with the quality of your effort or your product. If you find you have overcommitted yourself, tell him that you won't be able to have such and such done by the 15th, as you had promised—and don't wait until the 14th to tell him. Never let your assistance bring embarrassment to him: if he delivers a speech and the opposition attacks one of the statements in it, you had better come forward quickly with the correct information to back up his statement. If you haven't got it, you may not be welcomed back to his office. In the practice of politics, one mistake is all you get. Your friendly legislator must live by that rule and so must you. Second chances come rarely in politics. You should not expect to be offered one.

If the legislator journeys to your part of the state, away from his own district, to give a speech for you, he may do it free because he is genuinely concerned about the issue. But, by golly, if you have promised him 60 people, make good and sure that more than 15 show up. For all you know, the man is considering running for higher office and came in part because he hoped to build some grassroots support in your area or wanted press coverage for his name. And you have given him nothing.

Conversely, if you promise to write a speech for him, and provide a good one, which you afterward distribute to people on your statewide mailing list, you have done the legislator a great favor. By performing well when you promise to do something, you can bring him to the realization that you can indeed help him; and for your part, you can feel freer about asking him to do something for you another time. State lawmakers do not have the personal staff that members of Congress do; local board members have virtually none. That circumstance offers a crucial "in" to concerned parents: by doing the invisible, anonymous support work for a public spokesman, and doing it well, parents can bring out leadership among legislators, board members, and other public figures. Unless parents provide this support work, however, there is nobody to provide it. The education lobby, remember, is working on the other side of nearly every issue. And although a politician may be sympathetic, he is also very busy—usually too busy to undertake the work necessary to make a full-blown fight over a piece of legislation.

Marcia Sielaff of Phoenix, Arizona was a parent who trusted the schools but wondered why her youngest son could not read well. Eventually she came all the way around to political work. With the assistance of her fellow parents in Let's Improve Today's Education (LITE), she practiced this cardinal rule of winning friends in politics. The assistance Marcia and LITE provided State Senators Jim Skelly and, before him, John Conlan on the dull, tedious, repetitive, detailed work of going through, line by line, state guidelines and manuals and course requirements and policy statements enabled Conlan and Skelly to accomplish some substantive educational reforms in Arizona. They emerged as leaders in Arizona, and Arizona in turn became a leader in the nation for parents' rights in education. Without the backup work provided by the parents who kept their kitchen counters cluttered with paper but never received public mention, Conlan and Skelly could not have revised the course requirements for social studies in the state, or enacted a free-enterprise instruction law and written the course requirements and handbooks for it, or won a law requiring phonics instruction, or done a host of other things. Of course, the parents could not have succeeded without the leadership of Conlan and Skelly either. The name of the game is partnership.

So there *is* a proven method for political novices to make friends in the legislature. Finding the willing legislator is the first problem. Actually door-to-door lobbying of unknown lawmakers is not by itself the most efficient way to hunt for sympathetic souls. Comparing notes with other parent groups, or reading the newspapers closely, or even reading the educationists' newsletters to find out whom they dislike can give you leads to pursue. And once you have that mentor you can ask his guidance in learning your way around the capitol. Your own representative can be a source of simple factual information. He may not be sympathetic at all, but unless he is in a terribly secure position, he can't afford to treat you too badly. You live and vote in his district.

Suppose you hear that a committee of the legislature has scheduled a meeting to discuss graduation requirements for high school. Can you go? Can you get someone of your persuasion to testify? Find out what is necessary to be invited. To know ahead of time when similar opportunities will be coming up, you must check what bills have been introduced. Nominally, at least, the chairman of the committee issues invitations to testify, but in practice it is probably his staff and that of the ranking minority member on the committee. You must investigate this yourself, for often the facts of the situation do not square with what the handbooks tell you.

Deciding how to approach the person who hands out invitations is also a challenge. Be prepared to think circuitously. Perhaps the key figure, whatever his literal job description, is by some happy chance a former partner in a firm for which a friendly local board member in another town also works, and you can ask an allied parent group from that town to ask the board member to contact the key figure in behalf of your own parents' group. Or maybe you have heard that the one who issues invitations to testify is a deacon in the church where your friendly legislator's second cousin is a member. Your mind must work in roundabout ways like this. The possibilities may be unlimited—or they may be almost nonexistent. You have to work at it. And not only at getting an invitation to testify, but at getting an interview with an important commissioner, or a chance to speak to a state board hearing, and so on.

The intricacies of the legislative process guarantee that not much will get done in a matter of one or two days a year. The pace quickens during the legislative sessions, it is true, but in between you should not lose contact with the friends you are trying to develop. Nor should you cease to keep track of what your opposition is doing.

When a bill is due to come up for a vote on Wednesday, it is fine to be able to alert your people around the state on Monday to get in touch with their representatives. Having a statewide alert system is no mean accomplishment. But that should be the end of a long effort, not the beginning.

If the bill in question is undesirable, you should have known about it when it was introduced. Who introduced it? When was it referred to committee, and to which committee? You should have lobbied the members of that committee while they had control over the bill, and you should have gotten people from the members' home districts to lobby them. You should have found witnesses to testify against the bill, and secured invitations for them to testify. You should have lobbied the most receptive member of the committee to introduce amendments that would modify what you believed were the undesirable provisions of the bill. When the committee released its version of the bill, you should have followed it to the committee that cleared it for the floor, usually the rules committee. You should have lobbied members of that committee to stall the bill. At the same time you should have done a headcount of all the legislature and should have known who was supporting you and who was not. If some were undecided, you should have helped them to decide. If some on the wrong side seemed susceptible to argument and cajoling, you should have argued and cajoled, and gotten people from their home areas to argue and cajole as well. Also, you should have tried to find anybody—regardless of what committee he was assigned to—to introduce the modifying amendments that you believed were minimally essential or would create division in the ranks of the bill's supporters. By the time the bill came to the floor to be voted on, there should have been no surprises for you.

If you liked the bill in question, you should have gone through all the same steps, urging support for the measure instead of opposition. Meanwhile, you should have put local groups to work getting up publicity and other attention, if possible. That, and more, is what your opposition does continually.

Regardless of how the vote turns out, let your supporters know you appreciated their efforts, whatever they may have been. If a commission is to be created as a result of some legislation, try to see that good people are named to it. Keep track of its pronouncements. And so on.

There is one form of follow-up you absolutely must not

neglect. At regular intervals your friends in the legislature must be reelected. The moneyed education establishment probably will be working against them if they have been of help to your interests. You must make up the difference. With your volunteers you must go to work to make sure they are reelected. Enroll allies from other legislative districts as volunteers. Spare no effort: hold coffee hours in the neighborhood, go door to door distributing flyers, do whatever you are asked to do by your friend or his campaign manager. Reelecting your friend means more than almost any other fall project.

Is all this a big job? A tremendous one. And influencing the Congress is fifty times harder than influencing a solitary state legislature. Is all this impossible? Yes—for unorganized parents who are not willing to trust each other, and delegate tasks to each other, and perform delegated tasks, and follow directions from their leaders. But for organized parents who adapt the strategies of their opponents, training themselves along disciplined lines, allowing no time or place for vanity or egomania, planning carefully, and consolidating a base of support, victory is within reach.

Goals of the Parents' Rights Movement

What do parents want? Educators never tire of asking the question, but they can't quite believe the answer. Parents want control over their children's education. That is not the same thing as wanting control of the public schools (who in his right mind would seek that?). Even the liberal *Washington Star-News* has remarked:

> Since World War II and the detonation of a mass urban society, this choice [in the education of their children] has been diminished—not through any ominous conspiracy to impose a given set of values, but from pragmatism bred of sheer numbers. . . .

207

> To label all of this as but a mindless reaction, an eruption of a neo–Know Nothingism misses the point: it is expressive of a profound discontent.[34]

Parents, by and large, are perfectly content to delegate the routine chore of teaching multiplication tables, long division, verb conjugation, and the like to a school and a succession of teachers, provided that is what they teach. Today, though, there is no assurance of that. And so parents must interfere. It is not as if they had nothing else to do—quite the opposite, thank you—but a strong sense of duty compels them to take their time and make the effort to supervise and try to remedy.

Parents want schools to teach their children facts and mental techniques. They do not want schools to teach their children fuzzy standards of morality, radical political sympathies, biased interpretations of history, muddled psychology, and disrespectful behavior.

Mothers and fathers who teach their children that stealing is bad do not want their children to sit through a class discussion of "when it's O.K. to steal." Parents who believe the human body is the temple of God do not want their children to read Sol Gordon's irate declaration of his right to love anybody he wants to for as long as he wants to—certainly, they don't want a teacher handing their children such stuff to read. Patriotic parents do not want their children to be taught that America reeks of racism. If it is true, the children will discover it soon enough; if it is not, they will believe it because they are taught it. Teachers carry implicit authority in a child's eyes, partly because his parents urge him to respect his teachers. For a teacher to abuse this respect by teaching contrary to parental wishes is an intolerable invasion of privacy; to undermine the family unit, imperiled as it is in the modern age, by manipulating the minds of defenseless children is a form of tyranny.

To be more particular. Since their children are in the school system for a certain number of hours per day, for a certain number of years, parents want some say about what the children are exposed to during that time.

At the elementary level, parents often want phonics taught. They want supervised reading classes, including detailed reports to parents elucidating exactly what the child's competence is. They want handwriting taught, both printing and cursive, with practice in speaking and expressing ideas in an organized manner. They want spelling and the rules governing it taught and drilled. They demand that their children should know the basic rules of grammar: punctuation, sentence structure, parts of speech, syntax, verb forms, and other fundamentals. Parents would like a foreign language or two available to those students who are interested and capable of it. They want a simple, factual approach to history, usually in chronological order. They want taught an organized, complete concept of earth's geography and the solar system. They want science in its practical aspects such as weather, plant and animal life, geology, and the fundamental rules of physics. They want the basic skills of computation—adding, subtracting, multiplying, and dividing—learned so well that they become reflexes and no longer require laborious thought.

At the elementary level, there are specific things parents do not want. These include: effort-related grading ("Johnny's doing the best he can, so I gave him an A"), social promotion ("Even if he can't read, he'll miss his friends if we don't promote him to third grade"), and look-say reading and experimental alphabets. Parents object to machines that take the work out of learning, like typewriters and calculators for fifth graders. They object to "modified" grammar, and to a total lack of grammar. They don't like integration of "social studies" into a confusion of concepts strewn with selected facts. They don't like inclusion of sociological opinions, humanistic values, and political viewpoints in such a "social studies" program. Many parents object to the teaching of evolution as fact, rather than as theory. They don't trust "modern math," which expects abstract comprehension from arithmetically illiterate pupils. They don't care to have their children labeled for life, or mislabeled, as is more likely.

At the secondary level, parents want a continuation of intellectual discipline and development. They want their children to realize that, contrary to the instinct of adolescence, they do not know everything there is to know, and are not necessarily the greatest generation of thinkers ever to decorate the globe. For college-bound children, that implies the learning of a wealth of information in the sciences and liberal arts, a respectful acquaintance with the great literary, artistic, and musical accomplishments of Western civilization, and mathematical and scientific competence. In high school college-bound students should have experience doing research and learning about the resources that facilitate research.

Non-college-bound students should know what to expect in the working world. Mechanical and industrial skills needed on the job should be soundly taught. A general competence is needed as well, together with an ability to communicate intelligently. Parents expect high school to provide this much to students who are not likely to seek further education. Vocational education was one of the first causes of progressive education, yet it seems to have fallen from its former glory.

Since attitudes are formed during high school years more than in any other period of time, parents want their children to spend those years in an atmosphere favoring objective morality, common decency, free enterprise, unabashed patriotism, self-reliance, respect for duly constituted authority—all these, the traditional values of American society, should be held high in America's public schools. They do not have to be preached; they should be practiced. At the very least, they should not be ignored or insulted.

Parents do not want their teenagers taught "process learning," "discovery curriculums," "concept approaches," "interdisciplinary methods," the "new social studies," and other nonsensical inventions of professors of education. Most assuredly such things should not be taught to the exclusion of history, geography, and government. Parents do not want "preparation for family life" or "interpersonal relations" as a supplement or a substitute for nutrition, disease control, and hygiene. They do not want random "self-expression" instead

210

of a serious study of the disciplines of art or music. They do not want contemporary writers substituted for the giants of English literature. They do not want film study, multimedia explorations, self-discovery, and the like substituted for reading comprehension, literature appreciation, expository writing, and articulate self-expression. They do not want "community relations" courses to engender hatred of middle-class accomplishments, or "Mysticism of the Far East" to provoke contempt for Christianity, or trivia courses like "How to Succeed in College" simply to waste time. They do not want Transcendental Meditation, EST, Transactional Analysis, and other potentially dangerous fads to be clothed with respectability and academic credit. Parents object to interference with the inner thoughts of their children; they object to intrusive questions about home and family; they distrust soul-searching between or among students; they do not want their children's values "clarified" by the schools.

The list could go on endlessly; this enumeration reflects only the most common complaints of parents nationwide. Almost all the complaints are directed against pet projects of progressive professional educators. An educator reading the last several paragraphs would be nodding to himself, "Yes, yes, they're all Main Streeters; they're all backward and provincial. They don't know what's good for them. How desperately they need the very thing they resist." And as a member of the establishment, this educator is in a position to enforce his opinions on the children of those he despises. Is that justice?

Textbooks

Besides attempting to give parents a bigger say in the running of the schools, the parents' rights movement is imperatively concerned to cut back in every possible way the power of the education establishment.

The first step is to establish safeguards for parental prerogatives. As a result of the widely publicized confrontations in West Virginia in 1974–75, citizen review of textbooks before the school system buys or uses them has become a hot issue in many areas. Baltimore County, Maryland quietly decided to allow parents to inspect new books in the spring of 1977.[35] However, in 1976 a bill to require all Maryland school districts to display materials for 90 days before they could be used in the classrooms was killed in the House of Delegates. The ACLU objected to the bill because it would have put books "on trial" and would have reduced instructional content to the "lowest common denominator"[36] (as if dirty textbooks had not done so already). Suspicion is that Baltimore County took fright at the aggressive parent activism in neighboring Howard County and decided to save itself some trouble. If there is truth to the suspicion, it is very encouraging to know that school boards can learn from the difficulties of their peers.

Few states simply choose and then purchase textbooks for all the districts under their jurisdiction. Many states do prepare a large list of textbooks that local districts are authorized to buy on their own. This kind of system allows more opportunity for public participation—parents have a chance to be heard when the state is making its decisions and again when their local board is making its decisions, so the chances of successfully eliminating a thoroughly undesirable book are somewhat improved.

The statewide adoption policy works very well in Texas because the state board provides for extensive public inspection of materials before purchase. This is an exemplary policy. In Texas, too, many parents have organized to exercise their rights under the board's policy, and do so with great vigor (although it was not always so)—a factor as important as the policy itself. It would be preferable if the board's policy had the status of law, since the composition of the state board of education can change. About 21 states have some form of statewide textbook adoption. In these states a legislative guarantee similar to the Texas policy would be a worthwhile project for parents to undertake through their friendly legislators.

212

The Texas system is most vividly associated with the husband-wife team of Mel and Norma Gabler, who in 1962 began reviewing proposed textbooks out of concern for their son's education. Today they are known and respected by the publishers' representatives who come to Austin every year to defend their offerings from the criticisms of the Gablers and other parents and other groups. Parents all over the country write to the Gablers for assistance in evaluating textbooks.[37]

In Texas the state adopts books for all courses regularly offered by the public schools. This makes Texas the single largest purchaser of textbooks in the world. Usually, only a maximum of five and a minimum of two texts per subject are selected—a sacrifice of diversity in one respect: if a local district wishes to use as supplementary reading a book not purchased by the state, it must put up its own money. State-bought books tend to monopolize the schools because all districts are required to use them. In fact, the law stipulates that a teacher may be fined $50 a day for using a nonadopted textbook. Enforcement is lax, however.

The Texas Education Code provides that early in the year a 15-member textbook committee of "active educators" must be established. These educators represent the various areas of learning in which books are to be adopted that year. Because of the wide range of subject matter taught in Texas schools, the makeup of the committee changes every year. The policy of the state board of education is to let each textbook committee member choose up to five advisers in each subject—usually other educators. No textbook committee member may communicate with any publisher for about four months before the final decision of the state board of education. Earlier, however, the publishers' sales representatives wine and dine the textbook committee members and their advisers, who are required to keep detailed records of all contacts with the publishers' representatives. The education code also stipulates that no textbook committee member may have any personal or immediate family financial interest in any publishing company.

The state board of education sends out to the publishers

"proclamations" stating what is wanted, right down to specific characteristics of the materials. These proclamations can go into great detail about the content of the books, the type of binding, and so on. Three separate layers of bureaucracy—state, regional, and local—manage the Texas school system, so publishers are required to send complete copies of whatever materials they are submitting to all 20 of the regional service centers. This, plus providing copies to the members of the textbook committee, can be a costly procedure, particularly burdensome to a small company. However, the reward is great if a contract is awarded. Companies do not lack incentive. And how else, in a state as physically large as Texas, can the public have full and fair access to the materials? After the regional service centers receive the books and materials, such as teachers' manuals and workbooks, the public has approximately two months to scrutinize them. Citizens are allowed to check the materials out of the service center libraries for a period of time determined by each center.

A date is set for a public hearing before the textbook committee and the commissioner of education on the submitted materials. As much as a week is allowed, since everyone who writes in with objections (a "bill of particulars") is given a brief time on the floor in Austin. These hearings can be quite stormy as the publishers' representatives try to answer charges (the public and the publishers' representatives are also allowed to be present at the textbook committee meetings). In 1974 several housewives were sued for $30 million because the plaintiff company claimed that their objections at the public hearings prevented the granting of a contract to that company.

Publishers must agree to eliminate sections, add chapters, and make other major modifications in the texts at the request of the state board of education. For several years in the early 1970s the board of education, under pressure from women's liberation, had asked some publishers to tone down alleged "sexist" bias in their books; women's liberation groups, inspired by this, presented the state board with a list of 2,274 proposed changes for the 1975 textbook adoptions in spelling and mathematics.[38] Included were such changes as:

from: "The man climbed the telephone pole."
to: "The woman climbed the telephone pole."

from: "Carol was a bridesmaid at her sister's wedding."
to: "Carol played the guitar at her sister's wedding."

from: "I will help mother do the dishes."
to: "I will help father do the dishes."

The debate over these changes was a microcosm of the American system of self-government at work; it was a battle of the grassroots versus a vocal minority group. Eventually the mothers and housewives of Texas prevailed, and the state board eliminated more than half of the proposed changes.

To return to standard procedure: After the public hearing, the state board receives the recommendations and alternative recommendations of the textbook committee. Again, there are public hearings on this more selected list. The Texas Education Agency staff meanwhile reviews the bids of the publishing companies. The commissioner of education during this time may reject books on the list of recommendations from the textbook committee. The state board of education reads the public objections, in the bills of particulars submitted earlier, and meets again to hear more public testimony. Finally, the board votes on which books to purchase.

Thus, for most of the textbook selection process, parents of Texas schoolchildren can communicate directly with the elected state board of education. The Texas Education Agency has the initial responsibility of telling the board which subject areas need books, and some typical bureaucratic oversights occur: the free-enterprise course of study was adopted by law in 1973, but it was 1976 before the TEA got around to asking the state board to try to find books for the course (a goal unmet in 1976 too).

Any individual or organization can submit a bill of particulars objecting to a proposed textbook. Thus women's libera-

215

tionists have as much chance to influence the deliberations as the Women Who Want to Be Women club. The competition is good: it stimulates careful objections and meticulous attention to details, rather than sweeping ideological pronouncements.

Most states do not offer the opportunities for parental participation that Texas does. Nonetheless, parents and parent groups are more and more often given the chance to review a textbook—for a newsletter, for a local board, for a state commissioner, or whatever. Common sense is your guide. Take care in preparing the review: page numbers, line numbers, and complete quotations should precede the objection succinctly stated. Make your objections very specific; even a general critical summary of a book should contain specific references to the text. State your objections in language that will identify you with the best of America's educational tradition, and show where the objectionable passage deviates from generally recognized community values like patriotism, honesty, and so forth. By tying an objectionable book to anti-Americanism, parents can put those who purchase the book in the uncomfortable position of defending anti-Americanism. Of course, if a book is merely weak in content, you should say so and certainly should not "reach" for a charge you cannot substantiate.

The Gablers from Texas are willing to help parents in other states whenever they can. Another textbook review group is America's Future.[39] When citing America's Future as an authoritative source, however, be prepared to defend yourself against the charge that you are a "little old lady in tennis shoes." This is not because America's Future textbook evaluations are inaccurate—quite the contrary—but because the educationists know and fear America's Future, and universally try to pin derogatory labels on the women associated with it. For maximum effectiveness with a *liberal* school board, give a low profile to America's Future. The same caveat applies to the

216

Gablers, whom the educationists scorn as fundamentalist and provincial. "Sticks and stones may break my bones, but words will never hurt me" is not a motto to employ when you are dealing with a middle-class suburban school board. To be called a fundamentalist is no insult, but it will win you little respect from liberal board members. In an area populated by fundamentalists, the caution would of course not apply. These considerations are offered not to lessen respect for America's Future or for the Gablers, both of whom do yeoman service, but to suggest strategic considerations for concerned parents. The first hurdle parents must overcome is to be taken seriously by the educationists and the public, and a smear can rapidly destroy what respect your parents' group has earned by much hard work. When you can avoid it, don't give the enemy the ammunition for a smear!

Another source is available to parents researching or trying to evaluate new or proposed materials. The Ralph Nader of the education-industrial complex is the Educational Products Information Exchange (EPIE),[40] which researches and tests most of the 300,000 educational materials currently for sale in the United States. If federal truth-in-advertising guidelines were applied to educational products, EPIE feels, many would be taken off the market because hardly any of them have been tested before being sold, let alone revised in light of weaknesses discovered later.[41] EPIE offers its services to school boards, but not many subscribe. The NEA journal, *Today's Education,* runs a regular column by EPIE, which indicates that citing EPIE as an authoritative source would carry at least some weight with readers of *Today's Education.* Parents should encourage their local school boards to find out what EPIE has to offer, on the ground that the board is responsible for buying materials and should not want to buy worthless merchandise. EPIE's leanings are probably not those of concerned parents reading this book, but parents should nonetheless take a dispassionate look at its work. EPIE is not antiestablishment, but neither is it beholden to the educational-industrial complex. It

217

does not try to sell anything. It seems more like a gadfly to the establishment, and if parents can borrow its stinger from time to time, so much the better.

Legislation to Work For

Parents have been successful at obtaining, on both local and state levels, specific additions to the curriculum. For example, free-enterprise courses of study are now required by ten states. Educators dislike such measures, complaining that to require such a course diminishes the academic freedom of the student to take a more interesting course, and of the teacher to teach something he would prefer. There is, one must admit, little empirical evidence as yet that a course in free-enterprise economics makes a high school student understand or support the American free-enterprise economy. However, free-enterprise courses are not counterproductive; time spent studying free enterprise at least is time not spent studying variations on themes of radical politics or counterculture lifestyles. Who knows, some of the free-enterprise principles might rub off.

The same rationale can be applied to other parent-supported courses of study. In a number of states, however, parents are concentrating their legislative efforts on statements of principle, designed to give legal teeth to the moral rights of parents. A "Parents' Bill of Rights" has been proposed in several different forms in a number of different states. In some cases, only one section is introduced in a given year; in other cases, an idea from the "Bill of Rights" is incorporated in an amendment to another piece of educational legislation. It is unrealistic to expect any state to enact the measure in its entirety, given the political realities of the day, but the bill sums up quite well the demands of parents. Enacting any of its provisions into law would strengthen the legal status of parental rights. When concerned parents are accused of just being "anti," it is helpful to be able to present the proposals contained in the "Bill of Rights" as evidence of the positive side of their work.

Here are some excerpts from the draft legislation prepared by the American Legislative Exchange Council:

Section 1. [*Short title.*] This act may be cited as the Parental Rights Act.

Section 2. [*Purpose.*] This act is designed to protect the rights of parents and guardians in regard to their minor children enrolled in the public schools of the state. The educational well-being of the child is best served when there is mutual cooperation and confidence between parents and school personnel.

Section 3. [*Definitions.*] As used in this act, the term—

(1) "Academic test" means any instrument used to assess a pupil's academic achievement, including standard intelligence tests.

(2) "Instructional material" means any textbook, teacher manual, film, filmstrip, tape, and any other supplementary material used in a school.

(3) "Patron" means any legal resident of the school district.

(4) "Personality or adjustment test" means any test, scale, inventory, or other device, written or oral, for the collection of information relative to a pupil's personality, environment, home life, parental or family relationships, economic status, religious beliefs, patriotism, sexual behavior or attitudes, or psychological or sociological problems.

(5) "Pupil" means any student under the age of eighteen years enrolled in the public schools of the state.

(6) "Pupil records" means all information on

the pupil recorded and retained by the school, school district, or state, regardless of how the information is stored, and which is used or expected to be used in whole or in part by the school or any other school or official or agency of the state or federal government.

(7) "School" means any public school of the state.

Section 4. [*Access to instructional material and programs.*] The governing board of a school district shall keep on file and make available for inspection to parents, guardians, or patrons of the district all instructional materials used in the district. Such materials may be inspected at any time during regular office hours. Before placing a pupil in a program which is funded as an experimental, innovative, pilot, or research program, the board shall inform the parent or guardian that his child is being placed in such a program. If the parent or guardian objects, the board shall offer an alternative program or course of activities for the pupil.

Section 5. [*Testing procedures.*] No personality or adjustment test shall be administered except under the following circumstances:

(1) Reasonable notice shall be given to parents or guardians of the pupils of the intent to administer such tests.

(2) The tests shall be made available for inspection at the school where the test is to be administered.

(3) Parents or guardians shall be informed of the nature of the test and written consent shall be obtained from the parent or guardian prior to the administration of such a test to any pupil.

(4) The tests shall be considered voluntary and not a class requirement.

Section 6. [*Content of pupil records.*] Pupil records shall include an annual evaluation of the pupil's progress in the basic skills of reading, language, and computation. This evaluation shall be measured in terms of national standard grade level norms.

Section 7. [*Access to pupil records by parents.*] Upon confirming a parent's or guardian's identity, the authorized personnel of a school district shall, upon request, make available to the parent or guardian of a pupil the content of the pupil's records. The parent or guardian shall be permitted to be accompanied by any other person or persons of his choosing at such time as the parent or guardian reviews the contents of the pupil's records.

Section 8. [*Correction of pupil records.*] If any parent or guardian disputes the accuracy of any item in the pupil's records, he may give notice in writing to the principal, superintendent, or other designated school employee specifying in what manner he believes the records are inaccurate. Within fifteen days after receiving a notice of the alleged inaccuracy, the principal, superintendent, or other designated school employee shall, in writing, deny the alleged inaccuracy, admit the inaccuracy, or state that there has not been sufficient time to complete an investigation. If the school authority admits the item is inaccurate, he shall immediately correct the item in the records and inform anyone who has previously received a report containing such inaccurate information. If the school authority states that he has not had sufficient time to complete his investigation, then the school shall immediately investigate the

221

matter to determine its accuracy. At such time as the school does complete its investigation and determines whether the item is accurate or inaccurate, it shall so inform the parent or guardian. If the school determines that the item was inaccurate, it shall immediately correct the item in the records and inform anyone who has previously received a report containing such inaccurate information. The parent or guardian shall have a right to attach a written response to any disputed item that cannot be resolved.

Section 9. [*Permissible use of pupil records.*] Pupil records are confidential and shall be made available only under the following circumstances:

(1) To the parent or guardian of the pupil;

(2) To the professional staff of the school district in which the information was obtained;

(3) In response to the order of a court having jurisdiction to issue such an order;

(4) In accordance with written instructions of a parent or guardian to transfer the records to another school or institution; and

(5) In accordance with any other written instructions from a parent or guardian. No school employee may use pupil records for any personal reason.

Many parents are also looking with interest into a variety of "early exit" proposals. Curiously enough, some of these proposals have been made by educators who acknowledge the valid complaints about the custodial school. Most prestigious of the supporters of early exit is the National Commission on the Reform of Secondary Education, sponsored by the Kettering Foundation. To the surprise of many, the commission included in its recommendations a call for lowering the compulsory-attendance age to 14:

> To the rights the courts have already secured for American students, the Commission would like to add another: the right not to be in formal school beyond the age of fourteen. Compulsory-attendance laws are the dead hand on the high schools. The liberation of youth and the many freedoms which the courts have given to students within the last decade make it impossible for the school to continue as a custodial institution and also to perform effectively as a teaching institution.[42]

This sensible perception has irritated NEA, which can be counted on to take a strong position against anything that might free its captive clients.

Early exit means any arrangement by which a youngster can finish high school with credit before the age of 18 (dropping out has always been an option, but not a respectable one). Early exit carries an implication of satisfactory performance, generally on a minimum-proficiency test or other examination to determine that a given standard of learning has been attained. In California, under the proficiency-standard laws enacted in 1972 and 1975, a student may leave high school with a proficiency certificate at the age of 16. That certificate is as good as a diploma for admission to state colleges. Some criticize the early-exit system in California on the ground that the proficiency required by the exam is so minimal that it makes a high school diploma look ridiculous. This point has merit; however, high school diplomas do not necessarily guarantee competence anyway, and there was considerable objection to imposition of even those minimal standards. Academically serious students will probably not choose early exit, unless they are already capable of more challenging work than that offered by high school. The greatest benefit of the early-exit route is that those students for whom two more years would only be misery, provoking them in turn to cause misery for their teachers and fellow students, are now legitimately allowed to leave, without stigma. Another potential advantage is that early exit gives parents some clout to use in demanding reform of the high schools. Parents may legally argue, "If you don't clean up the sensitivity training (or whatever) in your junior and senior classes, our kids won't be around for you to count in your application for state aid." The schools, anxious to maintain a high average daily attendance figure in order to get large sums of state aid, may pay a little more attention to the parents.

Florida lowered its compulsory-attendance age to 14 in 1975, and also awards an equivalency diploma. Legislation to repeal this new law has been introduced, not surprisingly, by the "friends of education" in the Florida legislature. South Carolina considered a bill to facilitate high school exit in 1976, but to no avail. Likewise, Virginia considered lowering its required age to 16—a state legislative committee recommended it—but a bill to put the matter to the option of local districts failed in 1976.[43] It is to be hoped that these measures will be reintroduced in subsequent years, and that they will receive support from parents who want to decrease the amount of control exerted by the professional education establishment through the use of a long span of compulsory attendance. It is also to be hoped that educators who sincerely desire to improve their own performance will recognize that high schools do not function well as day-care centers for kids who have no interest in learning and who resent being there.

Even without early-exit provisions, requiring minimum proficiency of all high school graduates is a good idea, although NEA, predictably, worries that proficiency standards will cause a "shift away from individualized instruction."[44] In an uncharacteristic posture of fiscal responsibility, NEA points out that meeting the minimum standards will increase the need for costly remedial services in already hard-pressed schools. (Refreshingly, the organization does not try to argue

224

that there is no need for state-mandated minimum graduation standards.) That the public might like to spend more money to prevent the need for high school remedial reading courses, and less money on nonessential innovations, has apparently never dawned on NEA.

Many states are feeling pressure from dissatisfied citizens for some kind of minimum standards. Bills are pending in a number of legislatures, and some state boards of education have already acted on their own. New York State's board of regents, for example, now requires ninth-grade proficiency for a high school diploma. The educationists were opposed, naturally, but for once the will of the public was stronger. This trend shows signs of gathering momentum, and concerned parents should not let the opportunity pass to get on the bandwagon. Where agitation for quality control of high school diplomas has not yet started, parents ought to bring up the issue and work to raise the level of public awareness. New Majority–type politicians might want to latch onto this issue, and parent organizations can provide valuable help and guidance while fulfilling their own purposes at the same time.

The time is ripe. Parents are no longer alone in their protestations that the schools are not only failing at their primary purpose but are doing actual harm to the next generation. To question the divine right of the public schools to control a child's mind for 12 years or more is no longer madness or heresy. Almost everyone who must deal with students victimized by "affective education" or "education for the future" knows that the product of such fads is not worth hiring at the minimum wage. Employers find high school graduates inadequate as secretaries, whose typographical oversights may cost thousands of dollars, and unreliable as workers, whose skill is bad enough but whose attitude is worse. College teachers never cease to lament the low levels of written and spoken literacy, background, discipline, study habits, and other academic preparation in the college-prepared students produced under today's standards. Even the army is hard pressed to train the graduates of today's high schools. And everyone who owns a home knows that the costs of such education are increasing all the time.

How long must this continue? One generation has fairly completed its education under this program, and the nation is already suffering. It will continue to suffer until the next generation can make up the losses. Thousands, even millions, of parents have suffered and will suffer for the rest of their lives the grief of seeing their children psychologically maimed, or personally confused, or vocationally handicapped, because of an education that they, the parents, trusted to respect traditional social and moral standards and to inculcate traditional competence. Many are discovering too late that public education cannot be trusted to advance the child's best interests or to respect the parent's wishes for the child's formation.

Parents whose own children are grown up are concerned for their grandchildren; those whose children are nearly grown up are desperate to remedy whatever inadequacies they can. Even parents whose children are scarcely old enough for school are keenly aware that they must watch out for their offspring from day one of kindergarten. These young parents are looking for guidance; they are prepared to fight; and many of them are more sophisticated politically than their older compeers.

All over the nation, taxpayers are protesting the outrageous burdens they must shoulder. And, gradually, the message is getting to the ears of politicians, who ultimately are the only ones who can make significant changes in the chain of problems. But the fruits of grassroots efforts ripen slowly, and even slower is the harvest. Persistence, persistence: this must be the theme of concerned parents whose consciences will not let them ignore the problems. Their efforts will make the difference—in time.

226

6

Guidelines for Parent Activists

All along, this book has talked about concerned parents and parent activists. Who are these people? For what do they stand?

A concerned parent is any parent with a child in school— or a child out of school, for that matter—who suspects that all is not rosy in the big red-brick schoolhouse. This may be a dawning realization that something is wrong with her children's education, or a particular disapproval of school or school board policies, or a general suspicion of the continually rising tax assessment.

A parent activist is a concerned parent who recognizes that if he doesn't do something, nobody else will either. Thousands of parents across America have come to this conclusion —in Alaska and Arizona and Alabama, and Massachusetts and New York and Wisconsin. There probably is not a single state without at least one parent group, and some states may boast 20 or 30 or 50.

Parent activists are all kinds of people: working wives or full-time mothers, Ph.D.'s or sixth-grade dropouts, Christians or Jews or agnostics (though usually Christians), professionals or blue-collar workers, rich or poor (though usually middle

227

class), politically involved or heretofore oblivious to politics. They tend to be individualistic people who like to make up their own minds and who dislike paying homage to the pretensions of others. They are busy people who don't like to feel they are wasting their time (but because they are sometimes inexperienced, they are not always faultlessly efficient). Parent activists are mothers and fathers, but in contemporary society mothers generally have more time to take part in voluntary efforts. Their ages range from the twenties to the sixties and their levels of involvement from constant and heavy to occasional and sporadic.

In sum, parent activists are a heterogeneous crowd, about whom generalizations can be made only at the risk of sacrificing accuracy. No demographer has ever tried to write a "composite" of a parent activist. It would be impossible to do anyway, because there is no national network, no central point where parents check in and are registered. Mostly, parent activists cluster together as a result of some local issue. Local groups discover one another as a local issue becomes a state issue, and then a national issue. Local groups usually put out mimeographed newsletters, which rely in part for material on other local groups' newsletters. But they fall out of contact with each other as quickly as they found each other, and their coalitions are ad hoc. Former Congressman John Conlan admiringly described efforts at coordinating parent activists as a "floating crap game"—admiringly, because in spite of the informal organization, these parents do accomplish difficult tasks of not inconsiderable merit.

From time to time voices are heard urging that parents unite into a lean, disciplined national organization. And usually the consensus is that, yes, we need a unified voice. And since so much of our trouble comes from Washington, D.C., it would be valuable to have a representative there who could speak for us and keep us posted on what the education establishment was up to. But the parents' rights activists cherish their individuality, and there is no source of funds, so a nationwide coalition has not yet appeared. Perhaps someday parents' groups will get together to keep membership figures and mailing lists, and put out a newsletter, and answer inquiries, and draft position papers, but at the present time, desirable as that may sound, there are more important things to be done. One thing is for sure: overworked parents do not need another membership organization to consume their time. A research and information clearinghouse would be invaluable, to save hours and weeks of duplication of effort, but such a clearinghouse is even harder to set up than an umbrella organization. Some assistance along these lines is provided by the *Barbara Morris Report*,[1] which provides research from time to time, and the newsletter of Let's Improve Today's Education,[2] which is of scholarly value. *Education Update* from the Heritage Foundation[3] also provides useful references.

What do parent activists stand for? They want their children to have at least as good an education as they themselves had. They want the essentials stressed—reading, writing, and arithmetic. Concerned parents want their children to grow up with high moral standards, based on absolute moral values: secular humanists call this "reactionary." Concerned parents want the schools to develop their children's intellects and maybe their athletic skills, leaving the responsibility for social adjustment and personality development where it belongs—in the home.

Parent groups know pretty definitely what has put the public schools into such bad shape: federal funding and control, lack of discipline, neglect of the basics, affective education, and radical teacher activism. The solution they envisage? Ideally, the phasing out of federal aid. Locally, parent activists work for requirement of some courses and abolition of others, and establishment of minimum-content standards for all subjects. In general, they work for increased parent participation. Even if their own local public schools are so bad that they must send their children somewhere else, parent activists are not usually willing to give up on the public schools.

Parent activists are sometimes called *parents' rights* activists. The reason: parents bring children into the world and therefore have primary responsibility for their upbringing. Profes-

229

sional educators somehow manage to overlook the parental role, ascribing to themselves decisionmaking power over a child's future. Whether the decision is to adopt innovative courses, or to buy avant-garde textbooks, or to classify a student as "learning disabled" against the wishes of the parent, or to teach the child reading by look-say—these are decisions in which parent activists feel they have a right to be heard, in consultation with educators, perhaps, but ultimately in their own right. After all, as parents they are responsible for the consequences of those decisions. Educators tend to feel differently: by virtue of being practitioners of an arcane and difficult science, they need consult with mere parents only to affirm the ultimate authority of "the professionals."

It should not be forgotten that some parents and parent activists are at the opposite end of the spectrum of educational styles. Some parents feel that the public schools in general are too restrictive, engender undesirable competition, impart antiquated values, fail to respect student individuality and initiative, overemphasize irrelevant facts to the exclusion of preparation for the unknown world of tomorrow, and perpetuate local narrow-mindedness. Naturally, these parents have little in common with parents who worry that the schools are too undisciplined, teach radical new values, and are not responsive enough to local control. But the concerns of these parents are valid too: both groups assert their right to control the formation of their own children. Again, it is impossible to say how numerous or how well organized the innovation-minded parents are. It is enough to know that they are out there and that they also have a quarrel with the public education machine.

One surmises that these parents are wealthier and more influential than their conservative counterparts, but there is no reason why the two groups of parents must treat each other as enemies. Rather, they have a common enemy in the public education establishment.

230

Kanawha County, West Virginia

The first inkling that most of the nation had of anything resembling a parents' rights movement came in late 1974, when the Kanawha County (West Virginia) textbook controversy made front-page headlines.

In 1972, Kanawha County had hired a new superintendent, Kenneth Underwood, who was described by his friends as a "dedicated humanistic educator." Early in 1974 the school board had to adopt new language-arts books for kindergarten through 12th grade. The professional textbook committee appointed by Superintendent Underwood waited until five days before the appropriate board meeting to send in its recommendations. Alice Moore, who had been elected in 1970 on a platform of opposition to sex education, persuaded the board to withhold authorization for purchase until the board had seen the books for itself. Nonetheless, Superintendent Underwood went ahead and signed contracts with publishers to buy the books.

Mrs. Moore soon found herself alone in her objections, as the four other board members began to withdraw their initial criticisms. So she took the issue to the people directly, speaking to parents all over the county. Her husband is a minister, and soon ministers around the county were passing the word to their congregations about the profanity, blasphemy, and obscenity the school board was purveying to their children. Petitions were circulated, gaining thousands of signatures, and hundreds of citizens turned out to watch the board vote, after due consideration, 4–1 to purchase the texts.

Normally, that would have been the end of it. The education establishment would have gotten its way, and the public would have exhausted all avenues of appeal. But West Virginia is unique. Bleeding-heart liberals sneer at its "backwardness," its innocence. What annoys them, of course, is that the old-fashioned American virtues are still stubbornly alive in the Mountain State. The "creekers" and "hillbillies," as their detractors styled them, were not about to take this lying down. Protests erupted, schools were boycotted, demonstrations were held. In the middle of September the school board called a moratorium—the objectionable books were withdrawn from classrooms for 30 days, and parents were urged to calm down.

The bureaucracy went into action. A "review committee" was appointed. Assurances were given to Alice Moore that the "minority" viewpoint would be heard. The minority viewpoint turned out to be just that, because the Review Committee was stacked with 12 protextbook versus six antitextbook members. Concerned parents spent many hours preparing hundreds of pages of detailed and meticulously documented objections to the new books. Supposedly, the review committee was to study these objections. But the outcome was predictable: in November the school board, by the same 4–1 vote, reaffirmed its decision to purchase the books.

Again citizens responded in the only way left to them: rallies, demonstrations, town meetings, keeping children out of school, threatening strikes in the coal mines. Now the NEA sent in some investigators to see what was the matter. Their learned conclusion was that the hillbillies were bigoted Bible-thumpers who really needed multiethnic, pluralistic books to bring their children into the modern world. The American Library Association wailed that anti-intellectualism was running rampant and equated the citizen protests with McCarthyism.[4] Fretful businessmen wondered how the protests would affect the business climate. "Who wants to move to Charleston now if they have to put their kids in the public schools here?" asked the research director of the Charleston Chamber of Commerce,[5] in what was possibly an unwitting admission of the merits of the protesters' case.

At one point during the nine-week fall boycott, over 15,000 children out of the 44,000 registered were absent, according to Alice Moore.[6] The *Charleston Gazette,* which editorially favored the textbooks, conducted a poll and found opposition to the texts ran as high as 70 percent, from an early low of 40

232

percent.[7] Still, all the media referred to the "minority" who opposed the books. Since when does 70 percent constitute a minority? Mrs. Moore was flooded with mail from all over the country. Parents who had seen news coverage of the Kanawha County situation and had read between the lines recognized what was actually happening.

West Virginia parents did not content themselves with boycotts and protests. Parent groups sprang up like mushrooms, some to be short-lived, others to continue longer. Schools were started in homes and churches; unfinished garages were insulated and heated, and former schoolteachers went back on the job. Textbooks discarded as too old by other states were sent to these parent-run schools by friendly parents and groups elsewhere in the country. Parent groups from all over offered moral and even financial support. At least one lawyer came forward to defend parents charged with truancy, *pro bono publico.* Norma Gabler flew up from Texas to reassure protest leaders that their complaints were sound (the state of Texas had rejected some of the contested books.) The Business and Professional Peoples' Alliance for Better Textbooks was organized, and bought a full-page ad in the *Gazette,* quoting extensively from the profane books.

U.S. Commissioner of Education Terrel Bell, respected by establishment educators for his success at dissuading President Ford from slashing the federal education budget,[8] addressed the Association of American Publishers and reminded them of the rights of parents:

> Parents have a right to expect that the schools, in their teaching approaches and selection of instructional materials, will support the values and standards that their children are taught at home. And if the schools cannot support those values they must at least avoid deliberate destruction of them.
>
> . . . parents have the ultimate responsibility for the

upbringing of their children, and their desires should take precedence. The school's authority ends where it infringes on parental right.[9]

Future Congressman Robert Dornan, then working on behalf of Citizens for Decency Through Law, spent some time in Kanawha County urging parents not to waver in the defense of their rights.[10] In Congress a bill was introduced to withhold federal funds from any local school district that did not give parents a say in textbook selection—but even congressmen sympathetic to the parents of West Virginia were reluctant to interfere with local school management.

In time, Alice Moore prevailed upon the board to adopt these guidelines for future textbook selection:

1. Textbooks must respect the privacy of students' homes.
2. Textbooks must not contain profanity.
3. Textbooks must not ridicule the values and practices of any ethnic, religious, or racial group.
4. Textbooks must not encourage or teach racial hatred.
5. Textbooks must not encourage sedition . . . or teach that an alien form of government is superior.
6. Textbooks must teach that traditional rules of grammar are a worthwhile subject. . . .
7. Textbooks must not defame the nation's historical personalities or misrepresent the ideals and causes for which they struggled.[11]

And gradually, in the eyes of the rest of the nation, West Virginia quieted down. Most parents sent their children back to the public schools. (The truancy laws were vigorously enforced.) In January 1976 the Associated Press news wire carried a small item: Jack Boyer, who had kept his children out

234

of school for one-and-a-half years, was giving up and enrolling them in a local public elementary school.

> "Everybody wants somebody to fight this thing, but nobody wants to help," Boyer is reported to have said. "But I don't want anybody to get the impression that it's because I approve of the Board of Education. It's just that nobody is backing me and trying to do anything. I'm fed up with keeping my kids out of school while everybody else's are in school."[12]

So the Great Textbook War came to an anticlimactic ending, quietly fizzling away for lack of sustained support. Alice Moore's reelection to the board in April 1976 by 7,000 votes is a small indication that all is not forgotten. But the education establishment once again has its captive audience.

Was the West Virginia battle in vain? Not at all, although some parents who sacrificed the most might feel a residual bitterness. West Virginia woke up the rest of the country to the transformation in textbooks that had been occurring for about five years. The elementary–high school textbook industry grossed $548 million in 1973, only about one percent of the money spent on American schools that year.[13] The top publishers—among them Scott-Foresman, McGraw-Hill, Houghton Mifflin, Harcourt Brace, and Holt, Rinehart, and Winston—account for more than 50 percent of all sales, which means inevitably that there is a less than ideal amount of competition and diversity in the market. It takes time to put out a new textbook, however, and reportedly it is not unusual for five years to elapse between the idea for a new series and its arrival in the hands of a student.[14] What was being peddled in 1974 had been conceived in 1970, in response to complaints from educators in the late 1960s that textbooks did not reflect the fads and "in" topics of that era. It is probably safe to say that textbooks—like all of American society—changed more between 1965 and 1975 than between 1945 and 1965; parents who remembered their own books, or perhaps those of their first child in school in the early 1960s, assumed that things were basically the same and therefore there was no need to worry.

The Kanawha County conflict proved that textbooks *had* changed. Thrown on the defensive, the *American School Board Journal* published articles suggesting how school boards could avoid repeat incidents.[15] The recommended policies do bring citizens into the book-selection process, though not as much as some parents would like. Even that, however, is quite an improvement. In the 1972 edition of a standard text used by students of education, local adoption of textbooks is lauded because "it permits adaptability to local needs and interests. Furthermore, it permits participation in selection *by the teacher*" (emphasis added).[16] The author thought it unnecessary to mention parents or the public once in connection with the whole topic of textbook adoption. One hopes that the next edition will note that laymen care about schoolbooks too.

Local school boards are now taking a much more active interest in textbook selection, particularly when parents' groups encourage them, and give specific suggestions, and keep reminding them. Meanwhile, the intellectuals have wheeled out their heavy artillery to attack what they regard as parental interference. "Academic freedom" is the cry, the "right of each individual to read a variety of materials which are of value and interest to him."[17] NEA has passed a flurry of resolutions in favor of academic freedom, defined as the teacher's right to be the final arbiter of educational materials.

But the West Virginia battle did more than alert the country to the textbook crisis. Because it was so widely publicized, parents who had been toiling unrewarded in their local areas suddenly realized that they were not alone. After the media made West Virginia a national issue, stories began to filter in from Michigan and Maryland and New York and Pennsylvania—and many other states. Parent groups got in touch with each other across state lines. They began to see that *Man: A Course of Study* was a problem not only in Arizona, but also in New York, and that parents in New York might be able to convince their congressmen to vote for the measure proposed by the congressman from Arizona. Without West Virginia as a catalyst, it might have been years before parent activists recognized their potential impact.

Organization Manual I: Creating a Parent Group

A concerned parents' group starts with one person. All you need are yourself and another parent, and a name. When choosing a name, by the way, don't make it so ordinary that it will be readily forgotten, but don't make it so cute that a casual observer assumes that it's a joke either. A name should reveal something of the purpose of the group, and can be as specific as the organization. Thus, "Parents for Better Schools" is a good name, but "Parents Opposed to Secular Humanism" is more specific. However, the latter group, the acronym of which is POSH (don't neglect to consider acronyms), would be less justified in taking a stand on phonics instruction than would "Parents for Better Schools," the title of which suggests a broader purpose.

The only exception to the general rule about giving yourself a distinctive name is if you are trying to parody a parents' group on the other side of an issue. For instance: if the local pro-sex-education outfit is calling itself "Mothers for Modern Family Life," you could call your group "Mothers for Better Family Life" and try to sow some confusion. Only very rarely does such confusion benefit you, though, and it doesn't always harm the opposition, so be very careful about using this tactic.

Can there ever be too many parents' groups? Don't worry about it. Just because there already is a parents' group in your area does not mean you should not form your own, although it is generally recommended that you stay in contact with the prior organization, and work together with each other as you go along. A tried and true tactic of agitation and propaganda is to form a multiplicity of front groups. The education establishment keeps any number of professional educators' groups, research associations, parent-teacher groups, and so on in its stable to be trotted out for public statements or testimony as the need arises. At the state level, the same thing often is true as well. The different groups are not always independent of each other, financially, managerially, or in any other way. There is no reason parents cannot borrow a few tricks from the educationists.

A parents' group does not have to be huge in order to serve as a legitimate spokesman for the parental point of view. If you wait to make a statement until you have 50 active members, you will be forever silent. True, the opposition will try to discredit you if you cannot say that you "represent 15,000 elementary schoolteachers in the state," as it does. A handy way to avoid embarrassment at this point is by organizing a "coalition." On a typical issue, say phonics instruction, several parents' groups around the state may share the same sentiments. If one group manages to get itself invited to testify before the state board or state legislature, the chosen spokesman can easily say he represents 15 parent groups, active in 20 or however many counties. If questioned, the spokesman can say the groups are in contact with, say, 12,000 parents— 12,000 being the grand total of newsletters distributed by the different groups. No need to blush: you are not being deceptive. This method of calculating influence is commonly used by membership organizations of the highest respectability. Another way to avoid embarrassment at the inevitable challenge to your credibility is to deny that you represent anybody but your governing board, and affirm instead that you are a research group only, whose purpose is to study and advise parents who seek your advice.

Consider setting up a new club, rather than joining an old one, for this reason too: single-purpose organizations are often more effective than multipurpose ones. The better-textbook

238

group might not want to get tied up with the anti-sex-education organization, for example. The minimum-competence group might prefer to pursue that one topic alone for the time being, and stay away from bond issues. Parents' groups with "shopping lists" are often ignored. A group with a single purpose establishes its identity more quickly and can concentrate its efforts a little better.

Once you have selected a name for your group, find at least two other people to be officers. If you expect to handle any amount of money, you may want to open a bank account. Ordinarily to do this you need the signatures of two officers and a copy of the minutes authorizing the account. The complimentary checks the bank will provide you when you open a new account may last the life of your group, if its financial condition is like that of many.

If your group plans to be very controversial, you may not wish to put officers' names on your stationery. But an address, preferably with a phone number and at least one person's name, is important if press releases are to be put out on the stationery. Nothing is more underwhelming to a newsman than an interesting press release without a name or phone number, in case he wants to follow up on the story. For the same reason, if you are going to write letters to the editor or to legislators on this stationery, you should give a name and phone number because they lend an air of legitimacy. If nobody is willing to sign his name to something, a reader may well wonder why he should be expected to read it.

It is not necessary to buy an expensive letterhead. Most quick-copy places can make up a sheet and give you hundreds or thousands of copies at quite reasonable cost. Exercise a little forethought even at cheap prices, however. If your press releases and other documents will be mimeographed or dittoed onto sheets of your stationery, then obviously you need more of it than if you are going to offset or xerox complete copies from one original. If you foresee mailing a great deal to the public, it is wise to consider envelopes with your organization's name and address printed on them—it makes the envelopes look more businesslike and enhances their chances of being opened.

And in choosing a letterhead, make it simple. Unless you have a great commercial artist in your midst, who can design a striking logo, just use plain printing and no design at all. Nothing is cornier than a poorly drawn schoolhouse or liberty bell. Such emblems invite the skeptical reader to laugh you off before you've had a chance to get in a word.

If your group is fortunate, some member will from time to time have access to a photocopy machine. But that is rare. Consider yourself lucky if you can lay your hands on a mimeograph machine, and if one of you knows how to operate it. Few things create a poorer impression of your group and your cause than a barely legible, splotchy, unevenly typed sheet with crowded margins and no white space. When running off copies, and when typing up the ditto master, resist the temptation to be "inch wise and page foolish"—in other words, do not, in the name of economizing on paper, make your pages so unattractive and illegible that nobody reads them at all.

Organization Manual II: Recruitment

While you are planning your organization, you will of course be thinking about getting members. Not all groups want or need members; if you are such a group, you know it. In general, local parent clubs with broad multiple purposes should look for as many members as possible. Remember, you will be trying to impress the school board with how many parents are concerned about a given issue. That takes people. You may want to get active in school board electoral politics. That takes people.

Not many members are going to be indispensable, vital, contributing parts of your mechanism, nor should you expect everyone to be. But you should be able to plan on having enough members willing to do a few small tasks regularly or occasionally to fulfill all the obligations and activities you undertake. If you find that the activities are too many and the activists too few, maybe you are overextending your club, or maybe you are not paying enough attention to membership development. A new group, naturally, attracts members through the efforts of its founder; an established, ongoing group may allow itself the luxury of a membership chairman (or chairwoman, as the case may be: this book adheres to the traditional rule of grammar that the masculine pronoun prevails when gender is mixed or unknown). In either case, the basic strategies are the same.

1. *Using existing mechanisms.* Members of already existing parent groups may be interested in your cause. (If there is more than one group in the area, you can expect overlapping memberships, and should not find them a problem.) Local chapters, if there are any, of Women Who Want to Be Women (4 *W*s), Happiness of Womanhood (HOW), and other anti-ERA groups are fertile recruiting grounds. Folk of like mind tend also to belong to local chapters of Catholics United for the Faith (CUF) and to right-to-life clubs. Obviously, when you try to get people from such groups, you don't go to the local chairman and say, "Hi, I want to steal some of your members." You approach him and say perhaps that you would like to make a presentation at the next meeting on how the family life program in the district is teaching proabortion or liberationist sentiments. Then, after your presentation, pass around a tablet during the question period for interested people to sign their names, addresses, and phone numbers. Lo, you have increased your mailing list and your list of potential workers. Too, conservative churches often have women's clubs willing to hear of worthwhile projects they can undertake.

2. *Assaults on the public.* Find out what is involved in setting up a booth at the state fair, or the town carnival, or the like. During times when general interest is high, a table in a shopping center might net a few interested people as well. If you go that route, be absolutely sure that your booth or table is never left unattended, most especially while your literature is

there. It is better not to have a booth at all than to have your literature end up all over the fairgrounds, earning you the animosity of the manager. Obviously, for such occasions you want to limit your appeal to the simple, clearly understood issues: minimum competence for graduation, back to the basics, for example. Trying to explain secular humanism to a mother busy watching her kids while her own mind is on recreation can be painfully futile.

3. *Letters to the editor.* This is a good medium. Communications are transacted in writing, you have the opportunity for follow-up, and timely issues can be exploited.

Letters to the editor work two ways: you write them or you read them. If possible, assign one person to the duty of reading letters-to-the-editor columns in the daily and weekly papers, including community papers. When a sympathetic letter appears from somebody you do not know, answer it right away, preferably on your club stationery. Try to enclose a pertinent issues paper (if you have such a thing), or a brochure about your club (if you have such a luxury item), or a newsletter (if it looks good). Make the letter short and polite, and if you can, invite the stranger to your next function. Someone who takes it upon himself to write a letter to the editor is a near convert already, and you do not want to scare away such a person with a ten-page epistolary harangue, nor do you want him to remain in ignorance and misery, thinking he is all alone in the world.

When the need arises, your organization will want to work the other way around, by mounting a systematic letters-to-the-editor campaign. The crucial thing here is not to give the *appearance* of an organized campaign. Personally ask different "reliables" in your club to write a letter to the editor on a specific day on a specific aspect of the topic at issue. This is, incidentally, a good way of determining who in your club is a reliable and who is not. Ask the letter writer to send you a carbon copy of the letter. If possible, try to make sure that an address or telephone number appears under the signature when the letter is printed. That way, some other reader may be able to contact you—which, of course, is one purpose of the exercise. Another purpose of the exercise is to raise the level of public awareness, and to become a vocal majority, rather than a perpetually silent one.

One thing to watch for when you and your troops are writing letters: certain phrases very quickly become shibboleths. They prejudice the uncommitted reader and make it harder for you to get through to him. In 1971, during the child-development campaign, the phrase "Sovietizing of American youth" pigeonholed its users as right-wingers. Now that may not be so terrible in itself. However, a more desirable impression to give would have been that of nonideological objection to federal child care. In almost any case, you should avoid ideological overtones in favor of straight-from-the-heart, all-American gut reactions moderated with intelligent reflection.

Depending on your area and on other variables, you may not succeed in getting your letters to the editor printed. Nonetheless, you should still send out your press releases; you never know when somebody will be looking for a story and will want to follow up on a statement you made.

About press releases: keep the paragraphs short; keep the sentences short; keep the release short. Be absolutely sure that it is neat, legible, and clean. No smudges. Be absolutely sure that what you say in it is exactly what you mean. When you send it out, include a name and phone number "for further information." True, some people are afraid of being harassed if their name and phone number get spread around too widely. But without that vital information it is very hard to seem credible or responsible to an outsider who has no appreciation of your situation. Perhaps a special phone could be installed in someone's home, with a number to be used only for club business, if your club starts doing a good deal of visible work.

4. *Public meetings.* This is a bit ambitious for a small organization. Try it only if a number of other groups are willing to cooperate with you, or if your issue happens to be the subject

of widespread public concern. If you are well established and are gaining some attention for your cause, you might like to give the public a chance to get to know your group.

Line up a speaker on a date that suits most of your members. Avoid Christmas, Easter, Thanksgiving, and other holidays, as well as graduation and vacation times. Some people think that between February and April interest in schools peaks.

Talk with your local public library; many new ones have meeting rooms available for the asking. Also, they may put up signs for you if you are a nonprofit group. If one of your members has a husband in the Elks or the Knights of Columbus or a similar club, try to cajole him into getting their meeting hall free or at nominal cost. Church halls are usually available too. Set your date and reserve the place well ahead of time, at least a month if possible. Then start publicizing. Try to arrange for a refreshment period at the back of the hall after the meeting, since this encourages people to stick around and gives you the opportunity to meet and bring in new people personally. Not all meeting places are built to allow for coffee and tables of snacks, however.

When you do your publicity, be sure not to overlook the already converted. True, they don't need to hear your message, but if they come, they will help swell the crowd and impress those who do need to hear you. Getting notices into other newsletters and telephone/address lists from friendly groups can take time, so as soon as you know your date you should start negotiating. In return for the favor of using another club's list, you can promise to drum up publicity for their next meeting or do a mailing for them sometime. Rather than turning over to you the actual list, the cooperating club may ask you to furnish envelopes, flyers, and postage so their members can themselves address the envelopes and thus preserve the privacy of their list.

Publicity is more than sending out notices or press releases. It means making posters, and getting them into store windows; it means cajoling sympathetic pastors to announce your meeting from the pulpit; it means contacting radio stations that

244

run community-calendar bulletins as a public service. And it means getting on the telephone and calling every one of your members. Ask each to bring one other person, even if it is just a spouse or a visiting sister. If you have phone numbers from any of your borrowed lists, call those people. And don't call on the day of the meeting; call the day before or, better, the evening before, so the recipient of your message is less likely to forget it in the rush of fixing dinner. Those you phone should have received a notice in the mail not too long ago. Nothing else is more embarrassing than a meeting nobody attends. If it happens to you once, you will not want it to happen again.

What to do at the meeting? A guest speaker, if he is a good, lively talker, is an obvious suggestion. But if the speaker is not known to be lively, do not assume he is, regardless of how well he may write. If you have doubts, look for added interest: try a panel arrangement after the talk, for example, with a pro-MACOS parent or teacher and an anti-MACOS teacher or parent on the stage to ask the speaker questions. Inviting a member of the enemy camp can backfire if the intruder is given too much leeway or too much prominence on the program. Remember, you are holding the meeting to air your viewpoint. Because a few friends of the outsider are likely to come to support him, they will inadvertently give you a little free publicity. In addition, their presence might help make audience questions and answers lively, so it is worth considering. It also seems more "fair," and gives you something to point to the next time your group is accused of being close-minded and fanatical.

An out-and-out debate is good for building interest. A movie, preferably an objectionable movie used in the schools, is a good drawing card, if you can procure it (a friend in a private school might be able to borrow it through "official" channels and let you use it). During campaign years, members of and candidates for the school board will doubtless welcome an opportunity to address a public forum; the occasion also lets you ask some hard questions.

Public meetings may seem like too much work, but they aren't if you hold them infrequently. The organizational practice is very good. For one thing, you can assign different tasks to different members to see how well they perform. A cardinal principle of management is to make each individual feel important, so give every volunteer some task, no matter how small.

A public meeting is a perfect excuse to talk with newsmen. Call up the local papers. And, of course, the meeting may let you put a finger on the pulse of the community. Besides attracting new interest, and thus potential new members, a once-a-year public meeting is an opportunity for parents who know each other only over the telephone to meet face to face; in short, it is a morale booster. With this in view, your meetings could be geared regionally if your members are spread across the state.

During the meeting, do not forget to use the sign-in sheet. Invite everyone present to sign it as it passes from hand to hand during the program. Here are, you hope, new names for your mailing list, and new people to enlist in the cause. Also, use the refreshment time as an opportunity to meet new faces —you would be wise to assign a couple of "reliables" specifically to that task.

5. *Call-in shows.* Another method of getting free public attention is the radio call-in show. Frequently such programs are looking for guests, in which case, if you write a letter to the host, or have a chance to meet him, you may be invited on the show. Education is usually a hot topic these days. If the response to your appearance is good enough, you may be invited back. You can help bolster the response without telling the host that half the people who called in were your friends.

When a talk show features somebody you don't agree with, quickly call up a few of your reliables and get them to listen and call in as well. These shows like disagreement, especially if it's polite and rational, so don't be shy. The more response to a topic on education, the more likely the talk-show host is

246

to return to that or other education topics. Even if you are never invited to be the guest for the evening, your group can offer enough disagreement with the orthodoxies of the educationists, or enough agreement with education critics, to expose the public to the issues.

Organization Manual III: Routine Activities

To a large extent the routine activities of your club will be determined by the local issues. The following suggestions are offered as just that, with the expectation that readers will make the necessary adaptations locally.

In general, it is good to assign certain members to regular, ongoing jobs. This creates continuity and, since we all like to take pride in our work, gives the troops a chance to feel a deserved sense of accomplishment. Basically, there are several positions, which can be supplemented with a variety of monitors.

1. *Boss.* Call him what you will, this is the person who must take the blame, ultimately, for what the club may do wrong. Frequently, it is the person who started the club. Usually it is someone who can get along with a wide range of people, who is outgoing, is not "kooky," is articulate and a bit more experienced than most of his compeers.

2. *Treasurer.* Handles all money and dispenses it. Any and all can raise money, of course, provided they keep the treasurer informed. The treasurer keeps all financial records. Since so much of our "floating crap game" is played with individuals' out-of-pocket expenses, it is not a bad idea for individuals with such expenses to inform the treasurer, who will enter them on the records. This (a) gives recognition to the unsung; (b) swells the budget, for public relations purposes; (c) gives your members a break if you're tax-exempt (not generally recommended). Also, open records of who gave how much tend to buffer against infighting, which easily

degenerates into a contest to prove one's superior dedication.

3. *Newsletter publisher.* This job the boss can fill. He (or she, as we have noted before) determines schedule of publication and content, writes statements on behalf of the club, etc. To separate the jobs of publisher and editor is a protection for both.

4. *Newsletter editor.* This is the person with the day-to-day jobs of typing, dittoing, mailing, etc. He can portion out those tasks as he wishes, but his is the responsibility to see that it all gets out as scheduled. Since this is usually a big job, if you have a regular newsletter your editor should not be assigned anything else on a regular basis unless he happens to have worlds of time, is phenomenally well organized, and begs you for more work to do. He should be on the receiving end of several other mailing lists, such as the LITE newsletter, the *Barbara Morris Report,* the Coalition for Children alerts, and the newsletters of other clubs in the state.

5. *Public relations director.* This office can be separate, or can be combined with either (3) or (4) above. Duties: to coordinate the publicity work for public meetings and crisis-inspired blitzes, which is an all-hands effort anyway.

6. *Daily newspaper monitors.* The uses of the daily newspaper were discussed under "Recruitment." Besides keeping an eye out for letters to the editor, a newspaper monitor should take note of egregious misrepresentations of issues, as well as objectionable editorials, which he can answer himself or pass on to boss/publisher to answer, depending on the abilities of the individuals involved. Also, if you want to keep clippings of germane topics for newsletter use, or for research, political, or other purposes, this is the person to tell what you want, and he should clip and save. Articles are best preserved by pasting them on a sheet of paper—loose, oddly shaped scraps of newsprint are easily lost.

7. *Local school board monitor.* Each district should be covered. While many club members might wish to attend meetings from time to time, it is best not to rely on random attenders to keep the record. A separate monitor should be assigned to

go with the purpose of taking notes, which the club secretary (or editor, or boss, or whoever does the job in your club) should file for future use. Over the years these minutes will provide a very helpful record of the positions and performance of school board members. If a friendly board member offers to turn over to you copies of official minutes, fine; but also make sure you have your own. What you will note is not always what the secretary of the board will note!

Of course, you may not have enough people to assign a monitor to every school district, if your club is small and your districts are numerous. In that case, you will have to rely on members who go on their own. Make sure they go, and do not fail to get their notes from them within a couple of days, so you can call them while their memories are still fresh to fill in any gaps in the notes.

8. *State board of education monitor.* The individual who fills this slot should live in the state capital or be able to afford to go to the state board meetings. It is more a state function than a local one, but in the absence of a state organization, a local group does posterity a favor by taking upon itself this task.

9. *Liaison officer.* This will probably be the boss, but you can assign it to someone else if you want. Basically, it is more a task than a position. For parent organizations to work on anything larger than a local level, it is imperative that local groups keep in touch with state and national parent groups. There should be one member and one alternate in your club whose name, phone number, and address are given to other groups as their chief contacts. When an urgent call comes from the Coalition for Children, say, asking for letters to congressmen before a crucial vote on Wednesday next, that message must be relayed immediately.[18] Usually there is no time to put it into the newsletter. A phone-relay system is excellent, if it has been worked out in advance for such eventualities. Thus, your liaison officer would call five other reliables, each of whom would call two reliables and three other members, who will in turn call three other members and two other people, and so on down the line as far as you can go. It matters little

249

that some club member may receive duplicate phone calls; what matters greatly is that the congressman receives many letters and phone calls. The same principles, naturally, apply to state legislative issues. And remember, to generate 25 phone calls or letters, you should contact at least 75 people.

Organization Manual IV: Crisis Activities

Crises will not be frequent, one hopes, but since coping with crises is one of the reasons for organizing parents politically, you should have a plan of action.

1. *The phone relay.* Discussed above. This should of course be planned in advance to include not only members but fellow travelers ("fellow travelers" being defined as people who come to your meetings, give you encouragement, or maybe even a little money, but otherwise do nothing for the club, possibly because they're too busy with their own parallel organization, or their large family, or whatever.

2. *The flyer: preparation.* Write up one or two flyers. Obviously, do this only when you have a couple of weeks *minimum* lead time before the vote. Make the flyers brief, factual, and very readable; that means lots of white space, big headlines, and very short, succinct paragraphs. And *definitely* on only one side of a sheet of paper. You may use legal-length paper if necessary. Have the flyers printed or xeroxed on colored paper to add interest. Make sure the organization's name and mailing address are included somewhere on the flyer (phone numbers are not necessary for something intended for massive random distribution).

Be sure that you clearly set forth what you are asking people to do. It is not enough to say, "This bill is terrible; don't let it pass." You must say, for example, "H.R. 12345 is terrible. Write to Congressman John Smith, Washington, D.C. 20515, and tell him to vote against it. Call Congressmen Smith's local office, phone number 987–6543, and tell his staff how you feel about this bill." List as many congressmen's offices and their

250

phone numbers as there are congressional districts in your vicinity. Be as specific as you can in your plea for action.

3. *The flyer: distribution.* If finances allow, mail it to your regular list, and your special list, and press list, if such exist. If you can, enclose two copies, since your members and friends may want to give one away. If you can get permission to pass out the flyers in shopping centers, try to do so. Sometimes shopping-center managers will not grant permission to hand out "controversial" documents; then it pays to have a good friend. If the only person in the area who will allow you to pass out your flyers happens to be the manager of a local grocery store, beseech him for permission to stand outside his front door. And do stand. Don't set up a table and sit: customers coming in will find a way to bypass your table, but on foot you are much harder to avoid.

Pass out the flyers after church services, or place them on windshields during services. If rallies are planned, take plenty of copies to such events. Of course, you'll see a lot of them on the ground afterward; but don't forget, they passed through a pair of hands first, and if they had a catchy headline something might have penetrated. You can, if you have the energy and manpower to spare, pass out flyers door to door. But do husband your energy and resources: don't pull out all the stops for every bill coming up for a vote. Remember, a bill may start in the House and be passed there; then go to the Senate, and be passed in a different form there; then go to conference committee to be modified; and then go again to the House and again to the Senate. If it should happen to be vetoed, it goes again to House and Senate. Really significant bills may take a long time to get enacted into law; you may have plenty of chances to sidetrack a bad one. "Sleepers" are not unknown, however: when the bill slips through while no one is paying attention, as the child-development bill did in 1971. In that case, a last-minute frantic rush is essential.

4. *Letters-to-the-editor campaigns.* When you launch one, make sure that letters are sent by both the organization and individual members. Letters should not sound the same.

5. *Letters to officials.* Make sure your members write letters to the appropriate legislators or board members. It sounds silly, but sometimes in the flurry of moving the public to action you may forget to get in your own two cents' worth!

6. *Involvement by other groups.* Get other groups to issue their own statements, or launch their own blitzes, on the issue. Press releases from other groups should not use the same language as your press release, and should appear on a totally unrelated schedule.

7. *Public forums.* Seek them. Try to get on talk shows and other soapboxes. If the issue is local, send some people to a PTA or other meeting to try to bring up the matter there. At least those present won't be able to pretend later that they never heard of the problem. And if the crisis is prompted by an imminent school board vote, make sure that there are lots of citizens at the board meeting to watch the voting. If the issue is one that has cropped up elsewhere in the state or nation, and is likely to again, you may want to contact your state's Conservative Caucus for assistance or leadership. The national address of the Conservative Caucus is: 7777 Leesburg Pike, Falls Church, Virginia 22043.

Organization Manual V: Political Activity

Before your club can launch upon political activity, you should work out a plan for meeting crises. It goes without saying that if your club consists of only three dedicated people, you must scale down your expectations accordingly. It can be very, very frustrating to launch into a political struggle and realize that you are totally helpless and unprepared to make a "meaningful contribution." To spare yourself and your new converts or fledgling activists that bitter disappointment, don't try to salvage American education all at once. Recognize, and convey the insight to your members, who are most likely also your friends, that the purpose of your group will be amply fulfilled if you successfully do one thing, on one issue, at any one time. Even if that one issue does not turn out the way you would have liked, your group will have done its part, will have learned by doing it, and will be better prepared for the next challenge. By setting modest—and attainable—goals for yourselves, your local club will avoid high hopes and deeper disappointments, with the possible consequence of internal grumbling and dissension.

1. *Legislative activity.* If you are not located in or near your state capital, you probably cannot do much in this regard. Unless some other parents' group has blazed the way, or you know a legislative leader on the inside, you will be hard pressed indeed to get started. So don't set out to "influence the legislature." Just go along, doing your job, and you will sooner or later spot a chance to make your move.

Perhaps a newspaper article will offhandedly mention "Delegate Jones' bill to require ninth-grade literacy before awarding a diploma." You spring into action. You call Jones' office; you talk to his staff if he has one, to himself if you can, to find out more. If you like what you hear, you offer your assistance. It could be that Jones' bill is the compromise position, and that Delegate Smith has introduced a bill to require 11th-grade literacy. In that case, you would promptly get in touch with Smith, other things being equal. In any event, you come to your state capital sooner or later to do a little lobbying. Chapter 5 discussed state-level activism other than lobbying; now it is appropriate to back up and fill in details about this honorable activity. The same principles usually apply to the U.S. House of Representatives and Senate as well as to state legislatures.

First of all, a technical point. You are not really lobbying, as the law understands lobbying, because nobody is paying you to give your opinions to the legislators or to ask them to vote a certain way. You are doing it on your own, representing yourself and some friends.

When you go visiting legislators, bring a well-informed and articulate friend if you can. Rare indeed is the parent who does not feel a wave of shyness, and maybe a little awe, coming over him as he stands for the first time in the doorway of a legislator's office. This is quickly outgrown, but at the start it helps to have someone else with you—someone with whom to compare notes when all is over. If your friend represents another parents' association, with different membership, all the better: mention that fact to the legislator. Avoid taking more than two friends with you to a legislator's office, however; if there are more people who want to go, just divide into small groups and assign yourselves different offices to visit.

If you are going to Washington, D.C., plan ahead and take with you letters from other parent groups, authorizing you to speak on their behalf. You can visit several or all the congressmen from your state, and tell each of them that you are speaking to him on behalf of a parents' group in his district. That is the language a legislator understands best. Just in case you are challenged, have at your fingertips a letter on the stationery of that organization to prove that such a group does exist in his district, and that you are its representative. Never fear: such representation is entirely legal and aboveboard. (Of course, congressmen do come home from time to time and you can try to see them then. They always maintain one or more offices in the home district where you can call and voice an opinion. The Washington office usually talks several times a day to the district office, just to keep a finger on the local pulse, so don't overlook that less-expensive method of making yourself heard.)

When you talk to a lawmaker, or to his legislative aide (which in Washington you are more likely to do), limit your topics of concern to one or two. You may not plan to be in Washington again for a long time, but even so, you leave a confused impression if you rattle off eight concerns at once, when maybe only one of them is on the burner at the time. Bear in mind that congressmen (and senators) are very busy with many different things, and the same goes for their staff. Usually they can think only a very short while ahead, and on a limited range of subjects.

Bear in mind also that it does no good whatsoever, and

254

probably some harm to your image, to tell your U.S. congress-man that you think the state ought to reduce the school-leav-ing age to 15, or whatever. It does no good to tell your congressman he should oppose compulsory-attendance laws—the idea may be good, but it does not concern the U.S. Con-gress. Tell that to your state legislator; decisions like that are made at the state level. Likewise, don't tell your state legislator that he ought to support a federal law outlawing secular hu-manism. That, again, is something about which he can do nothing. If you are in the state capital in support of a bill to require public input into textbook purchase decisions, do not bother to mention the compulsory-attendance law either: it is not up for a vote next week. You want to leave as clear and distinct an impression as possible. Remember, you have much competition for the fellow's time and attention. You cannot afford to bring up irrelevant topics. Of course, knowing what is relevant requires some advance study.

Know ahead of time what you want to mention to the legislator. Tell him briefly that your group supports bill num-ber XX. Tell him why. Ask him to vote for bill number XX. Try to find out his feelings on the matter, and *after* you leave his office make a note of his response so you don't confuse it with somebody else's. It is all right to make notes in the presence of your local school principal, but a representative does deserve more courtesy. Before you leave the office, it is a good idea to leave a one-page summary of your position and your reasons. This is helpful to the office in keeping straight just who you are and what you said. And if the fellow comes around to your position, he might find your information useful at some future date.

If there is another pertinent issue you wish to bring to his attention and you will have no other more opportune time, wait until you have concluded discussion of the first issue before you bring up the second. That way there is less chance of confusion. Again, be brief, succinct, and prepared to answer questions. Leave a one-page summary of your position. Don't try to bring up a third topic. Before you depart, thank the

255

politician or his aide for taking the time to meet with you.

A general word about attitudes. Washington, D.C. and the state capital are often portrayed, usually with some validity, as bastions of the enemy. A subtle effect of this perception is that when you approach a congressman's office you may tend to feel either intimidated or irate. Neither attitude gets you or your cause very far. Keep reminding yourself that they are just human beings, and that you can talk to them civilly and persuasively, and that they ought to have some interest in listening to you. If they don't seem very interested, don't turn defensive. Instead, make yourself and your presentation as interesting as possible; establish eye contact and maintain it; use the legislator's title or the staff assistant's last name. Be yourself; don't be shy or nervous, because it will show. If you cannot restrain a spontaneous enthusiasm while talking, that's all right —provided it does not become a tirade and does not last very long. You can tell if it is too long by the facial expression of your listener. Again, you are not Daniel going into the lion's den when you visit your lawmaker. You are a citizen taking the Constitution at its word and exercising your rights of influencing your duly elected representative.

Don't forget to follow up your personal visit. After the vote, politely let the legislator know you are aware of the way he voted. Either thank him or tell him that you will be watching his future actions more closely to try to determine whether he deserves the support of concerned parents in the next election. Do not resort to direct threats, however. And certainly do not say, "We will work to defeat you in the next election" unless you can put some force behind that threat, either because there will be somebody else to work for or because this fellow is defeatable. Some incumbents just can't be beaten, and you gain nothing by trying.

2. *Electoral activity.* Liberals of all sorts have been decrying a drift to "conservatism" among Americans. Pollster George Gallup confirms these trends toward "conservatism" in his demographic explorations.[19] The last several years have seen an unprecedented organizing and coordinating of grassroots,

"responsible" conservatives into a political force. This force is yet young, but its potential is considerable. Both the Conservative Caucus and the American Conservative Union have state-level affiliates. The Committee for the Survival of a Free Congress works year-in and year-out to develop and assist conservative candidates in all states.[20]

These organizations represent part of what is called the "responsible conservative movement." Time was, "responsible conservative" was applied to people more of the center than of the right, because other conservatives were assumed to be wild men. Some tried to pin the wild-man label on Ronald Reagan in his 1976 primary campaign, but although he did not win the presidential primary, neither did the smear campaign succeed, because it was obvious that while Reagan was conservative, he was also mentally sound and, furthermore, *what he said made sense* to people who never would have thought of calling themselves conservative. That is the fundamental appeal of the conservative platform in general: *it makes sense to ordinary people.*

The complaints of concerned parents also make sense to most people; the garbled ivory-tower excuses offered by educators do not. Yet who are the allies of the educators, politically speaking? Jimmy Carter, Walter Mondale, Claiborne Pell, to name a few—who also support the liberal position on most fiscal, social, military, and foreign-policy questions. And what political figures understand and work for parents' rights? Carl Curtis, Orrin Hatch, Mickey Edwards, Bob Dornan, to name a few—who also take the conservative position on most fiscal, social, military, and foreign-policy questions. Defining the intrinsic meaning of *conservative* and *liberal* will not be attempted here; for practical purposes, the context and the general usage are sufficient to establish the meaning. Also useful is the adage about birds of a feather.

The criterion of making sense also distinguishes responsible from fringe conservatives, of whom, alas, there are some. Fringe conservatives usually refuse to cooperate with "movement" conservatives, being too purist in their outlook to align

257

themselves with anything popular. Ideological purity has its place, by all means. But it should not prevent diverse political groups from working together on issues they happen to agree about. Nothing is more frustrating than a three-way election: a liberal, a movement conservative, and a fringe conservative. This guarantees victory for the liberal. Yet the fringe conservative keeps running despite clear evidence that the movement conservative is stronger in the polls, better financed, and waging a better campaign. Why? Because the fringe conservative is "too pure" either to support the other conservative or to let his supporters do so.

Consensus-based politics is the only kind of politics that makes room for parents' rights issues. Conservatives believe in the family; they oppose the totalitarianism implicit in social engineering—the educationists' substitute for learning. Liberals are enamored of innovation; they await the dawning of a new day of human interdependence and understanding and fulfillment, based on a new economic order. Outworn social institutions must fade away. Common sense militates against such romanticism, but the typical liberal deep down hopes that it will all come true and wants to do everything he can to help it along by freeing the younger generation from the burden of the mistakes of its ancestors.

In pursuing their romantic dreams, liberals also redistribute your income and mine, bus other peoples' children, tell workingmen that they must sacrifice their promotions to workers whose ancestors were once persecuted, and declare that government knows better than the people what is good for them and their families. None of this makes sense. None of it wears well in practice. And more and more people are beginning to see the discrepancy between the utopian promises and the wretched reality.

People who oppose busing might not care too much about so-called consumer-protection regulations; workingmen who don't want to be forced to join a union might care little about government funding of secular humanism. But the antibusers and the right-to-work supporters are likely to agree on which

258

candidate they want to vote for. And chances are, it won't be the candidate endorsed by the NEA. Because the NEA won't be endorsing a candidate who believes in competition and individual responsibility, of which parents' rights are a part.

Consensus politics is the art of getting the different noncollectivist groups to see their common interests. When properly presented, these interests are easy to recognize. There is nothing arcane or obscure about parents' rights. Therefore, if your parents' group is working for a candidate and trying to attract supporters, it makes no sense to waste time on arguments over possible sinister implications of the symbols on a one-dollar bill. There is no need to advert to secret languages and secret meanings and secret societies that are controlling the country and destroying the world. There are enough perfectly obvious examples of educationist totalitarianism in everyday school life all over the country. Trying to explain the local school board's stupidity as part of a worldwide conspiracy makes extremely difficult a job that would normally be fairly easy to anyone who approached the point by appealing to the common sense of those who pay the tax assessments dictated by that school board. Enough said.

Because the conservative movement is growing and organizing itself, chances are that some conservative group acquainted with the overall picture already exists in most states. Politically interested parents should seek to cooperate with such groups whenever possible. Some parent activists may be precinct chairmen, and maybe an occasional one has been active in party politics, in which case those individuals should certainly continue their activities. But on the whole, parents can save time and energy by following the leadership of someone who has already gone through the tedious trial and error that otherwise they would have to experience for themselves.

There are, however, some ways in which parent clubs can serve the unique purposes of the parents' cause.

All along, the newspaper monitor for the club has been clipping articles pertaining to elected offices, both party and public. If you have the manpower to spare, a political monitor is nice to have. That person would automatically receive this political information. Someone—again, a political monitor is ideal, but a membership chairman can do as well—should keep track of the party preferences of the club members, so that if notice of a filing deadline for Democrat precinct chairman appears, he can notify a Democrat club member who might be interested. Ideally, it is desirable that each member's index card contain party affiliation, precinct, state and federal congressional district, and similar data.

If a club member should happen to run for local office, which is to be encouraged, naturally the rest of the club should be free to endorse him if they want to. Also, the club should be free to endorse candidates for office. If you are a tax-exempt group, however, don't do it.

The political monitor becomes an important person every other fall, when many club activities will be connected with electoral politics. The major task is to follow up on promises of support or opposition that may have been given earlier. Remember, *you must follow through,* or you will never earn credibility. An endorsement, or a promise of help, means nothing if it is not carried out visibly and enthusiastically. That means using your newsletter, putting out press releases, doing volunteer work for the candidate, and so on.

Equally important, if you have threatened (promised?) to work against some bad guy, make sure you do. If John Doe on the school board supports sex education, and your organization tells him it will oppose him, make sure John Doe *feels* that opposition. This should not be hard. Seed a candidates' forum with hostile questions. Put out press releases. Call everyone you have had contact with and say you oppose John Doe and why. Put it in your newsletter.

It may happen that John Doe's opponents are, in your opinion, no better. When that happens, be glad you told John Doe you would oppose him, and did not tell him you would defeat him. Your actual response to the situation depends on how badly you dislike John Doe. If you have indicated you are going to "get him," then you almost have to support an oppo-

260

nent, even if it's a yellow dog. The point is not so much to change the board as to *make a target of John Doe,* thus teaching future board members a cautionary lesson.

Needless to say, you should not rashly promise to ruin a candidate. Don't pick a 20-year incumbent who is president of the bank and whose son is chief of police, for example. Pick an easier target: maybe a carpetbagger if you live in the South, or a McGovern-type if you live in a hardhat area. Politicians with little seniority usually are the most vulnerable: they have the least power and name recognition. You are far worse off if you prove yourself totally ineffective—if John Doe gets reelected with 80 percent of the vote, for example. So be cautious.

The same principles apply when dealing with state legislators and congressmen, but when aiming at those offices, a local parents' club should cooperate with a statewide conservative organization. This does not automatically mean the Republican Party: some states have a conservative GOP; others do not. If there is no statewide conservative organization that endorses candidates and works for conservative victories, then parents' groups across the state are best advised to get in touch with one another, and with a national conservative action group such as the Committee for Survival of a Free Congress, before making decisions.

This cooperation is important for the following reason, among others: in your congressional district you may have a 30 percent chance of electing Mr. Good Man. But in the adjacent district there may be an open seat, and Mr. Better Man might have a 55 percent chance of winning. If you know about Mr. Better Man, your decision to withhold active support for Good Man and instead send volunteers into Better Man's district would be wise indeed. No matter how wonderful your local candidate may be, if you have good reason to believe he is not going to win the election, you cannot justify time and money wasted on his campaign—particularly when there is a winnable campaign not far away. Even a less than perfect candidate who can get elected is a better investment, and also is far more useful to the cause—especially when he gets elected with the help of parent groups, to whom he is then beholden. It may happen that there is in the whole state not a single candidate whom parent groups can support. In that case, finding and developing candidates for future elections becomes a high-priority task that the parents' coalition must begin as soon as the current election is over.

Max Rafferty, whose election as California commissioner of education made worldwide headlines in 1962, says he never thought of running for office:

> A small group of concerned parents had started a draft movement in my behalf some months before the 1962 primaries, and I had reluctantly consented to become a candidate. . . .
>
> As it turned out, all I had was the people. And they responded by the tens of thousands. . . . "Parents-for-Rafferty" clubs started to mushroom, and billboards, many of them homemade, began to blossom in vacant lots. My modest headquarters staff was completely unable to coordinate, much less control, the hundreds of volunteer committees that sprang up. . . . It was an amateur's campaign with a vengeance. . . . It was noisy and uninhibited, promising only a change in the state's educational philosophy and a better break for the kids. And it won, hands down.[21]

But he gives credit where it is due for his election.

Such is the potential electoral strength of parent groups. If it happened in California in 1962, it might happen again. Yes, the opposition is better organized and better disciplined now. But now more parents are also aware of the problems. And they are more politically conscious. If the government of the nation is truly to represent the people, the people must *work* to win that representation. Parents are as much "the people" as any other group of citizens.

With each passing year parents' groups find more opportunities to practice political organization. They have flexed their muscles a few times already. The 1971 child-development bill was vetoed and President Nixon's veto was sustained: most child developers agree, albeit reluctantly, that things would have been different if hundreds of thousands of parents had not written letters to the President and called their congressmen. The massive response by parents to the 1976 flyer on child-development legislation, while less significant than it might have been because the flyer was founded on factual errors, nonetheless was received by Congress as a sign to hold off for the time being. Federal child-development schemes will not go away. The next several years will provide many occasions to exercise and strengthen parent-activist muscle on this very issue.

Congressman John Conlan's amendment to restrict federal funding of secular humanism would not have passed the House of Representatives without the help of the parents' network. Groups located close to the nation's capital lobbied members of the House in person because time was too short for a regular letter-and-call campaign from all the states. Under the circumstances, unfortunately, the influence of parent wishes was not strong enough to persuade the Senate also to adopt Conlan's amendment. But, rather than being discouraged by failure, parent activists should look to the next available opportunity to get senators and congressmen on record for or against federal support of secular humanism. The more such votes are taken, the more easily the public can discern the true colors of its representatives in Washington, and the better informed will be the decisions on election days to come.

7

Alternatives Public and Private

There are, of course, parents who favor progressive education: education for the future world, unfettered by outmoded factual learning, that teaches the student how to manipulate human relations and all the rest. These parents probably think their public school is reactionary. They may detest what they regard as the backward theory and practice of the same schools that other parents decry as too innovative and too progressive. The question arises: Can the public schools serve both masters? Is the public system flexible enough to protect American pluralism?

The heritage of public education is the myth of the melting pot. Today more and more observers, scholars as well as ordinary folk, realize that the melting pot was precisely that: a myth. Ours is an age of neo-ethnicity. Blacks are proud to be blacks, and want their public education system to foster that pride in their offspring; Chicanos want Chicano language, customs, and attitudes taught to their children. Middle-class whites do not agitate for "white studies" courses; the equivalent demand is for traditional American and Christian values. Humanists are another subculture within this society of minorities; so are Jews; so are Roman Catholics. Not all are satisfied with the same offerings in the public schools, nor should they be. Yet all pay taxes to support the public schools and by rights deserve some kind of satisfaction from them.

No less respected a professional educator than the former dean of the Harvard Graduate School of Education, Theodore R. Sizer, recognizes the legitimacy of claims for diversity within the public school system:

> As a matter of public policy, education should move
> toward institutional pluralism. . . . We must lay to
> rest the bugbear that a diverse system is necessarily
> a corrosively segregated and unequal system. What
> we need is a smorgasbord of schools. . . .[1]

What Sizer is saying is that ultramodern parents and traditionalist parents should both be able to send their children to public schools, and be happy about it, just as members of racial minority groups should be able to choose their children's education within the public system.

Alternative Public Schools

The most common approach to this problem of satisfying parental pluralism has been that of "alternative schools" within the public school system. An alternative school is a public school within the local system, set aside by the school board to provide a different style of education: faculty are chosen, curriculum is designed, students are recruited, and the whole program is operated in accordance with one controlling viewpoint.

Schools can be "structured" (or "basic"), which implies phonics instruction, dress codes, achievement tests, firm discipline, letter-graded report cards, restricted experimentation, and similar features demanded by traditionalist parents. Or schools can be "open," which might mean a variety of things, such as flexible classrooms, nongraded report cards, pupil self-

265

direction, group learning activities, flexible grade-level determinations, and other innovations demanded by liberal parents. Alternative schools can lay special emphasis on multicultural awareness, if that is what the community demands, or on academics, or on music and art, or on mechanical/vocational training, according to the express wishes of the parents and the feasibility of the program. "Schools without walls" give students credit for work in the community; "continuation schools" meet the needs of dropouts and pregnant high schoolers or adults desiring diplomas; these are other kinds of alternative schools.

The idea of alternative schools—particularly the "basic" alternative school—is gaining popularity around the country. It seems to have been the brainchild of Pasadena, California school board member Henry S. Myers, Jr. The 1975 Gallup poll asked, "If you had children of school age," would you send them to a "special public school that has strict discipline, including a dress code, and that puts emphasis on the three Rs?" Fully 57 percent of those asked (the figure was identical for blacks and whites) agreed that, yes, they would send their children to such schools.[2]

School boards are discovering that alternative schools are a relatively easy way to satisfy what might otherwise be very troublesome parent demands. Establishing one or two alternative schools does not imply a challenge to the prevailing educational orthodoxy, as efforts to change policies districtwide might appear to do. And teachers are not all cast in the same mold; some are noticeably happier in an academic situation where they can teach rather than act as clinicians of one sort of another. The "basic" alternative school in Palo Alto, California no doubt pleased many parents when it reported that on average, one group of fifth graders in its program advanced two years, eight months in math during a period of nine months.[3] Much of that gain must be attributed to the individual teacher; without the support of the administration, however, the teacher could not have demanded the work that she no doubt did demand of her students. Intensive learning like

266

that doesn't usually happen in "everyday" public schools. Nationwide, at the end of the 1973–74 school year there were about 600 public alternative schools; at the end of 1974–75, about 1,400; and by now the number is probably in excess of 5,000.[4]

Some concerned parents are not satisfied with the principle of alternative schools within the public system, because the schools are still subject to the control of the school board, the federal courts, and HEW, as well as of the education establishment. But for parents who cannot afford a private alternative, the idea is timely. With a cooperative board and judicious planning and careful supervision, it can be a godsend.

The Voucher Idea

With or without the alternative schools, choice among public schools is small choice indeed. For parental freedom of choice to amount to more than rhetoric, private schools must be included in the range of available options. But how, if they must still pay taxes to support the public schools, can middle-class parents afford to send their children to private schools? This is the question of the day.

The voucher system comes closest to fulfilling the requirements of law and custom for nondiscrimination and nonsupport of religion, while simultaneously satisfying the demands of compulsory-attendance laws for the physical custody of students and the demands of parents for quality control in education. Regrettably, the voucher remains little more than a theory for financing better education, because professional educators are unalterably opposed to it. (See page 54.)

The Office of Economic Opportunity in the mid-1960s did set up a few pilot voucher programs. The most notable one was in Alum Rock, California, but that was not a true voucher experiment for various reasons. For one thing, only public schools could participate, and then only under a crushing burden of regulations and planned "compensations" that were

267

supposed to make poor or minority students more "attractive" to the schools. Efforts by Howard Phillips' OEO to test a purer voucher system in New Hampshire came to naught when the program was transferred to the National Institute of Education, which handled it with less enthusiasm.

Briefly, a voucher is an educational food stamp that parents can use like cash to purchase education for their children from the institution of the parents' choice. The institution would then be reimbursed (by the school district, say) in cash equal to the face value of vouchers collected. Milton Friedman, the chief advocate of the plan in contemporary times, suggests that the vouchers should be worth the per-pupil expenditure in the given locality. A parent could choose to send his child to a school which had a higher per-pupil cost than the average, but would have to make up the difference, if not out of pocket, out of scholarship moneys.

Friedman assumes that private schools would be eligible to participate in any voucher system; their participation would be essential to put into practice the principles of free-market competition. After all, if students merely go from one more or less conventional public school to another, how has diversity been enhanced? But if students can go to a private school, the self-protective instinct of the public education establishment will be alerted, and the establishment will have to modify and adapt itself to meet the wishes of parents who are finding greener fields in the private sector. Parents and students would no longer be captives; they would be more like customers, free to take their business elsewhere. For fear of just such a prospect, the public education establishment prefers to issue a blanket condemnation of vouchers. "Elitism," "subsidy for the rich," "racial discrimination," "quackery," and "church-state entanglement" are just a few of the accusations that have been leveled against the idea of vouchers. The last charge is particularly farfetched, since even the New Hampshire plan would have excluded religious schools after the 1973 Supreme Court decisions on school finance, and nowhere have vouchers been proposed to aid denominational schools.

268

In theory, the authority supervising and administering a voucher program could be the local school district. So far, however, the only encouragement even to try out the idea has come from the federal government. It has often been pointed out that the G.I. Bill established a sweepingly broad voucher system for higher education, financed by federal money. The G.I. Bill has worked quite well for the past 30 years, with no complaints about discrimination or church involvement, although a veteran may use his federal handout at any institution —even a religious seminary. Institutions of higher education, having a less secure source of funding and a less captive audience than the public schools, have been less scrupulous about the source of and theory behind the money that pays tuition fees and living expenses for their students. But then, colleges have all to gain, whereas public schools have something to lose, under a true voucher plan.

Interestingly enough, some liberals back the idea of vouchers as a social welfare measure. The Massachusetts legislature for several consecutive years has debated an "Adult Recurrent Education Entitlement Voucher Program" under which the state would reimburse educational institutions for the amount of the voucher entitlement used by the low-income, low-skilled, or unemployed individual who had signed over his voucher to that institution in return for some kind of education or training.[5] Alas, this sort of adaptation of the idea does not benefit the parents of children of compulsory school age.

Nor would all the concerned parents of the nation welcome the voucher with outstretched arms. Since many of the problems in the public schools result from federal and state influence, regulation, and supervision, enforced by federal and state financial support, some parents would view with suspicion any voucher program administered by either federal or state agencies. State and federal bureaucrats would be making educational decisions again, rather than parents. If the state were dispensing the voucher money, even though it was parents' tax money to begin with, would not the state also be able to exert control over the private schools that might participate in the program? Would not public money gradually turn the private schools into public schools? And would not this control be as undesirable as the other types of control that have caused problems already?

To win the full support of concerned parents, any voucher proposal would have to face and satisfactorily answer these questions. Once that was done, parents would no doubt be happy to take advantage of the program.

Established Private Schools

Sooner or later many concerned parents come to despair of the ability of any "system" to educate children. Where do they turn? One solution is to send the children to a school whose continued existence depends on parent satisfaction. That description fits most new and even some established private schools; the vast system of Roman Catholic parochial schools is also finding that its survival increasingly depends on parent satisfaction at the parish level.

Nonpublic is the word used in "pedagese" and "governmentese" to mean private schools. A semanticist might find diversion in contemplating the pejorative connotation of that term, which is comparable in its context to *unsaved, noncomplying,* or *uninsured.* It is a fact that the (public) education establishment dislikes private education with varying degrees of intensity. The antipathy is at least a century old but is fueled anew by the growing popularity of private education. At root it is the old tension between individualism and collectivism, between independence and public control, although ideological terms are rarely invoked. The establishment expresses its dislike for private education by lobbying and propagandizing against policy measures that might possibly benefit private schools, by discriminating against private institutions in the enforcement of state laws governing schools, by ignoring the existence of private education when making policy, and by frustrating the intent of laws meant to aid private school students. For example, one study that was made of ESEA's Title III, which is supposed to include private schools, found that while 22 percent of the sample group of private schools had 100 percent eligibility, only 2 percent had 100 percent participation.[6] Dr. Robert Lamborn, executive director of the Council for American Private Education, tells of a meeting of the prestigious Filer Commission on Public Needs and Private Philanthropy, at which a report was planned without even considering the role of private education in meeting society's needs—an oversight that Dr. Lamborn was able to remedy in the final report by personally convincing an influential member of the commission of the importance of the subject.

The Council for American Private Education (another CAPE) is a Washington, D.C.–based umbrella group for 11 associations of private schools, including the Association of Military Colleges and Schools of the United States, the Lutheran Church–Missouri Synod Board of Parish Education, the National Association of Independent Schools, the National Catholic Educational Association, and the National Union of Christian Schools. CAPE represents altogether about 92 percent of the private schoolchildren in the country, which in turn is about 10 percent of the nation's schoolchildren. CAPE is far from "militant." Its dual purpose is to promote the vitality of private schools and to enhance their contribution to American education and society.

CAPE establishes liaison with government bureaucrats, enabling its members the better to participate in federal programs. It follows developments in Congress and provides information about private education. It files *amicus* briefs in court cases. It tries to make friends with other professional education (establishment) groups. It encourages the private schools in each state to form state-level associations to do the same work, and is trying to set up a communications system among private and public education bodies. CAPE has received federal contracts, most notably to help conduct a survey of nonpublic schools throughout the nation. The Office of Education got poor cooperation from private schools when it conducted its 1970 survey, so it hopes to alleviate the suspicions of many private schools by working with CAPE. A harsh critic might call CAPE the "kept" private school association of the establishment for just such a reason.

To scold CAPE for providing useful services to its constituent associations accomplishes nothing, however. In the 1970–71 Office of Education survey of nonpublic schools, only 17.7 percent reported that they did not receive contributions from public agencies.[7] More Catholic schools (95 percent) took public aid than other religiously affiliated schools; and overall, nonaffiliated schools took less public aid than affiliated. Most public aid was for pupil transportation or lunch programs or student health services—it could have been either federal or state. But the crucial fact remains, that private schools in very substantial numbers take, and presumably depend on, public funds. The Council for American Private Education is helping those schools do what they would do anyway when it writes handbooks for participation in federal programs. Since those schools help support CAPE, criticism should be directed to the schools in question, and not to CAPE, which is only filling a vacuum. And from there criticism should go to the government policies that leave private schools in such bad financial condition that they have to seek and accept public moneys.

It must be stated, as blandly as possible, that sooner or later private schools will probably regret taking state or federal money. Inflammatory rhetoric on the subject is not necessary. The disenchantment with public money might come gradually: for instance, when the school can no longer bear the administrative burden of gathering the statistics and information required for participation in a hot-lunch program. Or the crisis may be abrupt. It may come to a head if none of the state-provided textbooks are acceptable to the private school, or if the content stipulated for a state-required course proves unpalatable to the parents who support the school. The 1970 Office of Education survey neglected to find out what percentage of private schools' budgets came from public assistance,

272

but it really makes little difference: the government can take punitive measures over $50 as easily as over $50,000.

When student health became a concern of the schools, and hence of the government, nobody foresaw that the definition of health would become a matter of ideological conviction. But such is now the case. A private school that balks at including "pregnancy-termination referral" as part of its health service just may find itself *forced* to include such a program. Already, HEW has forbidden parochial schools in Denver to require their female students to wear uniforms, allegedly because it is discrimination on the basis of sex. HEW is able to issue such a directive because the Denver parochial schools receive a federal subsidy to buy milk.[8] Nor is Denver likely to be the last case of its kind.

Ideally, the safest course for a private school to follow if it wishes to maintain its independence is simply that: independence. Do not accept any favors from any government body; do not try to curry favor with any either. This is not hostility; it is separation. Private colleges are discovering the truth of this maxim—very few in the nation have never received public assistance, but those are the very ones with the best defense now against government designs of compulsory affirmative action and other outrages against their independence.

Most private schools probably see the merits of a policy of independence. However, financial realities are compelling, and the urgent needs of survival must be met. If a school feels it will attract more paying parents if it is able to offer a hot lunch, the government subsidy that makes the lunch possible may indeed seem harmless. To take it is not likely to be regarded as a compromise of principle—at the time. Only the staunchest of the ideologically convinced can be expected to resist the allure of government subsidy during hard economic times.

And hard economic times are the lot of private schools in the 1970s, even more than in the 1960s. As government policies continue to punish the formation of capital and the giving of eleemosynary funds, and as inflation continues apace, and as taxation grows heavier, the financial condition of private education can only worsen. The well-insulated schools, the Phillips Academies of the private school world, will suffer the least, but they also will suffer.

On the optimistic side, as the public establishment becomes less and less satisfactory to parents seeking some substantive control over their children's education, the demand for private education will grow. Precisely that has been happening over the last ten years, despite the generally more difficult financial state of the middle class.

Most people know that Catholic schools lost nearly one million students between 1960 and 1970. Few realize that the experience of other denominations was just the opposite, so that the same ten-year span saw a 46.1 percent increase in enrollment in all other religiously affiliated schools. More interesting, the decade saw a 90.9 percent increase in enrollment among nonaffiliated private schools.[9] The absolute numbers in each case are well under a million, but the direction is quite clear, despite the purely statistical conclusion, biased by the massive Catholic numbers, that private schools taken as a whole lost 10.4 percent during the decade. Even within the ranks of Catholic schools, evidence is that the rate of decline is tapering off: in 1970–71 Catholic schools had 6.3 percent fewer students than the previous year, but by 1975–76, only 2.6 percent fewer.[10] The president of the National Catholic Educational Association does not expect enrollment to rise again until the decline in church membership has stabilized,[11] and that, for sure, is a question larger than education policy.

There is a need for religious education of children. So long as the public schools managed to feed children a watery pabulum of nondenominational Protestantism, parents with religious sentiments felt reassured. This reassurance has now been taken away and replaced with, at best, a course *about* religion, which is likely to put Christianity, Judaism, Hinduism, Buddhism, atheism, and voodooism more or less on a par. Probably more common is a vast religious void. At worst, the schools push "values education," which turns out to be situa-

274

tion-ethics indoctrination, and a variety of secular-humanistic tenets.

One of the most misleading statistics of recent times came out of a 1975 Gallup poll, "Public Attitudes Toward Education." One question was, "Would you favor or oppose instruction in the schools that would deal with morals and moral behavior?" The national totals were 79 percent in favor, 15 percent in opposition, 6 percent undecided.[12] The question did employ the word *morals* rather than *values,* but it did not specify what kind of morals were meant. The tendency of the typical respondent would be to assume that the question referred to "typical" morals, namely, the Judeo-Christian ethic, which is the set of morals probably subscribed to by about 79 percent of the population. Assuming that the schools would be teaching his own moral values, an unsuspicious citizen would naturally favor such instruction. Gallup did not ask whether the public favored the teaching of secular-humanistic situation ethics, which is quite likely the "morals" taught in public schools. Had he done so, the response would have been entirely different. The point is important to note because values educators allude to the Gallup poll as evidence of support for their position. Concerned parents should know that the allusion is weak.

The Christian School Movement

The values that parents want their children to learn are Lutheran values, Baptist values, Seventh-Day Adventist values, Episcopal values. In short, morals based on religion. In 1960 the Lutheran school population was 151,476; by 1970 it was 200,914. Jewish day school population was 39,830 in 1960 and 65,335 in 1970. Baptists taught 16,574 children in 1960; 35,098 in 1970. Other denominations enrolled 21,158 students in 1960, but had soared to 52,299 in 1970.[13] That last category includes a plethora of small fundamentalist schools, but in fact only very vaguely indicates the number of

275

children thus educated. The small, independent church schools are notoriously suspicious of state or federal prying, and many were not even on the mailing list used by the Office of Education to conduct its survey. And of the schools identified, by no means all returned the survey. This spirit of independence from government interference is deplored as noncooperative by the private education establishment, but it is the most interesting trend in private education in recent times. The next survey of nonpublic schools, says the Office of Education, will make special efforts to locate, identify, and enumerate those "unknown" schools and their student populations.

Though looked down upon by "establishment" private educators because of their nonconformist ways, the Christian schools have much to offer. Discipline is uniformly strict; in some areas, public school administrators have been known to visit the Christian school principal to ask how he does it. The three Rs receive due emphasis, and advanced curriculum programs are available, such as the Accelerated Christian Education (ACE) Program, which serves at least 1,500 schools. ACE is not an association of schools, but a curriculum program. And although the instruction may not be sophisticated enough for Ivy Leaguers, a parent may rest assured that the elementary-level education will be at least as adequate as the typical public school offerings and will be planned to reinforce Christian principles, not to ignore or undermine them. There is nothing silly, after all, about teaching second graders about plants and trees and at the same time inspiring them with respect for the God who created plants and trees. And surely even humanists will admit there is a great deal to be said for teaching children about foreign lands with the added instruction that God also made and loves the various races just as he loves the one to which you belong. Most Christian parents agree on creationism, so that is how anthropology will be presented in a Christian school.

Doctrinal bickering among Protestant denominations is, of course, legendary. But Christian schools that are not supported solely by one church—and many, if not most, serve families from several churches in an area—find it possible to emphasize their similarities rather than their differences. This is necessary for the continued existence of the schools, which depend on each child, and each parent's financial contribution. Indeed, some traditionalist Catholic parents, whose own parochial schools are unacceptably trendy and modernist, have put their children in local Christian schools and found them thoroughly acceptable for the first four or five grades. In an age that seems to be aligning itself along Christian versus anti-Christian lines, it is reassuring to see that Christians can bury the hatchet long enough to work together for the better education of all Christian children.

Christian educators are set apart from secular educators by their concept of the purpose of education: to a religious educator, the education of a child cannot be separated from the child's eternal salvation. To a secular educationist, education is a nice process that provides social services and prepares future citizens. (To some extent, this secular attitude has crept into the attitudes of educators of the large, well-established churches; accordingly, these pedagogues try to be "professional" rather than religious.) Given this basic divergence of viewpoint, one can easily understand why fundamentalist Christian schoolmen want nothing to do with any arm of government. It is equally obvious why the bureaucrats are suspicious of Christian schoolmen. Add to this in some cases a religiously based repudiation of worldly goals, and the stage is set for a showdown between the Christian school and government bureaucrats.

The "respectable" private education establishment scorns the Christian schools for refusing to cooperate with the government:

> Certain segments of the private school world try to achieve independence by not associating with any group . . . by not applying for tax exemption, by ignoring regulations and standards, and by being

openly opposed to the government schools. In my opinion, people who are attempting to preserve educational independence the most are at the same time their own greatest threat. That, in turn, is a threat to us all.[14]

This was said by an educator whose own denomination, the Lutheran Church–Missouri Synod, had decided in 1961 to accept public money for school-situated social services, but not for salaries, equipment, or textbooks.[15] A sister church, the Wisconsin Synod, held to a more strictly religious view of education and decided in 1963 to reject all federal aid and "all forms of governmental intrusion into church and religious practices, and regulations in areas not assigned to the state by God."[16]

The noncooperating Christian schools rock the boat, a valuable service to all parents. The Tabernacle Christian School in Ohio is now world-famous. Its pastor and principal, Rev. Levi Whisner, and 12 other parents were criminally prosecuted and convicted in 1974 for sending their children to Tabernacle Christian, which lacked a state charter because it failed to meet a long list of complicated requirements. In 1976 the Ohio Supreme Court reversed the conviction, ruling that private, church-related schools are exempt from the state's minimum standards, which the court found so pervasive as to eliminate distinction between public and nonpublic education. The Reverend Mr. Whisner had argued that fulfilling the minimum standards would leave no time for religious training in his school, and that some of the content standards for particular courses were unacceptably devoid of reference to God. It is unfortunate that the *Whisner* decision (the legal citation is 351 N.E. 2d 750) did not come down from the U. S. Supreme Court, which might yet rule the opposite way on some similar case. Until that time, parents in Ohio have won a smashing victory, thanks to the courage of the Tabernacle Christian Church.

By the way, if the Tabernacle Christian School had wanted

state funds for transportation, or library books, or even for a lunch program, it is highly unlikely that the state court would have found the school deserving of exemption from the minutiae of state licensing. As federal regulation of education becomes more exacting, it becomes apparent that no institution accepting benefits can be exempt from the consequences.

Noncooperation with the government does not necessarily mean noncooperation with other Christian schools. To the contrary, just as concerned parents are finding allies in the far corners of the nation, so also likeminded Christian schools are finding each other. One of the largest and oldest of several Christian school associations is the American Association of Christian Schools.[17] In September 1976 the AACS reported that it had 320 member schools with about 70,000 students; only four years earlier, in 1972, it had 80 member schools and 16,000 students. Also in 1976 an additional 125 schools were "affiliated," that is, they had not yet lifted their standards high enough for full membership. AACS is not just a "club" for Christian schools; it is a working organization dedicated to raising standards of Christian education. It issues certification for teachers and administrators, and accredits schools. The standards for certification and accreditation are not lax either. The AACS encourages and assists the founding of new schools, helps place teachers, and most recently has begun to take an interest in the goings-on in Washington, D.C. In 1976 the association testified at the Internal Revenue Service hearings on reform of the regulations governing "integrated auxiliaries." The IRS was proposing that for the future, only church buildings themselves should be exempt from taxation, whereas the "integrated auxiliaries" of a religious body, such as hospitals, schools, orphanages, publishing houses, and the like, should be taxed. Present regulations allow tax-exemption according to ownership of the property; the proposed new policy would punish churches large and small.

Membership in the American Association of Christian Schools is open to any group that agrees with its Statement of Faith, excluding those affiliated with the National Council of

Churches or the World Council of Churches. The Statement of Faith includes the following:

> We believe that the Bible, both the Old and New Testaments, was given by inspiration of God, and is our only rule in matters of faith and practice. We believe in creation. . . . We believe that all men are born in sin. We believe in the Incarnation, the Virgin Birth, and the Deity of our Lord and Savior, Jesus Christ. . . . We believe that He is personally coming again. . . . We believe that salvation is by grace through faith, plus nothing—minus nothing, in the atoning blood of our Lord. . . .

Roman Catholic Schools

At least schools affiliated with the American Association of Christian Schools can be counted on to adhere to a certain minimum line of doctrine. Many would complain that the same cannot be said of Roman Catholic schools. Since the Second Vatican Council concluded in 1965, the Catholic faithful have been in a greater or lesser state of turmoil almost incessantly. The council itself wrought few substantive changes, doctrinally speaking. Rhetorically speaking, though, much confusion was sown—and widely. In the wake of the council came calls to "modernize" the church, usually taken to mean that the church should become more worldly. Laymen were to be given a voice in church policy, and Catholic education was to be given a "relevance" it supposedly had lacked. Changes in the liturgy and in minor church laws also came fast upon the heels of the council. Nuns and clergy were caught in the cross-currents and began bailing out of their vocations; the convents and seminaries took this as a sign of their own inadequacy and began to innovate with more zeal than wisdom, so that within several years there were few candidates indeed for a religious vocation.

280

Parochial schools in the United States had been part of Catholic life since soon after 1884, when the Third Plenary Council of Baltimore, reacting to the messianic Protestantism that then dominated public education, decreed that every church should have a school nearby and required Catholic parents to send their children to those schools. The universal Code of Canon Law promulgated in 1917 reflected a concern for similar situations worldwide; it declared that "Catholic children may not attend non-Catholic, neutral, or mixed schools, that is, those which are open also to non-Catholics."[18] That canon was seldom enforced in the United States; nonetheless, parents made heroic efforts to obtain a Catholic education for their children. Thousands of nuns, staffing the schools for little more than bare room and often scanty board, made it possible. Critics today discount all this as a manifestation of the "ghetto mentality." It was more than that: Catholics recognized that Catholic teaching and Catholic culture were to be valued. Catholic parents wanted Catholic schools to teach their children to be Catholics, even though, or perhaps because, their own lives did not always meet that rigorous standard.

Catholics believe in the sinfulness of man but also in the forgiveness of God, so that no matter how many times you fall, God always invites you to the Sacrament of Confession, to try again. The world does not often give a second chance but God does, and Catholic parents very much wanted their children to have that divine hope from early in life. A result of the theological "modernization" of Catholic education after Vatican II was the tendency to turn students into socially concerned citizens, rather than into Catholics first of all. For parents whose own bent was progressive, the schools usually did not move quickly enough. For other parents, the schools moved too rapidly and too unwisely. Theologically uninterested parents might have sensed the change of emphasis and wondered why they were paying tuition charges for something their children could get just as well for nothing in the public schools. For some time, parents could have resolved their doubts by noticing that achievement scores and other indices of academic preparation were superior for Catholic schools. Although that superiority still prevails—on the whole—there are signs that relevance is elbowing out excellence.

Before the council, the pastor of the parish pretty much ran the parish school, under the ultimate control of the bishop. Sister Principal would ask Father about problems, and decisionmaking was clear and swift. But then the laity was given a voice—boards were set up to "help" run the schools, and boards were set up to "help" run the parish. The two boards were not necessarily the same, nor did they necessarily agree. At the diocesan level, lay boards were also established, with similarly nebulous functions, and almost instantaneously a management nightmare came true. The predicament of serving two masters was only a small part of the problem.

Simultaneously, population shifts left city schools with few Catholic families to attend them, and the "new theology" caused some to abandon Catholic education in principle. Also, the nuns were vanishing, with lay teachers being hired to replace them—at much, much higher cost. In 1957 Catholic schools had a full-time teaching force of 147,330, of which 35,129 were lay; by 1967 the teaching force was 206,959, but nearly half of it, 90,066, was lay.[19] By 1976 the AFL-CIO had taken notice: lay teachers in Catholic schools were ripe for unionization. The National Labor Relations Board upheld the right of Catholic schoolteachers to unionize, because of the predominantly secular nature of the schools. Yet five years earlier the U.S. Supreme Court had ruled out state support of "secular" courses in parochial schools because the schools were "permeated" with religion. Fortunately, the Supreme Court stuck to its logic and reversed the NLRB.

As long as Catholic schools attracted students primarily because of the religious factor, frugality could be practiced: nonessential items, lavish plant and equipment, and nonteaching staff could be kept to a minimum. It was not unusual for Catholic school costs to average 60 percent less than those of the public schools in the same area.[20] High pupil-teacher ratios and the unlicensed status of teaching nuns were perceived as problems only after competition with public schools had shifted to the terms set by the latter.[21]

As the Catholic aspect was downplayed and Catholic schools tried to mimic the public schools, material costs soared. When parochial school parents began noticing their children using new paperback textbook series, with several disposable workbooks for each child, and with audiovisual aids essential, it was a sure sign that things had changed. And it wasn't because the school had suddenly inherited a fortune. It was because hardnosed decisive management, devoted to providing essentials and providing them well, had been replaced by impressionable committees that could be sidetracked by frills, novelty, and high-pressure sales pitches.

Catholic schools reached a peak around 1966, when they were educating 77 percent of America's Catholic children.[22] By 1972 parochial schools were closing at a rate of two per day, raising costs to the public by $5 billion per year to do what the Catholic schools had been doing at no cost to the public treasury.[23]

There are, of course, private Catholic schools, unconnected with any parish. Private schools are usually run by a religious order, and high tuition fees must cover most costs. Parochial schools, on the other hand, are subsidized by the parish; diocesan high schools are supported by their diocese. Because of their special appeal, the private schools enjoyed a little insulation from the demographic disasters besieging the parochials. However, their costs rose unavoidably, and economic concessions like coeducation were widely introduced. Private Catholic schools, like any private school, are free to appeal to as specific an audience as they wish, and to raise their standards as high as they want. Opus Dei high schools, of which there are only a few in the country, can demand of their students four years of classical languages, four years of modern languages, four years of math and science, and find themselves flooded with applicants, while a diocesan high school several miles away dares not require its students to learn Latin for fear it will be branded "irrelevant"—but must scramble for enough students to justify its continued operation.

After several years of postconciliar disruption, the Catholic education bureaucracy, which imitates some of the worst aspects of the NEA, sought to legitimate its innovations. The result was a 1972 pastoral letter, *To Teach As Jesus Did*, calling for schools to become "communities of faith." Three steps were proposed to meet this goal: (1) proclaim the gospel message; (2) build community in homes, neighborhoods, the nation, and the world; and (3) serve by prayer and "direct participation in the cause of social reform." This was nothing new, although the National Catholic Educational Association (NCEA) made a lot of noise about it in 1972 and loudly congratulated itself in 1976 on how successfully it had put its own exhortations into practice.

Some examples of the supposed success: Jesuit High School in Portland, Oregon requires a nine-week "research and action" course in community involvement prior to graduation. Jesuit High in Dallas, Texas has a graduation requirement of 100 hours of social service; Jesuit High in Shreveport, Louisiana, requires a course on "social theology" supplemented by hospital or day-care volunteer work.[24] Jesuit schools are private, rather than diocesan, and can require such training only because the client parents are willing to go along with it. But Catholic school parents are finding their lot similar to that of public school parents: arrogance of power afflicts secular educators wherever they happen to teach—even in religious schools.

Little wonder that Catholic schoolchildren have come home and reported, "My religion teacher said that praying doesn't help anyway. God has created us—painted the picture—and then stepped out of the picture. We're really on our own."[25]

The history of Catholic education in the last 15 years would make a fat book by itself. What is its likely future? Maybe demand for Catholic schools, though lessened, will shift so that the specifically Catholic aspects of the education will be

284

emphasized again. There is reason to believe that the downward trend is bottoming out. The time may be coming when the only parents who still want their children to go to Catholic schools will want those children to wear uniforms, submit to discipline, learn the doctrines of the faith, appreciate Catholic culture—and acquire a traditional basic education. As the proportion of these parents in the Catholic school population grows, the principles of market operation suggest that they should swing more clout. That will mean an upgrading of the schools. Already one occasionally hears stories of how parochial schools that "went crazy" in the late 1960s have been "cleaned up." Catholic parents in large dioceses are organizing much as public school parents have done, in order to make their case to the school boards and bishop, and to try to wrest some parental control away from the cadre of professionals. Since attendance at Catholic schools is optional, concerned Catholic parents who organize to influence their schools should have an easier road ahead than public school parents. Now is the time for them to get moving!

In trying to solve their school problems, Catholics might learn something from the recent history of the Hebrew day school movement. Until the last 15 or 20 years, Jewish parents were satisfied to send their children to public schools and relegate religious training to a weekend class or several afternoon classes a week after school. In 1935 there were only 16 Jewish day schools in the country, half of them in New York City. But by 1965 there were over 300, and the number is still growing.[26] These schools commonly are not coeducational. The program is stern: Jewish studies for three or four hours in the morning, general studies in the afternoon. Graduates of Hebrew schools excel in the secular curriculum, which placates the fears of worldly parents who expected that too much Hebrew study would crowd out the history, math, and science regarded as standard fare.

Why this revival of what liberal educationists consider the "ghetto mentality," if that is what religious education is? Simple. By the 1960s it was obvious that Jewish children didn't take their religion very seriously. Intermarriage with Christians, assimilation into the broader Gentile society, falling away from Judaism—all were quite common, distressing rabbis and faithful alike.

"In order to raise a child to take his place happily, faithfully, and creatively in the Jewish community, you must give him a Jewish environment—at home *and* in the school."[27] The same can be said for Catholic children, Lutheran children, Presbyterian children, and children of any other denomination that comes to mind. Religiously affiliated schools that try to water down their distinctive religious aspects are doing themselves no favor, as the enrollment figures for liberal religious schools show, particularly when compared with the astounding growth of the fundamentalist schools.

Some may be alarmed that resurgent sectarian differences will take us back to the dark days before the melting pot heated up and blended everyone together as true-blue Americans. That concern is out of place: the melting pot never melted much besides economic differences anyway. Being a good American does not preclude being a good Catholic or a good Lutheran or whatever. In fact, the moral perspective of religion is needed today as never before in national affairs. Pluralism is the word to describe the contemporary socioreligious situation. Liberals invoke pluralism as one reason why the public schools must give time to the viewpoints of secular humanists, draft-card burners, racial revolutionaries, lawbreakers, sexual deviants, socialists, pacifists, abortionists, feminists, and other similar oddities on the American scene. Well then, if pluralism dictates that we must expose public schoolchildren to such baneful influences, why can it not also justify a religious education with all its beneficial influences?

Financing Private Education

The universal enemy of independent education, lack of money, may be the strongest weapon parents have to influence

286

the direction of their childrens' education in private schools. Statistician Andrew Greeley, for example, says that Catholic lay people would be willing to contribute $1.7 billion more each year to save their Catholic schools.[28] That such contributions are not forthcoming suggests a lack of satisfaction, if Greeley's finding is correct. All religiously affiliated schools face a financial problem to some extent. Even Jewish parents are finding it a strain to maintain the Jewish day schools, which are growing by leaps and bounds—so much of a strain, in fact, that some Jewish educators are rethinking their long-standing objections to government assistance to religious schools.[29] The Supreme Court, however, so far has not found any reason to rethink its long-standing objections to aid for religious schools.

Legal objections for the most part are based on the First Amendment, as interpreted by Justice Hugo Black in a 1947 dictum in *Everson v. Board of Education* (330 U.S. 1): "Neither [a state, nor the federal government] can pass laws which aid one religion, aid all religions, or prefer one religion over another." The same dictum was invoked in the school-prayer decisions. Ironically, that dictum was appended to a decision that upheld the constitutionality of a New Jersey plan to reimburse parents for their costs of using public transportation to send their children to school, including parochial schools.

Constitutional history reveals that the Founding Fathers, who eventually approved the First Amendment out of political necessity, feared that "the words might be taken in such latitude as to be extremely hurtful to the cause of religion."[30] Peter Sylvester of New York was more prophetic, fearing that the amendment "might be thought to have a tendency to abolish religion altogether."[31] Although hardly anybody short of Madalyn Murray O'Hair comes forward today to advocate the abolition of religion altogether, the trend in that direction is plain to see.

Traditionally, churches and private education have been given special treatment by means of tax exemption for their property and for donations to their work. Such a policy recognizes the service to society in general of private education, and the inviolability of religion. Today, however, one hears talk of doing away with this "preferential treatment" because it is no longer justified in a secular age. This attitude was anticipated by Charles Rice in 1964:

> I frankly expect these tax privileges to be invalidated in the early course of events. . . . Regrettably, restraint will have to be effected by Congress or by the people. . . . Unless such a check is placed upon the Court, we may fairly expect the abolition of all tax privileges accorded to religious activities of religious organizations. In which event, there will be "separation of church and state," but few churches.[32]

The IRS plan regarding "integrated auxiliaries" verifies Professor Rice's fears.

The professional establishment is adamant in opposition to any public aid for private education, and particularly against public aid for religiously affiliated private schools:

> A system of free public education is the chief means by which a free society continually regenerates itself. . . . It is a kind of fourth branch of government. . . . In this sense, the rights of free people in public education are prior to the rights of individual churches or of individual parents in private education.[33]

State after state has come up with schemes for aiding parochial education, and referendum after referendum has rejected the plans. New York finally did manage to allot $8 million in "mandated services" assistance to private and parochial schools, to reimburse those schools for their performance of certain state-required duties. A federal court found even this unconstitutional.[34]

The fact remains: parents who send their children to nonpublic schools are punished by double taxation. They pay to support the public schools and they also pay to support the private school of their choice. A parent who cannot afford that double taxation is thus effectively denied the right freely to practice his religion, or to pass it on to his children. For parents who are financially able, the burden is nonetheless a discouragement to religion. Does not the 14th Amendment require equal protection of the law for all citizens, regardless of race, religion, or economic condition? How, then, constitutionally, can state laws force parents to sacrifice their religious freedom in order to obtain "free" education for their children? The question has been raised only theoretically, because parents have yet to find an effective, vocal advocate who could convince the courts to recognize the right of parents to control the religious training of their children.

In the Republic of Ireland there is no such thing as a government school; all schools are under religious management, Catholic or Protestant or Jewish. The government pays teachers' salaries in all cases, and school construction costs with total disregard to which religion is the beneficiary. But, it must be remembered, Ireland (Eire) considers religion better than irreligion, which the United States officially does not, so it is only to be expected that policies will differ.

Those in the United States who ostensibly should stand to benefit from government aid to religious education are not entirely sure of the desirability of such aid, for reasons discussed above. Even a negative policy, like exemption from taxes, may soon be regarded as a form of direct aid that invites as much government interference and control as a cash grant does. Dr. George C. Roche, president of embattled Hillsdale College, has dug up an IRS memo that argues that tax exemption is a government-given benefit.[35] IRS has already made it

289

clear that tax exemption can be refused to schools with a racially discriminatory admissions policy.

A just and workable answer to the punishment of double taxation is a tax credit for parents whose children are enrolled in private schools. A proposal along those lines was first introduced in the 94th Congress (1974–76) by Senator Buckley and Congressman Delaney. While the bill as a whole, predictably enough, received no action, one provision was borrowed from it and attached as an amendment to the Senate's 1976 tax reform legislation. The Senate voted to allow parents a tax credit for each child whose tuition they were paying to a private college or university. Ultimately, the provision got lost in the shuffle of conflicting versions of the bill, conferences, political pressures, and shortage of time. While the measure would not have relieved the desperate financial plight of private elementary and secondary education, half a loaf would have been better than none.

In the 95th Congress the Buckley-Delaney proposal was revived and given influential support by Buckley's sucessor, Daniel P. Moynihan (D–N.Y.). Moynihan managed to line up half the Senate behind the proposal he and Senators Roth (R–Del.) and Packwood (R–Ore.) worked out to allow middle-class parents tax credits for tuition paid to private colleges, and eventually for private elementary and secondary tuition. The 1976 Democratic platform had promised tax relief to ensure "parental freedom in choosing the best education." Significantly, Democratic President Jimmy Carter and his HEW secretary, Joseph Califano, whose own children attend costly private schools, lobbied vigorously against the Moynihan-Roth-Packwood proposal. As this book goes to press (April 1978), the measure is very much alive, having been reported favorably out of the Senate Finance Committee. If the final legislation is everything it appears to be, parents should make tax credits for private education their highest congressional priority.

8

Around and Out
of the System

The Love Story (and Others)

C hristian schools are not the only private independent
schools being launched in this country. It is, in fact, impossible to calculate how many non-church-affiliated, independent proprietary schools are being established here, there, and
everywhere.

One of the foremost advocates of private education run
according to strict free-market principles is Robert Love of
Wichita, Kansas. Love believes that a school-as-business can do
a better job of educating children than a school-as-public-
welfare-measure. He is quite vehement about this:

> There is no need for parents to continue being frus-
> trated and angered over unsatisfactory education. It
> is a wasteful, draining exercise in futility. Instead of
> contending with the existing system, parents must
> take their lives into their own hands and educate
> their children on their own terms.[1]

This viewpoint is militant. It is also selfish, because it advocates that concerned parents simply flee the existing system, leaving the majority of the nation's children to their fate. As far as the education of a particular child is concerned, however, lifting him altogether out of the public school system may be the best solution to a multitude of problems—when, for example, a parent's activism is causing harmful reverberations from a classroom teacher. Parents must make such a decision on an individual basis.

Love invites parents who have decided to abandon the public system to follow the example of his Wichita Collegiate School. A similar offer is extended by Rev. Robert Thoburn, founder of the Fairfax Christian Academy in Virginia. Fairfax Christian opened in the fall of 1961 with 32 students. Ten years later it enrolled 532 students from kindergarten through 12th grade. It is still growing. Fairfax Christian has turned a tidy profit, most of which has been returned to the enterprise. And now Thoburn takes delight in reminding the citizens of Fairfax County that his school saves the public one-half million dollars a year, in addition to which it pays $40,000 a year in taxes. (His neighbors are evidently pleased: in 1977 they elected him to the Virginia House of Delegates.) Thoburn conducts seminars on the philosophy and mechanics of his free-market Christian school for those interested.[2]

Wichita Collegiate is not a Christian school; it proposes only to offer good education, defined as the owners agree to define it. Parents are regarded as customers, education as the product to be sold. Needless to say, the school has no interest in tax-exempt status. (Some other proprietary schools have gotten a tax break by incorporating two separate entities: one, a profit-making corporation that owns the land and buildings; the other, a nonprofit corporation that leases the land and buildings and runs the school.) Because Wichita Collegiate is a business in the strictest sense of the term, full-cost pricing is the name of the game. The budget is trim, but everything pays for itself, and Wichita Collegiate found that whatever its customers wanted, it was able to provide as long as they were

292

willing to pay. The school is not accredited, nor, like Fairfax Christian, is it interested in that rigmarole. Its standards are high; reputable colleges have not hesitated to accept its graduates. Any self-respecting college, after all, prefers a student who knows something to one who carries a meaningless "approved" diploma.

There was some harassment. For example, the Kansas High School Athletic Association would not let Wichita Collegiate become a member because it was not "accredited by the state." State laws guaranteeing that any graduate of a state-accredited high school will be admitted to state college naturally do not apply to graduates of the school either. But such tactics are trivial and are recognized as such by Wichita Collegiate's students and parents.

An essential ingredient for the success of a proprietary venture is team spirit. Wichita Collegiate has it. Unless students are willing to accept cheerfully the differences between their school and the public school, unless the parents are devoted to the idea and willing to sacrifice for it, and unless teachers are recognized as vital to the whole operation and treated accordingly, morale can quickly sink to a point of no return. On the other hand, when a venturesome spirit dominates the scene, starting a proprietary school can be an exhilarating experience for all concerned.

There are, without a doubt, many merits in taking the proprietary route, not the least of which is that neither the state, nor the federal, government can control the school. Every state has standards and codes governing public schools, which specify what must be taught, how many hours a week, in what kind of facilities, by teachers with what kind of preparation, and so on into a bottomless mire of senseless detail. Some states simply ignore teachers in nonpublic schools; others are not so helpful. In some states the amount of interest the state takes depends on whether the school has applied for state accreditation or not. Since proprietary schools generally follow a policy of totally separate existence, few are inclined even to apply for state accreditation if they can avoid it. In some states incorporation as a business is not enough to guarantee that the state education bureaucrats will not interfere; an education business may be subject to some kind of supervision regardless of clientele or management. In other states the leeway is much greater. These laws vary greatly, and any individual or group contemplating a proprietary school should seek out competent legal advice before making any plans.

Proprietary child-care centers, which have grown by leaps and bounds in recent years, have made a regrettable departure from the general rule of independence. Day care is not education in a strict sense, but the relation is close enough: errors in judgement by the day-care center can damage a child's education. Many privately owned profit-making day-care businesses are inviting their own destruction by participating in federally funded day-care projects. To qualify for a federal grant, they must be state accredited and must sooner or later satisfy the federal Interagency Day Care Regulations as well. By the time they qualify for federal money, day-care operators will discover that being the owner of the enterprise means nothing if you can't make any of the decisions—and the Interagency Day Care Regulations specify just about everything but the color of the walls.

High school accreditation bears scant relation to the caliber of instruction or the quality of students graduated by the institution. More attention is paid to the dimensions of the classrooms and the degrees of the instructors than to the quality of the actual educational product. A small old-fashioned Christian school may fail accreditation because it lacks a grand gymnasium while it may succeed in teaching children far more effectively than the accredited multi-million-dollar public school down the road. Fortunately, colleges are so desperate for good students that a student with good College Entrance Examination Board scores and good achievement-test scores, who can demonstrate competence in the English language, is at no real disadvantage for want of an "accredited" diploma. Colleges themselves must, as team players, pay lipservice to accreditation, but their need for students is urgent and promises to become even more so after 1980.

Nor is the situation entirely different at the elementary level. Several reasons are usually advanced by parents for not wanting to send their children to an unaccredited elementary school, but 20 years ago these reasons had more force behind them than they generally have now.

1. *The children won't learn as much.* What a child learns depends not on accreditation, but on the school. If a parent doubts a particular school's ability to teach—either from experience or hearsay or acquaintance with the school—his doubts would not be allayed by a piece of paper. Public schools are almost always "accredited," but children in them often learn precious little. To guarantee that your child is learning something, you as parent must keep in constant touch with his work. That is true in *all* types of schools.

2. *The children won't get into a good high school.* In the first place, the public schools cannot refuse a child on account of the irregularity of his elementary background, so a child can always go to some high school. At worst, he could be enrolled in a public school long enough to get a transcript established and then transfer out.

In the second place, parents interested in a private elementary school are not usually great supporters of the public schools to begin with. Private high schools are a little like colleges in their need for good students, except of course where "name" schools are involved, in heavily populated, affluent areas. Very often, if parents can pay the tuition and the student is competent, the accreditation status of the previous school is of little interest, even to "name" secondary schools.

Another factor to consider: it is common practice for private schools to add a grade a year to keep up with their students. If enough parents have been pleased with the job the school has been doing thus far, a high school may spontaneously grow out of the elementary school by the time the first class is ready for it.

Parent-founded schools need not be as ambitious as Wichita Collegiate and Fairfax Christian. Some may aim to provide an alternative for only the first, most impressionable years, and to fade away when their children have passed that stage. Some may find themselves involuntarily going out of business after several years, however. Observers of schools react instinctively with scorn for a school that "didn't make it" and with respect for one that "gets established." To a limited extent only is this reaction valid. True, long-term ventures tend to bespeak the planning—and the competence—of the individuals responsible. Likewise, involuntary failures usually result from deficiencies along those lines. But there, are other factors.

Parents who contribute their time, money, work, and other support to a private school venture have a personal interest in it. When their personal interest expires—usually when their children graduate—it is appropriate for somebody else with a compelling interest to step into the vacuum. If nobody else steps in, and the school has served the function desired by its founders, why keep it in existence merely because it is there? If there is no demand for its services, why should it exist? If it has done a good job and pleased its clients, it is likely to have built a good reputation; it will attract ample students to enable it to stay in business, provided the new crop of parents is willing to exert some personal effort.

One fact Robert Love neglects to emphasize in his otherwise very useful book[3] is that he and his cofounders of Wichita Collegiate were reasonably well supplied with funds. The school represented a business investment for its founders, as well as an educational venture. Unfortunately, very few concerned parents are affluent enough to undertake such a large business investment. More usual are the parents who are happy to have the checkbook balance at the end of the month. For these parents, a private school represents mere satisfaction of the letter of the law for only as long as their children are subject to it. These parents cannot be expected to continue to support a school after its usefulness to them has passed. Unlike the supporters of a regular business, patrons of education are a transitory group.

Nevertheless, it must be admitted that schools do fail even when there are parents ready, willing, and able to make the necessary sacrifices, and when other circumstances would seem favorable. Perhaps the most common cause of failure is a combination of excessive optimism and insufficiently critical selection of the people in charge. A school should not count its chickens before they are hatched: if a junior high is going to be added to an elementary school, it should be planned for slightly fewer students than are currently enrolled in the sixth grade. If more students have registered by September, well and good. Neither should a school assume that, because busing is being introduced in the adjacent urban complex, enrollment is going to skyrocket. It may happen, but the registrations and fees should be in hand before any irreversible decisions are made under that assumption. If the headmaster assumed there would be 50 students, and rented space for that many, and hired teachers for that many, and only 25 show up when school starts, the problems are big.

Parents cannot do everything in a large school: responsibility must be delegated, so a headmaster must be hired to handle administration. Resist the temptation to fill this position on the basis of "he's a fine young man," or "he goes to our church," or "he has a fine education," or "his dad's a good lawyer." Those statements may give good reasons to like the young fellow, but they do not give good reasons to think he can do the job. The questions you must ask are: Is the man well organized? Can he keep 15 balls in the air at one time without dropping any? Can he assume responsibility? Can he meet strangers and make a dynamic impression? Has he a head for details? Is he acquainted with financial and economic realities? Can he hold someone to a commitment? Does he clearly understand the gist of a conversation, or is he likely to misunderstand what is said to him? Is his a strong personality that commands respect? These questions must be answered on the basis of the individual's demonstrated ability—and not on the

297

basis of his apparent or assumed ability. Errors in basic judgement are fatal to a small, struggling enterprise of any kind, but more particularly to a venture that needs to create demand for its services.

There are schools that never face the problem of hiring an administrator because they never get big enough to need one. There are even schools that don't get big enough to need to hire teachers. The Holy Innocents schools are an example of a shoestring operation. This movement was begun under the aegis of Catholics United for the Faith,[4] an association of lay Catholics dedicated to preserving the traditional teaching of the church in the face of the innovations of the late 1960s. Holy Innocents schools sprang up as they were needed, around the country here and there, and faded away as their usefulness expired. Some still exist, and CUF welcomes renewed interest as a new generation of post–Vatican II Catholics comes of elementary school age. These ad hoc schools show what can be done with minimal resources. The staff was usually parents volunteering their time; the plant was likely to be someone's basement; the tuition fee may have been paid in hours of instruction. Because few people were involved, arrangements could vary widely from school to school.

There are also lay-controlled Catholic schools that are independent of CUF. Two outstanding examples are Seton School in Manassas, Virginia, and the Colorado Catholic Academy of the Holy Rosary in Denver.

Begun in 1973 with $18,000 seed money, the Academy of the Holy Rosary now has all 12 grades and about 100 students. "Professional" educators would be appalled at the limited staff of five full-time and three part-time teachers, but all of the first graduating class were accepted by the college of their first choice, and one student won the state VFW speech contest. The school buys secondhand textbooks and uses the McGuffey Readers in the early grades. It is a tax-exempt corporation in the state of Colorado, but has no traffic with the federal government at all. Tuition is relatively high: $189.00

298

per month per family—but that is regardless of the number of children the family sends to the school.

Seton School in Manassas, Virginia, outside Washington, D.C., is more moderately priced: $40 per month for the first child, $20 per month for the second, and $10 per month for all subsequent children. After a year and half of existence, the school had 53 students, mostly in grades 7 through 10, with a combined 11th and 12th grade. This population is served by two full-time and two part-time teachers, devoted to the school as an apostolic endeavor and able to accept minimal salary. This is an uncommon occurrence, and it does help keep down the overhead. Actually, as the unemployment for young Ph. D.'s and other scholars continues to rise, more well-qualified teachers may be available to teach at sacrificial wages. Anne Carroll, the founder of Seton School,[5] could not find a book that presented world history in an acceptable manner, so she wrote her own, *Christ the King, Lord of History,* which is used also by Holy Rosary and other parent-run Catholic schools.

Not all parent-controlled Catholic schools are biased in favor of tradition. In New England, for example, there is a Catholic Pentecostal school, run primarily by lay people who want their children to experience this kind of education. Because the established Catholic schools are so thoroughly progressive, it is not necessary for Catholic progressivist parents to break away to start their own schools, except perhaps in a few of the more old-fashioned dioceses of the United States.

Parents of all ideological and religious persuasions are banding together to start schools for their children. If a few sympathetic parents are willing to put out the effort, a smorgasbord of education is a real possibility. The "establishment," naturally enough, deplores such diversity and may eventually seek legal action to halt this "underground railroad" in education. In some states punitive action is already under way, so parents should apprise themselves fully of the situation in their state when planning a new school. Two documents are worth consulting. In 1975 the U.S. Office of Education funded a survey entitled *State and Federal Laws Relating to Nonpublic Schools.* The work was done by Bascomb Associates, 7961 Eastern Avenue, Silver Spring, Maryland 20910. And in 1974 the National Institute of Education funded a study, done by the Lawyers' Committee for Civil Rights Under Law, a Washington, D.C. think-tank, entitled *A Study of State Legal Standards for the Provision of Public Education.* This latter study is available through the Educational Resources Information Center (ERIC) of NIE, a system to which many major libraries have access. Taken together, the two documents reveal the dreary uniformity of public education from state to state and the obstacles to the establishment of "legitimate" alternative education. It may be enough to make parents want to take matters into their own hands.

Better Late Than Early

In Chapter 5 early-exit programs were discussed as one way to shorten the excessively long span of mandatory school attendance. Meanwhile, educationists are continually advocating the lowering of the compulsory entry age and are winning enactment of their proposals in more and more states. Most states now include kindergarten in the public education program; increasingly, educationists are demanding mandatory kindergarten; legislation has been introduced in Congress to define public education as beginning at age four. To no small degree, extended mandatory education is advanced as a means of employing surplus teachers. And because teachers have been organized into an effective lobby, they have a good shot at reaching their goals—despite a respectable and growing parents' rights lobby working against them.

Many mothers doubt the wisdom of sending their barely five-year-old children, particularly boys, off to school. Too often their doubts have been confirmed as their sons became frustrated and began to hate school, then became poor students or disciplinary problems—patterns likely to be permanent. It is common knowledge that girls usually do better in school than boys of the same age, and that boys are more often the discipline problems. That the former is often a factor in the latter is less commonly realized. Experienced mothers know that little girls tend to talk at younger ages than little boys, and to pay better attention younger, and to concentrate on small toys or detailed games at earlier ages than their brothers. Biological and psychological findings validate these everyday observations and strongly suggest that boys would benefit from later attendance at school and would benefit also by being separated from girls during their early years of formal education. After all, if you are giggled at every time you stand up to read, you are not likely to enjoy reading, especially if your eyes cannot distinguish the letters as clearly, so that you cannot help yourself from making the mistakes.

Yet school policy insists on packing little boys and little girls into the same elementary school classrooms when their ages are identical. And school policy expects them to perform equally, even though their developmental disparity may be as much as 9 or 12 months.

The Gesell Institute of Child Development is very concerned with "developmental placement," which is to say, ignore the calendar and the education code, and start or continue a child in school on the basis of his or her individual maturity. "Our own figures, as well as those arrived at by many other educators throughout the country, agree that the older children are when they start school, the better they tend to do," says one spokesman of the institute.[6]

The institute has formulated an individual behavior examination to determine the proper grade placement for children. Of course, this exam cannot be administered to everybody, and it even may not be much more reliable than the person who administers it. But at least such a test does exist, and it is a tangible, fairly objective criterion by which to measure such an elusive quality as maturity. It is useful because the common sense of parents only rarely convinces professional education bureaucrats of anything. Unfortunately, the Gesell examinations are not readily available everywhere.[7] As a means to the end of delaying a child's entrance into a destructive school system, though, the Gesell examination may be able to offer assistance.

One of the long-standing beliefs of the Gesell school, that "slow teething tends to go along with slow development of behavior,"[8] has recently been corroborated by an education professor at New York State University College at Fredonia. Dr. John Silvestro studied a number of first- and second-grade students, and found that the more permanent teeth first-grade boys have, the better they perform on tests that predict future reading success. Silvestro's theory is that when the permanent teeth come in, 95 percent of the head development is completed, a biological sign that the brain is mature and can absorb enough to begin learning to read.[9]

Ophthalmologists have long been of the opinion that early reading is injurious to the eye, particularly before age seven. The chief of pediatrics at the Harbor General Hospital in Los Angeles maintains that only 25 percent of kindergarten children are neurologically ready to read: the eye may receive the image, but the connection between what is seen and what is understood is simply insufficient.[10] Neurological maturity rarely exists at so young an age.

Dr. Raymond S. Moore of the Hewitt Research Center in Berrien Springs, Michigan is a specialist in the matter of school readiness. Moore first came to public prominence when he advanced objections to universal day-care proposals. Day care may be good for deprived or handicapped children, Moore argues, but to send all children to day care is "like sending all healthy kids to the hospital to be sure they get the same benefits as sick ones."[11]

The reasons for objecting to universal day care are the same as for objecting to universal early school entrance: precisely what young children do not need is systematic, formal academic training. What they do need is a sound foundation for

302

physical and emotional stability and development, without which mental and social development cannot come later. But the best foundation for emotional stability is the home, where a child has warm, intense attachments, abundant interaction with a constant mother (or surrogate mother), and a free but protected environment. It is well known, and has been abundantly demonstrated scientifically, that the most important single factor in all future development is a child's first, basic emotional relation with mother. The human being is a very slow-developing creature, and the satisfaction of that primary emotional need takes much time. Birds do not throw their young out of the nest before they are ready to fly; yet people have been convinced that they do well to throw their young out of the secure home environment before they are really old enough to benefit by it, or even, perhaps, to endure it.

Nor is the home solely a place of emotional satisfaction; it is also a place to learn. Says Moore:

> Simply by being herself, a concerned loving mother usually can do more for her normal child than a teacher can. By using the framework of everyday home activities in a practical way, she can help her child learn as much as possible about the things around him.[12]

Admittedly, it is not easy to turn home life into a planned learning experience, but neither is it overwhelmingly difficult. In their book, *Better Late Than Early,* Moore and his wife offer numerous practical suggestions.

Moore speaks frequently of the integrated maturity level (IML):

> Early childhood education must take into account the development of the child's brain, vision, hearing, perception, emotions, sociability, family and school relationships and physical growth. For each of these factors, there appears to be a level of matu-

303

rity at which most children can, without serious risk, leave normal homes and begin typical school tasks. When we bring these factors together, we have an index to total maturity that we call the child's integrated maturity level (IML).

On the basis of a comprehensive review of many research findings . . . we believe that the IML is seldom if ever achieved earlier than ages 8–10.[13]

And until the IML is attained, the best possible environment for a child is his home, and the best teacher his mother.

No less an authority within the establishment than the dean of education of the University of California at Los Angeles admits that elementary school students could learn as much in three well-planned hours as they usually do in five and a half.[14] Planning three hours of learning for a child should not be a major effort for a mother, who, after all, is accustomed to planning 24 hours for her children and family. Both the child and the parent will enjoy and benefit more from three hours together than from six or more at school. The child's education is more important than having a spotless house; a maternal conscience can relax on that score. Besides, having the child help with housework is an excellent learning opportunity for him. Nor should working mothers automatically disqualify themselves from home education of their children; the president of the National Parents League can tell of several working mothers who have successfully done it.

Despite the accumulation of research indicating that it is inadvisable, state after state continues to lower the age for school attendance. And enforcement of the laws is tightening. Even Mississippi is likely to reenact a compulsory attendance law.[15] In May 1976 the city of Baltimore announced that it was hiring 100 new truant officers. This force is needed to keep track of the estimated 30,000 students per day who are absent from the public schools.[16]

It would seem that those 30,000 youngsters are trying to tell

304

the school system something. But because the main part of the student body is from lower-class minority groups, the school system can ignore or distort whatever the message might be. NEA is perturbed that 10 percent of all the high school diplomas awarded in 1973 were issued on the basis of General Educational Development (GED) exams. That year more than 250,000 citizens, who had completed an average 9.8 years of formal school, received GED diplomas. Had those citizens stayed in school and gone the usual course, an additional 58,645 certified teachers would have been needed to educate them—"a fact of some interest to unemployed teachers," as an NEA memo laconically states it.[17] Unfortunately, had many of those citizens stayed in school and gone the usual course, the chances are they would not have learned very much, and, worse, would not have wanted to learn very much. The point is, our schools are so bad that even the students know it and make every effort to get out of them as soon as they can. So why are parents allowing the state to compel their children to start school at ever-younger ages?

Even "respectable" academics are beginning to ask these questions. Professor Edward Banfield of Harvard University some time ago recommended lowering the school-leaving age to 14 so that the nonlearners would have the incentive and the opportunity to learn something of use to themselves and of benefit to society.[18] Social critic Ivan Illich shocked the intellectual world even more in the early 1970s when his book *Deschooling Society* was published. That book made the unheard-of point that universal schooling and the deification of formal education are not desirable, good, or necessary. Illich is a thoroughgoing nonconformist, with mostly leftist sympathies; recently he has moved on to problems of health care, attacking schemes for nationalized medicine on grounds that they denigrate man's ability to care for himself and exalt technocracy.

He leveled the same basic criticism against education. Although Illich's book was radical when it first appeared in 1970, its theme was shortly picked up by a group of American

305

critics, among them Paul Goodman and John Holt. The bias of these writers has been against American public schools because they are incompetent at, and perhaps incapable of, promoting social reforms desired by the intellectuals. Here is a case of the right solution to the wrong problem, perhaps.

Between the extreme positions of no schools at all and schooling from cradle to grave must lie some happy medium, waiting to be discovered. For the nonce, at least, the Illichians have opened up the discourse, so that the merits and short-comings of compulsory-attendance laws can be honestly debated. The discussion is given impetus by parents who take matters into their own hands and keep their children out of school.

Every so often—and more often in 1978 than in 1968—one hears of parents who have decided that late entry is not feasible or acceptable for whatever reason, and cannot wait out the years until early exit becomes possible. So they have decided to educate their children at home. In some cases the parents do the teaching themselves; sometimes they pool with other parents; sometimes college or graduate students are hired to supplement the parents.

The Scoma family of Chicago is a case in point. Richard and Julie Scoma are what you might call part of the counterculture: both are artists, and Richard doesn't believe in competition, so he does not hold a regular job. Financially, the family's existence is marginal. The two daughters started in the Chicago public schools, but as the parents learned more about what went on inside the school, they objected. One daughter was a gym monitor, with the task of checking whether the other kids' uniforms were complete: "a little Gestapo person," her father described it. The other daughter was sensitive to the competition of other children, and would cry when she was not first in her class.

After consulting with the school board and school district officials to try to get official approval of a plan for home instruction, the Scomas removed the two girls from school and began to follow the home-instruction plan anyway. The truant

306

officer came to visit. The family moved quickly, and their lawyer immediately sought a federal district court ruling that the girls could not be forced to return to public school, and that the Illinois compulsory-attendance law was unconstitutional.

The ruling was not granted, and the federal legal-services resources the Scomas had planned to use for further appeals were not available. However, Lizabeth and Nicole were secure for the time being, at least: no school official tried to force them back into public school.[19] The Scomas' prompt offensive legal strategy may have given the education bureaucrats cause to think twice before pursuing the matter further.

In other cases, by the time parents resort to teaching their children at home—for it is usually a measure of last resort—they have made veritable nuisances of themselves with their local school administration and board. The local bureaucrats may be so happy to see them go that they are willing to blink at the compulsory-attendance statutes. Of course, another set of bureaucrats may respond to a similar situation with mohammedan zeal and prosecute the case to the fullest extent of the law. If the truant officer never knocks, fine. But if he should, and official harassment appears in the offing, parents should wait no longer. Being the first on the legal battlefield is often a distinct advantage psychologically, if not necessarily legally. It is no guarantee that parents will win, but it is an unmistakable sign that they take the matter very seriously. Because so many people are beginning to question compulsory attendance, a legal challenge that goes to the heart of the matter is a can of worms that most educrats are quite happy to leave unopened.

No less a chronicler of liberal orthodoxy than the *New York Times* has allowed a parent educator to tell her story. Patricia Heidenry has four children. She was appalled at the waste of time and the suppression of youthful vigor and imagination practiced by ordinary schools. Because the family was moving across the country—indeed, across the Atlantic—when the first child came of school age, it was easy to keep off the education treadmill. In England she found a school that showed a real love for its students and treated each individually, so for three months the two oldest enjoyed what the school had to offer. Back in America, Mrs. Heidenry enrolled the three oldest in a local public school—primarily, she admits, because having time to herself while the children were in school had spoiled her. But that enrollment was for one year only. She couldn't bring herself to send them back to waste their time. For the next year, she drew up a course of study and family life became organized around it. Eventually a social worker came to inquire why the children were not in school. She was so impressed with the home education that she ended up by recommending that the family be left alone, because the children were obviously well adjusted and receiving a good education. As of the date of the *New York Times* article, the local public education authorities had accepted the social worker's recommendation. Publishing the article was a good offensive strategy for Mrs. Heidenry, as well as a good intellectual defense of home education.

> My desire to educate the children at home is based essentially on my belief that it is almost immoral for the children to spend a large portion of their youth in one building with more than a thousand other children and teachers in an environment that is lifeless and not life-giving. I use the word "immoral" to emphasize how strongly I feel about the time that is wasted by children in school. And I use it to indicate that this time wasted is something more important than children's I.Q.'s.[20]

There is no organization as such of parents who are educating their children at home. The National Parents League[21] does provide a curriculum program for parent-run schools, together with standardized tests—for schools that belong to the league. Results of those tests are on occasion remarkable: some students with one year of home teaching improve as much as three grade levels in a given subject. The NPL curriculum is designed to make parents fully autonomous as teachers. They are not slaves to a "system"; the curriculum only guides them. From experience with this curriculum comes evidence that parents are quite competent as teachers: one mother with a sixth-grade education herself used the NPL guidelines to put five children through high school!

Legal Aspects of Home Instruction

Legal precedent in home-instruction-versus-compulsory-schooling cases is scanty and contradictory. The recent case of Barbara Franz in New York City is typical: the burden of proving that their home is not inferior to a school rests with parents. In other states the burden is upon the state to demonstrate that the home is inferior.

Mrs. Barbara Franz, a widow who objected to having her son taught the look-say method of reading, as a last resort kept the boy home and taught him herself. She had tried to get the method of instruction changed, but had received no satisfaction from the school hierarchy. Arrested and brought to trial, Mrs. Franz procured expert testimony at her trial to demonstrate the wisdom of her action. The judge, however, ruled against her, not because she was incapable or because the child was being harmed, which were the charges made by the school district, and which the judge specifically denied—but because she was violating the letter of the law. With New York City's grim truancy problems, one would expect school officials not to waste their time persecuting a concerned mother whose child is being cared for and educated adequately. However, Mrs. Franz was used as an example. For her to be allowed to teach her son at home might have loosened the bars on the windows for other children whose parents also would be ready, willing, and able to teach them at home. To allow one parent successfully to defy the public school establishment might well have encouraged similar defiance from other par-

309

ents—and that general invitation to insubordination New York school bureaucrats cannot afford.

The wording of state laws regarding school attendance varies. One observer has noted that there are basically two kinds of laws: the "cookie cutter" law and the "other guy" law.[22] The latter type is easier to live with: it is worded so as to punish those parents (the "other guys") who might willfully neglect the education of their children, out of sheer laziness or whatever. Such people are not common, but because they do exist, a law is around to ensure that their children get an education. Under an other-guy law, parents who seek and find responsible alternative means of education have the chance to demonstrate that they are not the other guy against whom the law is directed, and can hope to receive a hearing on the merits of their case.

The cookie-cutter law seeks to standardize all children according to some vaguely perceived notion of what an American citizen should be taught to be. Under a cookie-cutter law, individualism is precisely what is legislated against, so individual education plans stand slight chance. Laws like this are likely to form the basis for criminal convictions: the parents are supposedly depriving their children of "social interaction." Education, remember, is not what the cookie-cutter law wants to ensure for all children; standardization is. And peer conformity is an important part of standardization.

The state of Virginia has enacted a unique variation on the theme of compulsory education: a parent with a genuine conscientious objection can exempt his child from compulsory schooling or a certain required course of study.

Parents considering the ultimate in passive resistance to the school system should acquaint themselves with their state's laws before planning on home education. If the law allows leeway for "equivalent education" of an unspecified nature in lieu of public education, then the parents would be well advised to obtain the state guidelines for instruction at the grade levels in question, and to prepare proof that the instruction in their home includes at least that much content. Using text-

310

books similar to those used in public schools is another way to establish "equivalency," as is the administration of tests from time to time to keep track of achievement. If the state law stipulates that only a public or recognized private school satisfies the attendance requirement, parents might consider forming a legally recognized corporation as a school. They should also give thought to the peer-association factor, which the state may deem essential to the definition of a "school."

The basic constitutional right of parents to fulfill compulsory-education laws other than by sending their children to public school was established in 1925 by *Pierce v. Society of Sisters* (268 U.S. 510). Beyond that, however, the legal position of home instruction is far from clear. No challenge to the constitutionality of compulsory-schooling laws has reached the Supreme Court. Even within a single state, different cases have been treated differently under the same law.

A 1959 Washington State case[23] found that teacher, pupils, and a place were the necessary components of a school and that the parents were not qualified teachers, so that their home instruction program could not be regarded as "school." On the other side, an Illinois case in 1950[24] approved a home instruction plan because the mother had taken "some pedagogy and educational psychology" in her two years of college, and maintained regular hours and proper subjects, with evidence of her daughter's good progress. New Jersey courts in 1937 and 1950[25] found against a home education program on the grounds that the program lacked opportunities for free association with other children. However, the judge who presided over a 1967 case in the same state[26] read the education code in a different light and permitted home education on the basis of academic equivalency.

Compulsory Attendance: Bane or Boon?

The American public, it must be noted, is remarkably submissive to the dictates of compulsory-education laws. Probably

311

this is because most people *believe* in compulsory school attendance. And to be sure, the tradition of mandatory schooling goes back to the early New England settlements.

The Puritan fathers wanted mandatory education in order to promote uniform religious sentiments among the colonists. Martin Luther had advocated the same idea in his time. The ancient city-state of Sparta had prescribed a mandatory education for its boys, and then had proceeded to plan a man's life. In Prussia, where the practice of universal compulsory education was perfected, the purpose was unabashedly political: to create and maintain political loyalties, and to erase dissent. When a regime they dislike gains control of the public schools, whether in Germany forty years ago or in Chile in recent times, liberal educators in America condemn that regime as totalitarian because it would control the minds of the young. Yet is that not what the American education establishment, in partnership with the federal bureaucracy, has done and intends to continue doing?

In the 19th century, Massachusetts school superintendent Horace Mann admired the Prussian system and plumped for it in the United States. Care must be taken, Mann said, to "regulate the will of the people."[27] The established classes at the time saw public education as their best protection against the immigrants of the middle and late 19th century—how else to purge them of their alien heritage than by "Americanizing" their youth?

Social workers were just then beginning to influence public education, and they agreed fully with this purpose. It became an article of faith of progressivism. In Chicago, for example, the Immigrants' Protective League, an offshoot of Hull House, obtained the names and addresses of all children between the ages of 6 and 16 who came to Illinois by way of Ellis Island, and referred them to their local school authorities.[28] That kind of crusading spirit did not die with Jane Addams either, although the rationale for it gradually evaporated.

The popular defenses of compulsory education are not very strong, when examined critically.

Compulsory-schooling laws have made education possible for many who might otherwise never have gone to school. This is a standard argument. However, all that the laws have actually done has been to compel physical attendance at school; learning cannot be compelled. If a youngster does not want to learn anything, he is not likely to do so ("You can lead a horse to water but you can't make him think"). But under compulsory-attendance laws, he must remain in school, a drain on the taxpayers' money and a distraction to other students.

Without compulsory-attendance laws, we would be a nation of illiterates, instead of having the highest educational standards in the world. Well . . . are we a nation of illiterates or not? There seems to be some dispute. The evidence offered earlier in this book seems to indicate that compulsory-attendance laws have failed to rub out illiteracy.

In the absence of compulsory attendance laws, the public would spend less money on education than it does under the pressure of such laws. Now that may be true. But why is it necessarily bad? The present system of giving state and federal funds to a local school district on the basis of average daily attendance works hand in glove with compulsory-attendance laws. But is that a defense of the laws?

Certain groups of children—bilingual, migrant, handicapped— would miss out on formal education unless the law required it. Aside from the thorny question of what benefit such children derive from formal education, we are told that even with the compulsory-attendance laws such groups are not receiving "equal education." Else why all the agitation for "compensatory education" and special programs for the various categories? Clearly, something more than—or other than—compulsory-attendance laws is needed to ensure equal education, whatever that may be, if today's militants can even agree on a definition.

One argument that does hold true is that *compulsory-attendance laws have helped decrease unemployment.* This is not surprising, but it is unrelated to the question whether public education prepares youngsters to be better workers or to be more employable. It could be simply because the absolute number of potential workers has been reduced thanks to the attendance requirement. Naturally, the proportion of employed workers is going to increase under this artificial restriction, so Labor Department statistics will reflect less unemployment. The statistics always show unemployment rising in the summer, when teenagers are out of school. It is not inadequate education so much as the minimum-wage laws that keep young people out of jobs. Labor leaders know that compulsory-attendance laws are good for them: the fewer people in the job market, the better the chance that those already there will land jobs. The draft also decreased unemployment, simply because it lowered the absolute number of job seekers. Is that a good defense of the draft?

Compulsory-attendance laws became widespread after the Civil War. Few will dispute that during frontier-taming days and the days of heavy immigration, mass education had some merit. On the frontier the schoolhouse was a civilizing influence, because the schoolmarm did not worry about "education for living." If she had, she would have taught her charges how to fire a sixgun, break a horse, or lay railroad track. Instead, she tried to pass on a little history and culture, and to teach certain basic skills. That was what the patrons of her school needed and wanted. Such teachers earned respect for formal education in America. Among the immigrants, education was necessary to teach the language and give some orientation in Anglo-Saxon Protestant culture.

What is arguable is whether education had to be made compulsory. Had the state not stepped forward to assume the mantle of supreme educator, parents who wanted an education for their children (most parents) and people who wanted one for themselves might have pursued their goals independently, relying on themselves, their parents, their churches, their communities, and other individuals more learned than they to guide them. Their education would have excluded nonessentials: if two years of English and American literature were of no interest or use, people would not have wasted their

314

time studying literature. As it was, compulsory-attendance laws eliminated self-reliance in education and created instead a dependence on government. If government was responsible for education, naturally it had to stipulate what courses were to be taken, who could teach them, and how long the school year would be. In other words, government came quickly to monopolize education.

The line between universal education and mind control is a thin one. As one libertarian thinker phrased it:

> The student is confirmed once again as an item of public property by virtue of his compulsory attendance at a government-accredited structure which preserves records. . . . The tie that binds the school to the state, and the students to the school, is the tie that binds the student to the state.[29]

So the fundamental argument against compulsory-attendance laws is simple: such laws are coercive, and coercion is not acceptable. Some libertarians assert that forcing students to attend school is a violation of their 14th Amendment right to equal treatment under the law. Married students below school-leaving age are exempt from compulsory attendance— why should somebody be penalized for being single? Other observers argue that compulsory education as it is now practiced fails to provide the individualized attention really needed by disadvantaged students. The right to privacy, seldom invoked outside of sexual freedom cases, may also be violated by compulsory-schooling laws.

Stephen Arons has suggested in the *Harvard Educational Review* that *Pierce v. Society of Sisters,* read in the context of the First Amendment, could be a precedent for demonstrating the unconstitutionality of compulsory-attendance requirements. The First Amendment includes the words: "Congress shall make no law respecting an establishment of religion or prohibiting the free exercise thereof; or abridging the freedom of speech. . . ." Observes Arons:

The result of [reading *Pierce* as a First Amendment case] is that it is the family and not the political majority which the Constitution empowers to make such schooling decisions. A First Amendment reading of *Pierce* suggests, therefore, that the present state of compulsory attendance and financing of public schools does not adequately satisfy the principle of government neutrality toward family choice in education. . . .[30]

Arons recognizes that education cannot be value-neutral, that many parents object to the values inculcated either implicitly or explicitly in public schools today, and that not all such dissatisfied parents can afford to send their children to private schools. If a parent's right to choose his child's education—the right specifically clarified by *Pierce*—cannot be served by the public schools, where does the parent turn for relief? Arons concludes that the combination of compulsory-attendance laws and local taxing arrangements does not allow real freedom of choice in education and may not be constitutional, because "any conflict between public schooling and a family's basic and sincerely held values interferes with the family's First Amendment rights."[31] In other words, if the values inculcated by the local public school conflict with your religious values, and you cannot find alternative formal education but are forced under pain of criminal sanctions to send your children to that public school, your constitutional rights have been violated.

Several Supreme Court decisions have established crucial parents' rights in education, but none has been so sweeping as Arons would like to see. In 1923 *Meyer v. Nebraska* was decided. Nebraska had passed a law forbidding instruction in any but the English language; a teacher who persisted in teaching in German was brought to trial. Eventually the U.S. Supreme Court held that the state law was an unreasonable interference with the natural right and duty of parents to give their children a suitable education, and therefore was unconstitutional. The 1925 case *Pierce v. Society of Sisters* was similar. The state of Oregon had passed a law requiring all children to attend public schools only; the Catholic order of nuns that continued to teach was brought to trial. The U.S. Supreme Court held that the Oregon statute was an unconstitutional violation of the liberty of parents to direct the upbringing and education of their children.

The year 1971 brought victory for the Amish—after decades of persecution—who won the right to withhold their children from compulsory schooling after eighth grade. The Supreme Court again upheld the sovereignty of parents in determining the education of their children. Although *Wisconsin v. Yoder* dealt with the Amish in particular, no case challenging compulsory attendance by ordinary, middle-class children has made the trip to the Supreme Court yet. Should such a case reach the Court, the parents seeking vindication will have to convince the justices that the education bureaucracy is denying them their right to control their children's education.

Professor Arons has defined the problem pretty accurately; but an inappropriate remedy could do irreversible damage. Establishment liberals who recognize some of the educational problems of the day might prefer, as a remedy, to reform the school-financing laws so that the government would subsidize all education, through vouchers, parochiaid, or whatever. Obviously, such a solution would be the beginning of the end of choice in education. In time the government would exercise total control over education, private as well as public.

A far simpler remedy would be to remove the proximate cause of the unconstitutional coercion—namely, the compulsory-attendance statutes. Without a criminal law compelling parents to subject their children to whatever education was available, it would be no crime for parents to provide personally tailored alternative education that might easily turn out superior to standardized formal education. This is a radical solution, literally; *radical* means going to the root. But such a solution is just what the doctor ordered.

317

The Phantom of Equal Education

Why are educators so powerful? Because they have a captive clientele, students; because they have a captive source of funds, taxes; because they can threaten that without the high school diploma issued under their auspices, a person will get nowhere in life. Browbeaten, the public dutifully furnishes the taxes and the students. In the name of the magic principle of "equality," parents are forced to deny their own children a decent education.

A taxpayers' revolt is mushrooming across America today. A parent and student revolt is growing also. Many people, including some independent-thinking educators, are turning sour on school-as-day-care-for-teenagers. They are looking for ways to dodge the traditional requirement of so many years of physical presence in a classroom. Similarly, millions have discovered that a college education is not necessary for a good career, while employers and young people alike are discovering that a high school diploma is not necessarily related to a person's ability to perform a job. It is ironic, in what we are told is an age of increasing technology and specialization, that these things should be happening. But they are. Recent legal cases as well as the experience of many young people are weakening the customs and laws that make a high school diploma a prerequisite for unskilled or semiskilled employment.

Deep in the American mind lurks a belief that schools should serve a social purpose and ensure somehow that no child grows up without the advantages of other children—as if, somehow, differences in social standing were by definition undemocratic. Perhaps they are, at least according to the current understanding of democracy.

The latest phantom the nation is called to pursue is that of "equal education." What is equal education anyway? For two children to spend the same number of years in school, even in the same school, or in the same classes, does not guarantee them an equal education. One child will end up knowing more

318

than the other. For education to be truly equal, every child would have to grow up under the same influences and stimuli from conception onward (including the same maternal nutrition). All children would have to read the same books, take part in the same conversations, see the same movies, watch the same television shows, eat the same foods, swallow the same vitamins—in short, have the same families, lead the same lives, have the same interests, and, to eliminate the ultimate genetic inequalities, have the same parents. Clearly, then, literal equality is absurd.

In practice the demand for educational equality merely means raising the bottom rung of American society a few steps and abolishing discrimination on the basis of sex, race, social class, etc. But as the bottom level rises, the top will probably also rise. So much for equality. Granted that there is a need to improve the education of the lowest socioeconomic groups, how will we know whether, or when, it actually *has* been improved?

The only way to know whether a child knows more than he did a year ago, or more than another child, is to test them both on objectively measurable facts, skills, and fundamental processes of reading, writing, and computing, and to compare the results of the one with those of the other, and then to compare the combined results with those of other children who took the same tests. Only by watching the results of objective tests can it be known for sure whether an individual or a group has increased in knowledge over a span of time.

But where do the loudest condemnations of objective testing come from? From the NEA, which is also loud and clear in demanding equal education. The professional educators, ironically, are the very ones who make equality impossible to achieve by depriving it of definition. Not only is the goal—equality—vague to begin with, but there is no way of knowing whether progress is being made toward achieving it.

Even if, for the sake of argument, everyone could agree on what constitutes an equal education, how to go about it would become the next problem. What makes some students perform better than others? Not the size of the school budget, as previous parts of this book have indicated. Not innovative gimmicks and learning strategies, not psychological intervention and behavior modification. The greatest influence on learning is exerted by the family—the home. And that factor cannot be equalized.

No massive program of equalizing education can succeed, nor should we expect it to. Education is an individual experience, not a collective one. The only goal appropriate to education is to improve the individual being educated: to broaden his horizons, to deepen his understanding, to hone his intellectual skills, and to exercise his mind. Whatever practical benefits society may gain from the education of an individual are incidental. If individuals are well educated, the nation will by definition be well educated. But massive federal efforts to educate the nation have resulted in an illiterate and discontented population of individuals—a result that could and should have been foreseen.

In Closing

It is not the thesis of this book that compulsory-attendance laws must be abolished tomorrow, and that all children should be taught by their parents at home. Rather, my belief is that educational options must be dramatically widened; private schools, ad hoc schools, home education, apprenticeship education—even no education at all in the formal sense—should be among the choices available to American children. Public education as it now exists is not only a failure but a nuisance and a threat to the continuance of an ordered society. Past wrongs should be righted: because public education has ignored and denigrated parents in the past, it must strictly respect parental prerogatives from now on. Parents and taxpayers will no longer tolerate the excuse that ninth graders cannot read and write because of "larger social changes." Parents must take the matter into their own hands; if public schools are unsatisfactory, parents must find means of educating their children that *are* satisfactory. The moral obligation of parents is stronger than any legal obstacles the education establishment may care to throw up.

This book has attempted to show concerned parents how to work not only outside, but around and within "the system." Because the system is controlled by educationists and their kept politicians, it is not, as a rule, responsive to ordinary parents in its normal course of operation. But until you have tried all avenues of approach and found them wanting, it will not be honest or truthful to say that the system is unacceptable. Parents have won some impressive victories here and there—for example, in Arizona—and these should encourage renewed resolve. Exceptional individuals have won the victories, with the help of exceptional persistence and sacrifice.

Concerned parents need to develop some political savvy. They must learn to go for the jugular. They must study the enemy until they know him as well as the friend. Fight in the open if you can win that way, or in the committee rooms if success lies there. In the glamour of electoral politics, never forget that you are seeking to influence the legislative process.

A political movement grows out of the enthusiasm of hundreds of thousands of individuals sharing, spontaneously and genuinely, the same concerns. Parents have been organizing at the grassroots for at least a decade. It is time for leaders to step forward at the national level—leaders respected and trusted by the rank-and-file. We need a leadership that can build a broad, united front, bringing together many different parental dissatisfactions. Moral objections, ideological objections, and practical objections to the state of the schools must all be exploited. When a phonics advocate is given a (rare) public hearing, he must not scorn to mention the moral concerns of parents as well as their concern over illiteracy.

The greatest danger the parents' rights movement faces is despair. There are two kinds of despair, one brought on by fatigue, the other by ideology. When defeat follows weeks of ceaseless effort, and frustration piles on top of frustration,

321

naturally a person is going to ask whether there is any chance of winning, what this fight is all about anyway, and why not be like other people and watch TV instead of writing irate letters to Congress. This fatigue will pass, in the normal course of events, but its victim is most susceptible to the second kind of despair while under the influence of this first.

The second kind of despair asks: Why bother to continue to fight, since the outcome is always predetermined, the problems are all the same, everywhere, because a force larger and stronger than any we could muster is in control of the whole scene? To succumb to this despair is to surrender to the progressive-liberal establishment. Regardless of any conspiracy, real or imagined, only those political activities conducted through the usual channels of a representative system of government will have any impact. War-weary parents must not forget that.

This book is intended as a road map for parents seeking to become politically active in behalf of their rights. It points concerned parents to the problems they need to know and the possible and promising means of resolution. Ten years hence, let us hope, there will be no need to write such books—because parents stood up and fought.

Notes

Chapter 1

1. *Education Daily,* August 18, 1976.
2. Vermont Royster, "The Tools of Thought," *Wall Street Journal,* December 4, 1974.
3. *Education Daily,* July 19, 1976.
4. UPI story in *Washington Post,* January 18, 1975.
5. "GPO Draws the Line on Obscenities," *Human Events,* June 19, 1976.
6. "South St. Paul Bans Sex Textbook," *Minneapolis Tribune,* September 21, 1974, p. 1–A.
7. "Newsbriefs," *Phi Delta Kappan* 57, no. 5 (January 1976): 361.
8. *Long Island Press,* January 14, 1976.
9. A very personalized account of the Gracey family is C. Stephen Hathcock, "With the Graceys," *Triumph,* January 1971, pp. 16ff.
10. *Let's Improve Today's Education* (newsletter), September 1974.
11. "Newsbriefs," *Phi Delta Kappan* 57, no. 7 (March 1976): 490.

12. *Education Daily,* July 26, 1976.

13. Frank Armbruster, *The U.S. Primary and Secondary Educational Process* (Croton-on-Hudson, N.Y.: Hudson Institute, 1975), p. 122.

14. *Ibid.,* pp. 209–10.

15. International Reading Association, *Annual Report,* 1974–75, p. 43.

16. Oluf M. Davidson (of the American College Testing Service), quoted in *Monitor,* newsletter of NEA Instruction and Professional Development Division, July 30, 1976.

17. This study, by Robert C. Nichols and John Loehlin, is covered as a news item in *Education Daily,* September 8, 1976, pp. 3–4.

18. Two University of Michigan researchers, Zajonc and Markus, advance this theory, reported in "Newsnotes," *Phi Delta Kappan* 57, no. 9 (May 1976): 631.

19. *Ibid.,* 57, no. 7 (March 1976): 486.

20. Albert Lynd, *Quackery in the Public Schools* (Boston: Little, Brown, 1952), p. 14.

21. *Ibid.,* p. 21.

22. "Newsnotes," *Phi Delta Kappan* 57, no. 5 (January 1976): 355.

23. Mary A. Golladay, *The Condition of Education, 1976* (National Center for Educational Statistics, March, 1976), p. 263.

24. H.G. Good, *A History of American Education,* 2d ed. (New York: Macmillan, 1968), p. 354.

25. Bertram S. Brown, "Behavior Modification: What It Is and Isn't," *Today's Education* 65, no. 1, (January–February, 1976): 67.

26. The three aforementioned innovations are funded with ESEA Title III funds, and are listed in *Innovative Education Practices* (see n. 42 for more data on *IEP*).

27. *Education Daily,* August 18, 1976, p. 4.

28. The case was *Mercer v. Michigan State Board of Education;* news coverage was *Education Daily,* August 23, 1974, p. 5.

29. Quoted in the *Barbara M. Morris Report,* May 1973, p. 3.

30. "Innovative Education Held to Make Little Difference," *Washington Post,* December 23, 1976, p. A1.

31. From report of Committee on Social and Economic Problems, published separately as *A Call to the Teachers of the Nation;* quoted by Lawrence A. Cremin, *The Transformation of the School* (New York: Knopf, 1961), p. 263.

32. *Ibid.,* p. 269.

33. Terrel Bell, quoted in "Washington Report," *Phi Delta Kappan* 57, no. 6 (February 1976): 422.

34. Jane Addams, *Democracy and Social Ethics* (1902), pp. 180–81; cited by Cremin, *op. cit.,* p. 62.

35. Quoted by Cremin, *op. cit.,* p. 276.

36. *Ibid.,* p. 275.

37. *Ibid.*

38. Quoted by Anne Lewis, "The Bell Legacy at the USOE," *Phi Delta Kappan* 58, no. 2 (October 1976): 217.

39. Stevanne Auerbach and Peter Levine, "Child Care Services: Should the Public Provide Them?" *Phi Delta Kappan* 57, no. 8 (April 1976): 514.

40. "Newsnotes," *Phi Delta Kappan* 57, no. 8 (April 1976): 562. The researcher was Peter Bogdan, of the Center on Human Policy at Syracuse University.

41. Arlene Silberman, "If They Say Your Child Can't Learn," *Reader's Digest,* July 1976, p. 150.

42. Several such projects are listed in the *Innovative Education Practices,* Vol. 2 (October 1974), of the National Advisory Council on Supplementary Centers and Services, a now defunct division of the Office of Education.

43. *The Gallup Polls of Attitudes Toward Education, 1969–1973,* ed. Stanley Elam (Bloomington, Ind.: Phi Delta Kappa, 1973), p. 26.

44. George H. Gallup, "Eighth Annual Gallup Poll of the Public's Attitudes Toward the Public Schools," *Phi Delta Kappan* 58, no. 2 (October 1976): 189.

45. *Ibid.,* p. 190.

46. *Ibid.*

47. *Ibid.,* p. 196.

48. Copies of past polls can be ordered for a small fee from Phi Delta Kappa, Eighth & Union, Bloomington, Ind. 47401.

Chapter 2

1. B. J. Chandler, et al., "Teaching as a Profession," in *Education and the New Teacher* (New York: Dodd, Mead, 1971); reprinted, *Resource Book,* Iowa Governance Packet, Iowa SEA and NEA, June 1975, p. 14.

2. David D. Darland, "Preparation in the Governance of the Profession," *Teachers for the Real World* (Washington, D.C.: American Association of Colleges for Teacher Education, 1969), chap. 11.

3. Stephen K. Bailey, *Education Interest Groups in the Nation's Capital,* (Washington D.C.: American Council on Education, 1975), p.6.

4. W. Vance Grant and C. George Lind, *Digest of Education Statistics,* 1975 ed. (Washington, D.C.: U.S. Government Printing Office, 1976), p. 26.

5. Michael Kirst, *The Politics of Education at the Local, State & Federal Levels* (Berkeley, Calif.: McCutchan Publishing, 1970), p. 153.

6. *Education Daily,* October 6, 1976, p. 3; October 7, 1976, p. 4.

7. George Meany, "1976 Quest Consortium," April 24, 1976; address at the conference on education and the economy, reprinted by American Federation of Teachers.

8. Code of Ethics of the Education Profession, adopted by the 1975 NEA Representative Assembly, Principle II.

9. John Ryor, "Down with Bargain Basement Blues," *Today's Education* 64, no. 3 (September–October 1975): 5.

10. James Browne, "Power Politics for Teachers, Modern Style," *Phi Delta Kappan* (October 1976): 161.

11. *Ibid.*

12. *Ibid.,* p. 180.

13. Wayne G. Sanstead, "From the Classroom . . . and into Politics," *State Government* 47, no. 1 (Winter 1975): 14.

14. *Ibid.,* p. 15.

15. *Ibid.*

16. "NEA: A Peculiar Hybrid," *Congressional Quarterly Lobby Report,* June 1, 1974, p. 1415.

17. *Ibid.*

18. *Education Daily,* November 8, 1974, p. 1.

19. Lorraine H. McDonnell, "The Internal Politics of the NEA," *Phi Delta Kappan* (October 1976): 185.

20. *Education Daily,* October 7, 1976, p. 4.

21. *Ibid.,* October 22, 1976, p. 2.

22. *Congressional Quarterly Lobby Report,* June 1, 1974, p. 1415.

23. Browne, *op. cit.,* p. 161.

24. "Newsnotes," *Phi Delta Kappan* 57, no. 4 (December 1975): 289.

25 "Newsbriefs," *Phi Delta Kappan* 57, no. 10 (June 1976): 708.

26. *Ibid.*

27. *Education Daily,* September 30, 1976, p. 4.

28. *Ibid.,* October 18, 1976, p. 1

29. *Ibid.*

30. Telephone conversation with Mr. Oliver, AFT's Office of Collective Bargaining, in August 1976.

31. *Education Daily,* July 1, 1976, p. 3.

32. *Ibid.,* September 7, 1976, p. 3.

33. "Newsnotes," *Phi Delta Kappan* 57, no. 9 (May 1976): 634.

34. For a copy of this report, contact: Public Service Research Council, 8320 Old Courthouse Road, Suite 430, Vienna, Va. 22180.

35. Browne, *op. cit.,* p. 180.

36. Roscoe Martin, "School Government," in *Government & the Suburban School* (Syracuse, N.Y.: Syracuse University Press, 1962); reprinted in Kirst, *The Politics of Education.*

37. John Chamberlain, "New Jersey Congressional Candidate Takes on Courts," *Human Events,* July 10, 1976.

38. Grant and Lind, *op cit.,* p. 37.

39. Mortimer Smith, *A Citizen's Manual for the Public Schools* (Washington, D.C.: Council for Basic Education, 1959), p. 51.

40. Bruce S. Cooper, "Collective Bargaining Comes to School Middle Management," *Phi Delta Kappan* (October 1976): 202.

41. National Education Association, Teacher Rights Division, "A Textbook Study in Cultural Conflict," Inquiry Report of Kanawha County, West Virginia, February 1975, p. 47.

42. *Ibid.,* p. 46.

43. *Education Daily,* December 2, 1974, p. 4.

44. Helen Bain, "Self-Governance Must Come First, Then Accountability," *Phi Delta Kappan* (April 1970); in *Resource Book,* Iowa Governance Packet, p. 98.

45. *Ibid.*

46. Dan C. Lortie, "The Balance of Control and Autonomy in Elementary School Teaching," in *The Semi-Professions and Their Organization* ed. Amitai Etzioni (New York: Free Press, 1969), p. 25.

47. *Education Daily,* March 13, 1974, p. 3.

48. Unidentified article, *Today's Education* (September–October 1975); reprinted, Iowa Governance *Resource Book,* p. 45.

49. "What Does Governance Mean?" *Today's Education* (December 1971); reprinted, Iowa Governance *Resource Book,* p. 7.

50. Kyle Crist, "Professionals Should Run the Schools, Not Parents," *Christian Science Monitor,* August 16, 1976, p. 19.

51. Donald A. Meyers, reprint from *Decision Making in Curriculum and Instruction,* in Iowa Governance *Resource Book.*

52. Neil Sullivan, "How Did We Lose the Wheel?" *Saturday Review/Education,* September 16, 1972.

53. *Ibid.*

Chapter 3

1. Charles Riborg Mann, et al., *Federal Relations to Education: Report of the National Advisory Committee on Education, Part I: Committee Findings and Recommendations* (Washington, D.C.: 744 Jackson Place, 1931), p. 37.

2. *Ibid.*, p. 95.

3. *Ibid.*, p. 96.

4. Edgar B. Wesley, *NEA: The First Hundred Years* (New York: Harper, 1957), p. 52.

5. *Ibid.*, p. 306.

6. "Federal Aid—What Kind? How Much?" *Senior Scholastic*, February 1, 1961, pp. 6–7; reprinted in Ronald Steel, *Federal Aid to Education* (New York: H.W. Wilson, 1961), p. 45.

7. John F. Kennedy, Education Message to Congress, February 20, 1961, in *New York Times*, February 21, 1961, p. 22; in Steel, *op. cit.*, pp. 50 ff.

8. *Ibid.*, p. 51

9. *Ibid.*, p. 49.

10. *Ibid.*, p. 51.

11. Sam M. Lambert, statement before the General Subcommittee on Education, Committee on Education and Labor, U.S. House of Representatives, 87th Cong., 1st sess., March 14, 1961, pp. 170–92; in Steel, *op. cit.*, p. 61.

12. Roger Freeman, "False Claims in School Control Drive," *Nation's Business*, March 1961, p. 3; in Steel, *op. cit.*, p. 72.

13. "A 'Deeper Commitment' to Public Schools," editorial in *Fortune*, April 1961, pp. 109–10; in Steel, *op. cit.*, p. 80.

14. Freeman, *op. cit.*, p. 68.

15. *Ibid.*

16. *Ibid.*

17. Sidney C. Sufrin, *Issues in Federal Aid to Education* (Syracuse, N.Y.: Syracuse University Press, 1962), pp. 57–58.

18. John Sherman Cooper, in *Advance* 1 (April–May 1961): 11–13; in Steel, *op. cit.*, p. 76.

19. Sufrin, *op. cit.,* pp. 58–59.

20. "Masters of Our Schools," editorial in *New Republic,* January 9, 1961, pp. 3–4; in Steel, *op cit.,* pp. 87–88.

21. Myron Lieberman, "Four Myths Cripple Our Schools," *Nation,* February 28, 1959, pp. 179–83; in Steel, *op. cit.,* pp. 89–94,

22. Clayton D. Hutchins, Albert R. Munse, and Edna Booher, *Federal Funds for Education, 1958–59 and 59–60* (Washington, D.C.: Department of Health, Education, and Welfare, Office of Education, 1961), p. 19.

23. Martha V. Gottron, "Education Block Grants: Little Interest Seen," *Congressional Quarterly,* April 24, 1976, p. 968.

24. *Ibid.*

25. *Appendix to the Budget for Fiscal Year 1977,* 94th Cong. 2nd sess., House document no. 94–344. Office of Education funds are included, pp. 344–56; NIE funds, pp. 357–58; Office of Assistant Secretary funds, pp. 358–59; Special Institutions funds, pp. 376–78; Human Development funds, pp. 378–80.

26. Stephen K. Bailey, *Education Interest Groups in the Nation's Capital* (Washington, D.C.: American Council on Education, 1975), p. 36.

27. House Republican Study Committee, "The Elementary and Secondary Education Act (H.R. 69)," Fact Sheet, Washington, D.C., March 8, 1974.

28. Peter Rossi, review of *Education and Reform: The ESEA of 1965, Title I,* in *Harvard Educational Review* 46, no. 2 (May 1976): 263.

29. "The Elementary and Secondary Education Act (H.R. 69)," p. 7.

30. "The Efficiency of Educational Expenditures for Compensatory Education—An Interpretation of Current Evidence" (Palo Alto, Calif.: Stanford Research Institute, 1972), pp. iii, 32; quoted in "The Elementary and Secondary Education Act (H.R. 69)."

31. "Newsnotes," *Phi Delta Kappan* 57, no. 7 (March 1976): 485.

32. "The Elementary and Secondary Education Act (H.R. 69)," p. 3

33. For a fine analysis, including considerable evidence of widespread federal funding of affective education programs, see Joan Janaro, Rita Lucas, and Gail McGuire, "A Description and Evaluation of the Magic Circle" (Pittsburgh: City Council of PTA's, 1974).

34. National Public Radio, *Options in Education*, Program No. 56, "Compensatory Education: Part I," December 10, 1976, transcript p. 18.

35. "High Schoolers Decide Goofing Off Pays Big in Federal Funds—Sometimes," *Buffalo Courier-Express*, June 2, 1973, pp. 1 ff.

36. Edith Green, "The Educational Entrepreneur," *Public Interest*, no. 28 (Summer 1972): 13

37. W. Vance Grant and C. George Lind, *Digest of Education Statistics*, 1975 ed. (Washington, D.C.: Government Printing Office, 1976), p. 159.

38. *Education Daily*, September 13, 1976.

Chapter 4

1. Nicolaus Mills, ed., *The Great School Bus Controversy* (New York: Teachers College Press, 1973), p. 8.

2. Editorial Research Reports, "Busing Reappraisal," December 26, 1975, p. 948.

3. *Ibid.*

4. *Ibid.*, p. 951.

5. "A Judge Becomes an Advocate," editorial in *Detroit News*, June 8, 1976.

6. "Newsnotes," *Phi Delta Kappan* 57, no. 4 (December 1975): 289.

7. Cited from *Keyes v. School District No. 1,* in James Bolner

and Robert Shanley, *Busing: The Political and Judicial Process* (New York: Praeger, 1974), p. 33.

8. Nick Thimmesch, "Busing: The Hypocrisy in Washington," *Saturday Evening Post,* April 1976, p. 40.

9. These figures were cited in a speech by Sue Mills, chairwoman of the Prince George's County Board of Education at a meeting on March 22, 1976, of the Parents Action Committee of New Castle County, Del. News coverage was provided in a *Newark* (Del.) *Weekly Post* article, "PAC Members Air Maryland Busing."

10. *Ibid.*

11. Carmen Roberts, member of the Detroit Central Board, in testimony before the 1976 Republican Convention Platform Committee. Quoted in *Bulletin No. 1* of the National Association of Neighborhood Schools, September 1976, p. 3.

12. *Ibid.*

13. Thimmesch, *op. cit.,* p. 84.

14. *Ibid.,* p. 85.

15. *Ibid.,* p. 39.

16. Editorial Research Reports, *op. cit.,* p. 961.

17. Christopher Jencks, "Busing—The Supreme Court Goes North," *New York Times Magazine,* November 19, 1972; in Mills, *op. cit.,* p. 26.

18. "Desegregation Without Turmoil," conference sponsored by U.S. Department of Justice and National Center for Quality Integrated Education, May 19, 1976; George Meany sent a filmed message to this conference, which was reprinted as an AFL-CIO press release.

19. All of the mentioned individuals are referred to in Thimmesch, *op. cit.,* pp. 41–42.

20. Norman Miller and Harold Gerard, "How Busing Failed in Riverside," *Psychology Today* (June 1976): 100.

21. *Ibid.*

22. David Armor, senior social scientist at Rand Corporation, quoted by Thimmesch, *op. cit.,* p. 39.

23. Mills, *op. cit.,* p. ix.

24. Burns W. Roper, "Roper Poll," *New Castle* (Del.) *Sunday News Journal,* August 1, 1976.

25. *Education Daily,* October 21, 1976, p. 5.

26. Alexander M. Bickel, "Untangling the Busing Snarl," *New Republic,* October 23–30, 1972; in Mills, *op. cit.,* p. 35.

27. The national address of NANS is: P.O. Box 19252, Westwood Station, Denver, Colo. 80219. Executive director is James Venema.

28. This testimony of Mayor Harvey I. Sloane is referred to in the 1975 *Congressional Quarterly Almanac,* (Washington, D.C.: Congressional Quarterly, 1976), 94th Cong., 1st sess., p. 660.

29. Johannes Gaertner, "How to Avoid Busing and Other Hassles," *Education* 97, no. 2 (Winter 1976): 158–61.

30. Charles E. Rice, *The Supreme Court and Public Prayer* (New York: Fordham University Press, 1964), p. 15.

31. *Ibid.,* p. 55.

32. Quoted *ibid.,* p. 77.

33. Paul A. Freund, "The Legal Issue," Burton Lecture, published as *Religion and the Public Schools* (Cambridge: Harvard University Press, 1965), pp. 23–24.

34. Rice, *op. cit.,* p. ix.

35. *Torcaso v. Watkins* (367 U.S. 488), fn. 11.

36. Eleanor Blair, "Humanist Manifesto II Offers a Survival Philosophy," *New York Times,* August 26, 1973, pp. 1, 51. This news article extracts highlights of both Manifestos and lists the initial signers of Humanist Manifesto II.

37. This point and others of value are raised by Barbara M. Morris in "Why Are You Losing Your Children?" *Barbara M. Morris Report* (Ellicott City, Md., 1975).

38. *Ibid.,* pp. 17–21.

39. The best study of MACOS available is by Susan Marshner, *"Man: A Course of Study:* A Prototype for Federalized Textbooks?" (Washington, D.C.: Heritage Foundation, 1975).

40. Concludes a research study funded by NSF: "The new math courses are blameless for the falling scores because they

are fundamentally sound and because the spirit and substance of such courses have not been extensively implemented in U.S. classrooms" ("Newsnotes," *Phil Delta Kappan* 57, no. 5 [January 1976]: 357).

41. John Conlan, "National Science Foundation School Programs Should Be Abolished," *Human Events,* December 27, 1975, p. 8.

42. The parents' group involved in this case is: Citizens Coalition, P. O. Box 1765, Albany, N.Y. 12201.

43. The organization most involved in this aspect of the challenge to secular humanism is: Parents Rights, Inc., 12571 Northwinds Drive, St. Louis, Mo. 63141.

44. Quoted by Onalee McGraw, "Secular Humanism and the Schools" (Washington, D.C.: Heritage Foundation, 1976), p. 26. Dr. McGraw's pamphlet is an excellent summary of the present situation and brief analysis of the teaching of secular humanism in American public schools.

Chapter 5

1. Jacob Javits, interview in "Gifted Children in the Schools," *Options in Education* (National Public Radio), Program No. 31, 1976.

2. Rousas J. Rushdoony, *The Messianic Character of American Education* (Nutley, N.J.: Craig Press, 1972).

3. *Ibid.,* p. 29

4. *Ibid.,* p. 34

5. *Ibid.,* p. 104

6. "Much of the real impetus for educational innovation and improvement springs from the well-financed suburban school districts. . . . The highest teacher salary schedules and the highest expenditures per pupil are typically found in suburban school districts" (Chris De Young and Richard Wynn, *American Education,* 5th ed. [New York: McGraw-Hill, 1964], p. 125).

7. This was the Johns Hopkins Study, financed with federal

money in Howard County, Maryland. The best account of how parents organized in response to this invasion of privacy was written by the leader, Kris McGough, "Can One Parent Change the School System?" *Potomac Magazine* of the *Washington Post,* August 1, 1976, pp. 5–23.

8. Ellen Lurie, *How to Change the Schools* (New York: Random House, Vintage Books, 1970), pp. 43–44.

9. This was a personal account given to the author.

10. David Selden cites this passage in "The Future of Community Participation in Educational Policy Making," a speech prepared for the October 1974 Conference on Community Participation in Education at the University of Wisconsin (Madison). Draft of speech available in megafile in Instruction & Professional Development Division, NEA headquarters, Washington, D.C.

11. Lurie, *op. cit.,* p. 134.

12. Selden, *op. cit.*

13. *Education Daily,* August 13, 1976, p. 4.

14. Selden, *op. cit.*

15. Personal letter to the author.

16. Michael Kirst, *The Politics of Education at the Local, State & Federal Levels* (Berkeley, Calif.: McCutchan Publishing, 1970), p. 159.

17. The "Seven Cardinal Principles" are enumerated in De Young and Wynn, *op. cit.,* p. 183.

18. Harold Shane, "The Seven Cardinal Principles Revisited," *Today's Education* 65, no. 13 (September–October 1976): 57–62.

19. Mortimer Smith, *A Citizen's Manual for Public Schools* (Boston: Little, Brown, Atlantic Monthly Press, 1965), p. 6. Originally published in 1959 by the Council for Basic Education, this book remains a valuable handbook for the cause of basic education, a cause admirably defended by the council, which is located at 725 Fifteenth St., NW, Washington D.C. 20005.

20. *Education Daily,* September 8, 1976, pp. 3–4.

21. Frank Armbruster, "The U.S. Primary and Secondary Educational Process," (Croton-on-Hudson, N.Y.: Hudson Institute, 1975), p. 275.

22. Kyle M. Crist, "Professionals Should Run the Schools, Not Parents," *Christian Science Monitor,* August 16, 1976, p. 19.

23. Lurie, *op. cit.,* p. 120.

24. Jo Goul, "Boise Likes Its School Volunteers," *Today's Education* 64, no. 4 (November–December 1975): 72–73.

25. Walter D. St. John, "Dealing with Angry Adults," *Today's Education* 64, no. 4 (November–December 1975): 82.

26. "Child Care Scare," *Newsweek,* April 6, 1976, p. 77.

27. *Education Daily,* July 13, 1976. p. 5.

28. Selden, *op. cit.,* p. 17 of the draft.

29. In De Young and Wynn, *op. cit.,* p. 122.

30. *Ibid.,* p. 131.

31. *Education Daily,* June 23, 1976, p. 4.

32. De Young and Wynn, *op. cit.,* p. 133.

33. American Legislative Exchange Council, 600 Pennsylvania Ave., SE, Ste. 204, Washington, D.C. 20003.

34. "A Plan with Potential," editorial in *Washington Star-News,* December 8, 1974. The editorial was approving the Prince George's County "basic alternative" plan.

35. Antero Pietila, "School Book Review Set in County," *Baltimore Sun,* November 14, 1976.

36. "Trials for Textbooks Defeated," *Washington Star-News,* February 26, 1976.

37. Mel and Norma Gabler, Educational Research Analysts, P.O. Box 7518, Longview, Tex. 75601.

38. "Landmark Decision," flyer no. T-442, from the Gablers.

39. America's Future, 542 Main St., New Rochelle, N.Y. 10801.

40. Educational Products Information Exchange, 463 West St., New York, N.Y. 10014.

41. "How to Tell Whether Your Schools Are Being

Gypped," *American School Board Journal* 162, no. 1 (January 1975): 38–40.

42. Quoted in "Alternative Schools," NEA Briefing Memo No. 6., August 1974, from NEA/IPD (Instruction & Professional Development Division).

43. "Changing High School Requirements," NEA/IPD Briefing Memo, no. 11, June 1976, pp. 1–2.

44. *Ibid.,* p. 3.

Chapter 6

1. *Barbara Morris Report,* 8925 Chapel Ave., Ellicott City, Md. 21043.

2. Let's Improve Today's Education, 15221 N. 29 Drive, Phoenix, Ariz. 85023.

3. Heritage Foundation, 513 C Street, NE, Washington, D.C. 20002.

4. John Mathews, "More and More Parents Battling 'Dirty' Textbooks," *Washington Star-News,* November 17, 1974, p. B-1.

5. Ben A. Franklin, "West Virginia," *New York Times,* January 5, 1975, p. 5.

6. Letter from Alice Moore, "Dear Friend," December 31, 1974.

7. *Ibid.*

8. George Neill, "Washington Report," *Phi Delta Kappan* 57, no. 10 (June 1976): 707.

9. Terrel Bell, "Schools, Parents, and Textbooks," speech before Association of American Publishers, School Division, Cherry Hill, N.J., December 2, 1974. Copy provided by U.S. Office of Education.

10. Elmer L. Rumminger, "You Shall Not Do This to My Child," *Faith for the Family* (magazine), January–February 1975, pp. 6, 10.

11. *Ibid.*

12. AP story, January 4, 1976, in *Bluefield* (W. Va.) *Telegraph*.

13. Edwin Barber, "Birth of a Textbook: Much Labor and Risk," *New York Times,* March 23, 1975, p. 16E.

14. *Ibid.*

15. "Textbook Battles: They're Brewing and Bubbling," *American School Board Journal,* July 1975, pp. 21–26.

16. Chris De Young and Richard Wynn, *American Education,* 5th ed. (New York: McGraw-Hill, 1964), p. 396.

17. Resolution of the International Reading Association, 1975.

18. The Coalition for Children is the primary Washington-based parent group in touch with other groups in the country. Its address is: 6542 Hitt Ave., McLean, Va. 22101.

19. Kevin P. Phillips, "Polls Show Conservative Trend," *Human Events,* June 26, 1976, p. 11.

20. Committee for the Survival of a Free Congress, 6 Library Court, SE, Washington, D.C. 20003.

21. Max Rafferty, *What They Are Doing to Your Children* (New York: New American Library, 1964), p. 88.

Chapter 7

1. Theodore R. Sizer, "Education and Assimilation: A Fresh Plea for Pluralism," *Phi Delta Kappan* (September 1976): 35.

2. George H. Gallup, "Seventh Annual Gallup Poll of Public Attitudes Toward Education," *Phi Delta Kappan* (December 1975): 237.

3. Barbara Ballou, "Parents Demand, and Get, Back-to-Basics School," *Christian Science Monitor,* August 9, 1976, p. 19.

4. "Newsnotes," *Phi Delta Kappan* 57, no. 5 (January 1976): 358.

5. *Education Daily,* April 22, 1976, p. 4.

6. "The Nonpublic Schools and ESEA Title III," a special

report by the National Advisory Council on Supplemental Centers and Services, April 1975, pp. 12–13.

7. Diane B. Gertler and Linda A. Barker, *Statistics of Nonpublic Elementary and Secondary Schools, 1970–71* (U.S. Department of Health, Education & Welfare, Office of Education, National Center for Educational Statistics, 1973), DHEW publication no. (O.E.) 74–11420, pp. 22–23.

8. *Eagle Forum,* October 1976, p. 1.

9. Gertler and Barker, *op. cit.,* pp. 27–28.

10. Jane Peckham Stoever, "Schools as Faith Communities," *National Catholic Reporter,* October 22, 1976, p. 8.

11. *Ibid.,* p. 10.

12. Gallup, *op. cit.,* p. 240.

13. Gertler and Barker, *op. cit.*

14. Summary prepared by CAPE, "Private Schools: Fact and Future," conference, Washington, D.C., July 24–25, 1976, jointly sponsored by CAPE and USOE.

15. Walter H. Beck, *Lutheran Elementary Schools in the United States,* 2nd ed. (St. Louis: Concordia Publishing House, 1965), p. 465.

16. *Ibid.,* p. 464.

17. The address of the association is: 6601 N.W. 167 St., Hialeah, Fla. 33015.

18. *Codex Juris Canonici,* Canon 1374.

19. Albert Koob and Russell Shaw, *SOS for Catholic Schools* (New York: Holt, Rinehart & Winston, 1970), p. 84.

20. *Ibid.,* p. 63.

21. Andrew M. Greeley and Peter H. Rossi, *The Education of Catholic Americans* (Chicago: Aldine Publishing Co., 1966), pp. 217–18.

22. "Newsbriefs," *Phi Delta Kappan* 57, no. 9 (May 1976): 635.

23. William F. Buckley, *Four Reforms* (New York: Putnam's, 1973), p. 79.

24. Stoever, *op. cit.,* p. 7.

25. Virginia Black, "Paper Crosses Are Everywhere," *Wanderer,* January 29, 1976, p. 6.

26. Judah Pilch, ed., *A History of Jewish Education in America* (American Association for Jewish Education, 1969), p. 210.

27. Joseph Kaminetsky (national director of the National Society for Hebrew Day Schools), quoted in George Riemer, *How a Private School Can Help Your Child* (New York: Association Press, 1971), p. 63.

28. Andrew Greeley, interview, "Catholics Prosper While the Church Crumbles," *Psychology Today,* June 1976, p. 51.

29. Pilch, *op. cit.,* p. 212.

30. Charles S. Hyneman and George W. Carey, *A Second Federalist* (New York: Appleton-Century-Crofts, 1967), p. 274.

31. *Ibid.*

32. Charles E. Rice, *The Supreme Court and Public Prayer* (New York: Fordham University Press, 1964), p. 103.

33. R. Freeman Butts, "Public Funds for Parochial Schools? No!" *Teachers College Record* 62, no. 1 (October 1960); in August Kerber and Wilfred R. Smith, *Educational Issues in a Changing Society* (Detroit: Wayne State University Press, 1962).

34. *Education Daily,* July 13, 1976, p. 2.

35. George C. Roche, "Will IRS Cripple the Independent Institutions?" *Human Events,* July 10, 1976, p. 17.

Chapter 8

1. Robert Love, *How to Start Your Own School* (New York: Macmillan, 1973), p. 2.

2. The Reverend Mr. Thoburn may be contacted at Fairfax Christian Academy, 11121 Pope's Head Road, Fairfax, Va. 22030.

3. Love, *op. cit.*

4. The address of Catholics United for the Faith: 1291 North Ave., New Rochelle, N.Y. 10804.

5. Anne Carroll, 16006 Tiffany Lane, Haymarket, Va. 22069.

6. Louise Bates Ames, *Is Your Child in the Wrong Grade?* (New York: Harper & Row, 1967), p. 10.

7. The exams may not meet the approval of all parents anyway. The author does not mean to imply endorsement of the Gesell exam or agreement with all Gesell theories.

8. Ames, *op. cit.,* p. 53.

9. *Education Daily,* July 13, 1976, p. 6.

10. Eda LeShan, *Conspiracy Against Childhood* (New York: Atheneum, 1967), p. 108.

11. Raymond S. and Dorothy N. Moore, *Better Late Than Early* (New York: Reader's Digest Press, 1975), p. 117.

12. *Ibid.,* p. 21.

13. *Ibid.,* p. 35.

14. *Education Daily,* August 4, 1976, p. 3.

15. "Newsnotes," *Phi Delta Kappan* 57, no. 10 (June 1976): 711.

16. "Newsbriefs," *Phi Delta Kappan* 57, no. 9 (May 1976): 634.

17. "Alternative Schools," NEA/IPD Briefing Memo, no. 6, August 1974, p. 3

18. Edward C. Banfield, *The Unheavenly City* (Boston: Little, Brown, 1968), pp. 148–52.

19. Gary Wisby, "This Couple's Running a School for Two in the Attic," *Chicago Sun-Times,* January 19, 1975, p. 20.

20. Patricia Heidenry, "Home Is Where the School Is," *New York Times Magazine,* October 19, 1975, p. 80.

21. National Parents League, P.O. Box 3987, Portland, Ore. 97208.

22. These terms were coined by Robert P. Baker, "Statute Law and Judicial Interpretation," in William F. Rickenbacker, ed., *The Twelve-Year Sentence* (LaSalle, Ill.: Open Court, 1974), an excellent collection of essays on compulsory attendance.

23. *State ex rel. Shoreline School Dist. No. 412* v. *Superior Court*, 55 Wash. 2d 177, 346 P2d 999 (1959).

24. *People* v. *Levisen*, 404 I.U. 574, 90 N.E.2d 213 (1950).

25. *Knox* v. *O'Brien*, 7 N.J. Super 608, 72A 2d 389 (1950).

26. *State v. Massa*, 95 N.J. Super 382, 231 A2d 252 (1967).

27. See Murray N. Rothbard, "Historical Origins," in Rickenbacker, *op. cit.*

28. Lawrence A. Cremin, *The Transformation of the School* (New York: Knopf, 1961), p. 71.

29. Robert LeFevre, "The Anti-Human Public School," *Occasional Review* 3 (Summer 1975): 92.

30. Stephen Arons, "The Separation of School and State: *Pierce* Reconsidered," *Harvard Education Review* (February 1976): 78.

31. *Ibid.,* p. 84.

Index

ABC (Association for Better Citizenship), 62
Abington Township School District v. Schempp, 74, 147
"Academic freedom," definition of, 236
Accelerated Christian Education (ACE) program, 276
Accreditation, 293–95
ACLU, 212
Addams, Jane, 30, 32, 312
Adult Recurrent Education Entitlement Voucher Program (Massachusetts), 269
Advisory Committee on Education (F.D. Roosevelt), 94–95
AFT. *See* American Federation of Teachers
Alabama Education Association, 69
Alternative public schools, 265–67
American Association of Christian Schools (AACS), 279–80; Statement of Faith, 279–80
American Association of School Administrators, 48

American Conservative Union, 257
American Education Fellowship, 28, 31
American Federation of Labor–Congress of Industrial Organizations (AFL-CIO), 46–47, 69, 136, 282
American Federation of School Administrators, 78
American Federation of Teachers (AFT), 46, 47, 48, 49–50, 64, 68, 69, 78, 101, 107
American Issues Forum, 130
American Legislative Exchange Council (ALEC), 201, 219
American Library Association, 232
American School Board Journal, 236
American Teachers Association, 50
America's Future, 216–17
Amish, and compulsory-education laws, 317
Armstrong, Bill, 117
Army, educational standards of, 20–21
Arons, Stephen, 315–16, 317

Association of American Publishers, 233
Attendance age, opposition to lowering, 299–305
Awakening the public, 71–72

Bain, Helen, 80
Banfield, Edward, 305
Barbara Morris Report, 229, 248
Bayh, Birch, 137
Behavior modification, 16, 25, 27
Bell, Terrel, 33, 233–34
Better Late Than Early, 303–4
Biological Sciences Curriculum Study (BSCS), 154
Black, Hugo, 287
Block grants, 114, 115. *See also* Revenue sharing
Board of Vocational Education, federal, 90
Boston, 58; busing in, 134, 135, 140
Brennan, William J., Jr., 148
Brown v. Board of Education, 50, 97, 129, 130, 133, 143, 147
Buckley, James, 290
Bundy, McGeorge, 176
Business and Professional Peoples' Alliance for Better Textbooks of Kanawha County, West Virginia, 73, 233
Busing, 53, 54, 79, 113, 115, 127, 128–45; Congress and, 140–44; Miller and Gerard study of, 138–39

Califano, Joseph, 290
California Teachers Association, 61
CAPE. *See* Council for American Private Education
Carroll, Anne, 299
Carter, James G., 161–62
Carter, Jimmy, 34, 143, 257, 290
Catholics United for the Faith (CUF), 298

Certification of teachers, 80–81
Charles Kettering Foundation, 36, 222
Charleston Gazette, 232, 233
Child care, 56, 128, 302; proprietary centers, 294
Children: gifted, 35; handicapped, 34–35
Christ the King, Lord of History, 299
Christian schools, 275–80
Citizens for Decency Through Law, 234
Civil Rights Act (1964), 102, 128, 129
Coalition for American Public Employees (CAPE), 69
Coalition for Children, 248, 249
Code of Canon Law (1917), 281
Coleman, James, 130–31
Collective bargaining, 69, 74
College Board Advisory Panel on Score Decline, 21
Colorado Catholic Academy of the Holy Rosary, 298–99
Commager, Henry Steele, 20
Committee for Full Funding of Education Programs, 46, 47
Committee for the Survival of a Free Congress, 257, 261
Committee on Political Education (COPE), 64
Common Cause, 64
Community-control movement, 168–70
Comprehensive Child Development Bill, 189
Compulsory-attendance laws: defenses of, 312–14; history of, 311–12, 314; opposition to, 306–17
Congressional Record, 16, 189
Conlan, John, 155–57, 204, 228, 263
Conservatism, 257–58
Conservative Caucus, 252, 257
Constitution, U.S., 141, 143, 146, 148
Cooper, John Sherman, 105–6

Council for American Private Education (CAPE), 271–72
Council for Basic Education, 177
Cranston, Alan, 61
Curtis, Carl, 257

Daley, Richard J., 131
Dashiell, Dick, 69–70
Delaney, James J., 290
Democratic Study Group (DSG), 125
Deschooling Society, 305
Detroit Federation of Teachers (DFT), 68
Developmental placement, 301–2
Dewey, John, 24–25, 151, 174
Discipline in schools, need for, 36, 74
Dornan, Robert, 234, 257
Douglas, William O., 148

Eagleton, Tom, 137
Early exit, 222–24, 300, 305
Economic Opportunity Act, 100
Education: a big business, 44; declining standards of, 37; diversity in, desire for, 264–65; federal interference in, 32–35; homogeneity of, 70; messianic roots of American, 160–63, 281; "modern," 22–28; "new," 23; parenthood, 35; problem of, causes for, 21–22; progressive, 23, 28, 30–33; as social reform, 28–36, 81
Education, federal role in, 89–126; general-aid-to-education bills, 95–102 *passim,* 157
Education, local control of, 70–73, 116, 134–35, 136, 158–60, 193–95
Education establishment, 37, 38, 41–70, 79, 168, 230, 235, 238, 168, 270; opposition to private education, 270–71, 288, 299–300; totalitarian control by, 312

Education for the Handicapped Act (1976), 123
Education Update, 229
Educational Opportunity Program (EOP), 124–25
Education Products Information Exchange (EPIE), 217
Educational Research Council of Greater Cleveland, 107
Edwards, George, 130
Edwards, Mickey, 257
Eisenhower, Dwight D., 97, 98–99
Elementary and Secondary Education Act (ESEA; 1965), 32–33, 40, 62, 100, 101, 102, 113, 115, 116–18, 119, 129, 160, 271; critical analysis of, 121–24; and federal educational involvement, 102–7; titles of, 110–13, 118
Emergency Committee for Children, 189
Engel v. Vitale, 74, 147, 148
Equal education, 318–20
Equal Rights Amendment, 51, 53
Esch, Marvin L., 140
ESEA. *See* Elementary and Secondary Education Act
Everson v. Board of Education, 287
Ex Parte McCardle, 142
Exploring Human Nature, 154

Fairfax Christian Academy, 292, 296
Family environment, influence of, 29, 302–4, 308, 320
Fauntroy, Walter, 137
Federal Advisory Council on the Arts, 99
Federal child-care programs, 34–35, 56
Federal Election Commission, 63, 64
Federal Emergency Relief Administration, 95
Federal Housing Authority, 133

Federal Paperwork Commission, 126

Fike, Elmer, 73

Filer Commission on Public Needs and Private Philanthropy, 271

Ford, Gerald, 115–16, 142, 233

Ford Foundation, 169, 176

Franz, Barbara, 309

Fraser, Donald, 138

Free enterprise, courses in, 198, 204, 210, 218

Freedmen's Bureau, 90

Freeman, Roger, 104

Freund, Paul, 148–49

Friedman, Milton, 268

Functional illiteracy, 18–21, 86

Gabler, Mel and Norma, 213, 216–17, 233

Gaertner, Johannes, 144–45

Gallaudet, Rev. Thomas, 18

Gallup polls, 36–37, 128, 256; "Public Attitudes Toward Education" (1975), 266, 275

Gardner, John, 101–2

Garfield, James A., 92

General Accounting Office, 123, 125

General Educational Development (GED) exams, 305

Gerard, Harold. See Miller, Norman and Harold Gerard

Gesell Institute of Child Development, 301–2

G. I. Bill. See Serviceman's Readjustment Act

Gong Lum v. Rice, 129

Goodman, Paul, 306

Gordon, Sol, 208

Great Depression, 20

Greeley, Andrew, 287

Green, Edith, 125–26

Gubbins, Joan, 200

Harcourt Brace (Jovanovich), 235

Harris survey (on busing), 139

Harvard Educational Review, 122, 315–16

Hatch, Orrin, 257

Hathaway, Bill, 62–63

Head Start, 34–35, 100, 121

Health, Education, and Welfare, U.S. Department of, 26, 34, 101–2, 131–32, 273; Assistant Secretary for Education, Office of, 120; Assistant Secretary for Human Development, 121; Civil Rights Office, 129

Hebrew day schools, 285–86, 287

Heidenry, Patricia, 307–8

Hellman, Dr. Louis, 26

Heritage Foundation, 229

Herndon, Terry, 61, 68

HEW. See Health, Education, and Welfare, U.S. Department of

Higher Education Facilities Act, 100, 114

Holt, John, 306

Holt, Rinehart & Winston, 235

Holy Innocents schools, 298

Home instruction, legalities of, 309–11

Hoover, Herbert, 91

Horton, Frank, 126

Houghton Mifflin, 235

House of Representatives, U.S.: Commerce Committee, 96; Democratic Study Group, 100; Education and Labor Committee, 96, 97, 98, 115; Republican Policy Committee, 143; Republican Study Committee (RSC), 122; Rules Committee, 98, 99, 100; Science and Technology Committee, 155, 157

Housing Act (1950), 97

Hudson Institute, 178

Humanist Manifestoes, 151–52, 155, 199

Illich, Ivan, 305–6

Illiteracy. See Functional illiteracy

IML. See Integrated maturity level

Immigrants' Protective League, 312
IMPACE, 65
Individual Science Instructional System (ISIS), 154
Institute for Political and Legal Education, 26
Integrated maturity level (IML), 303–4
Integration, school, 52–53, 97–98, 114, 119, 128, 130–31, 133–45. *See also* Segregation, school
Interagency Day Care Regulations, 294
International Reading Association, 21
International Society of Professional Bureaucrats, 126
Ireland (Eire), school policies in, 289

Javits, Jacob, 137, 160
Jencks, Christopher, 135
Johnson, John, 176
Johnson, Lyndon, 100, 102, 111, 129

Kanawha County, W. Va., textbook dispute in, 16, 73, 78–79, 150, 212, 231–35, 236
Kennedy, Edward, 137
Kennedy, John, 97, 99, 100, 102–3, 105
Kennedy, Robert, 137
Keyes v. School District No. 1, 132
Kohlberg, Lawrence, 153

Lamborn, Dr. Robert, 271
Landgrebe, Earl, 116–17
Lanham Act, 95
Lawyers' Committee for Civil Rights Under Law, 300
Lear, Norman, 176
Learning disability, 35

Lent, Norman, 16
Let's Improve Today's Education (LITE), 203–4, 229, 248
Letters, writing, 239–40, 242–43, 251–52
Levi, Edward, 142
Libraries, 111, 123
Library Services Act, 100
Lieberman, Myron, 107
Lincoln, Abraham, 90
LITE. *See* Let's Improve Today's Education
Look-say reading method, 18–19, 209, 309
Louisville, 134, 144
Love, Robert, 291–292, 296
Luther, Martin, 312

McCarthy, Eugene, 137
McCollum v. Board of Education, 74
McFarland, Stanley, 64–65
McGovern, George, 137
McGraw-Hill, 235
MACOS. See *Man: A Course of Study*
Man: A Course of Study (MACOS), 127, 154–55, 237
Mann, Charles Riborg, 91
Mann, Horace, 161, 312
Manpower Development and Training: Act, 100; Administration, 108
Marburger, Carl, 61
Marshall, Thurgood, 137
Meany, George, 50, 136–37
Meyer v. Nebraska, 316
Michigan Education Association, 61
Miller, Norman and Harold Gerard, 138–39
Milliken v. Bradley, 132
Minimum-proficiency standards, 224–25
"Modern" education, 22–28
Mondale, Walter, 34, 114, 121, 138, 190, 257

Moore, Alice, 231, 232–33, 234, 235
Moore, Dr. Raymond S., 302, 303–4
More Unfinished Stories, 19
Morrill Acts, 90
Moynihan, Daniel P., 131, 290
Muskie, Edmund, 137
Myers, Henry S., 266

NAACP. *See* National Association for the Advancement of Colored People
National Academy of Sciences, 121
National Advisory Committee for Education, 91–93, 113; *Federal Relations to Education,* 91; "Tentative List of Contemporary Activities," 93
National Association for Neighborhood Schools (NANS), 144
National Association for the Advancement of Colored People (NAACP), 20, 46, 47, 129; Legal Defense and Education Fund, 47, 137
National Association of Professional Educators (NAPE), 69–70
National Association of Secondary School Principals, 116
National Catholic Educational Association (NCEA), 271, 274, 284
National Catholic Welfare Conference, 101
National Center for Family Planning Services, 26
National Citizens' Committee for Education, 61
National Commission on the Reform of Secondary Education, 222–23
National Congress of Parents and Teachers, 175

National Council of Churches, 101, 279–80
National Defense Education Act, 98, 100, 108–10
National Education Association (NEA), 19, 23, 32, 46, 47–48, 49, 50–67, 68, 69–70, 73, 79, 80, 84, 92, 95, 101, 103, 113, 162, 171, 175–76, 177, 181, 223, 224–25, 232, 236, 257, 305, 319; on assuaging parents, 185–86; Bicentennial Committee, 175, 177; Commission on Reorganization of Secondary Education, 175; Government Relations Department, 65; inflationary positions of, 58; noneducational issues, involvement in, 59–60; Political Action Committee (NEA-PAC), 51, 62–65, 118; political goals of, 50–60; political tactics of, 60–66; Representative Assemblies, 50–53, 54–58
National Foundation for the Improvement of Education, 65
National Institute of Education, 114, 120, 128, 131, 268; Educational Resources Information Center (ERIC), 300; *A Study of State Legal Standards for the Provision of Public Education,* 300
National Institute of Mental Health, 155
National Labor Relations Board, 282
National Parents League, 304, 308–9
National School Board Association (NSBA), 46, 47
National Science Foundation, 20, 96, 97, 109, 127, 154–55, 156–57; *Man: A Course of Study,* 127, 154–55; other programs of, 154; Science Information Service, 109
National Teachers' Exam (NTE), 81

NDEA. *See* National Defense Education Act

NEA. *See* National Education Association

Negative checkoff, 63–64

New Jersey Education Association, 61

New Republic, 106–7

New York Public Employment Relations Board, 68

New York State Regents' Prayer decision, 146, 147

New York State School Boards Association, 106

New York Times, 307–8

Nixon, Richard, 97, 119, 129, 189, 263; education proposals of, 114–15

Northwest Ordinance, 89

NSBA. *See* National School Board Association

Office of Economic Opportunity, 108, 113, 115, 119, 267

Office of Education, U.S. (USOE), 27, 32, 92, 101, 119–20, 126, 271–72, 276; 1977 programs of, 119–20; *State and Federal Laws Relating to Nonpublic Schools*, 300

Office of the Handicapped, 35

O'Hair, Madalyn Murray, 287

Operation Bruce, 25–26

Packwood, Robert W., 290

Parent activism, 163–226; accuracy, need for, 188–91; through the administration, 182–91, 196–97; awakening, 163–67; behavior at interviews, 185–87; follow-ups, 183, 187–88, 256, 260–61; groups, beginning, 166–74; groups, importance of, 184–85, 187; lobbying state legislatures, 200–207, 253–56; local boards, 193–97; note-tak-ing, 184–85, 187; parent sove-reignty, 171–72; "Parents' Bills of Rights," 218–22; at state and national levels, 191–93, 197–200, 249, 253–62; the teacher, 179–81; volunteer work, 181–82

Parent activists: activities of, 247–62; creating groups, 237–47; goals of, 219–30; unifying, 228–29, 236–37; who they are, 227–28. *See also* Parents' rights movement, goals of

Parental Rights Act, 219–22

Parenthood education, 35

Parents: critical attitude of, 36–38; rights and duties of, 37–38, 233–34

Parents' groups: creating, 237–40; crisis activities, 250–52; jobs of, 247–50, 259–60; political action by, 252–62; recruiting for, 240–47

Parents' rights activists. *See* Parent activists

Parents' rights movement, goals of, 207–11. *See also* Parent activism; Parent activists

Parker, Francis W., 162

Pell, Claiborne, 62, 137, 257

Percy, Charles, 137

Phillips, Howard, 119, 268

Phonics, 18, 194, 208, 265, 321

Pierce v. Society of Sisters, 311, 315–16, 317

Plenary Council of Baltimore, Third, 281

Plessy v. Ferguson, 129

Pluralism, 286

Population education, 26–27

Powell, Adam Clayton, 98

Prayer, in-school, 74, 127, 145, 149, 287

Press releases, 239, 243

Prince George's County, Md., school integration in, 133–34

Private schools: Christian, 275–80; failures of, 297–98; growth

in non-Catholic, 274; independent proprietary, 291–300; Jewish, 285–86, 287; opposed by "establishment," 270–71, 288; and public funds, 271–74, 287–90; Roman Catholic, 270, 272, 274, 277, 280–85, 287, 298–99
Professional self-governance, 79–88
"Professionals," educational, 31, 32, 33, 41, 57, 80–85, 168, 198, 211; objections to, 176–77; usurpation by, 229–30
Progressive education, 23, 28, 30–33
Progressive Education Association, 28, 31
Public education: alternatives in, providing, 265–67; goals of, 175–76, 177–78; voucher plans, 267–70
Public Service Research Council, 69
Public Works Administration, 95

Quie, Albert, 113–14, 115, 116

Rafferty, Max, 61, 70, 188, 262
Raspberry, William, 188
Reagan, Ronald, 257
Reeves, Floyd, 94–95
Religion in schools, defending, 149–50. See also Prayer, in-school
Religious education, need for, 274
Revenue sharing, 114, 115, 116
Ribicoff, Abraham, 137
Rice, Charles, 147–48, 288
Right-to-work laws, 69
Riverside, Calif., busing study of, 138–39
Roche, Dr. George C., 289
Rockefeller, David, 176
Roman Catholic parochial schools, 270, 272, 274, 277, 280–85, 287, 298–99

Roosevelt, Eleanor, 97
Roosevelt, Franklin D., 94
Roper poll (on busing), 139–40
Roth, William V., Jr., 290
Rousseau, Jean-Jacques, 161
Rowan, Carl, 137
Rushdoony, Rousas J., 161
Ryor, John, 60, 61

St. John, Walter, 185
SAT (Scholastic Aptitude Test), 81, 86
School boards, local: control by, 73–88; limiting of, 86; powers of, 74
School Desegregation Standards and Assistance Act, 142
School districts, consolidation of, 75
School Lunch Program (federal), 96
School systems, echelons of, 191–92
Schooling, length of, 24. See also Attendance age, opposition to lowering; Early exit
Scoma, Richard and Julie, 306–7
Scott-Foresman Company, 19, 235
Secular humanism, 146, 150–55, 275
Segregation, school, 95, 97–98, 114, 129–30, 131–33. See also Integration, school
Senate, U.S.: Finance Committee, 290; Labor and Public Welfare Committee, 96; Subcommittee on Education, 62
Serviceman's Readjustment Act (G.I. Bill), 95–96, 269
Seton School, 298, 299
Sex education, 17, 26–27, 55
Shanker, Albert, 67
Shriver, Sargent, 137
Sielaff, Marcia, 203–4
Silvestro, Dr. John, 302
Simon, Sidney, 153
Sizer, Theodore R., 265

Skelly, Jim, 200, 204
Smith, Mortimer, 177–78
Smith-Hughes Act, 90–91
Society for College and University
  Planning, 20
Spellman, Francis Cardinal, 97
Standardized tests, 21, 23, 36, 37,
  81, 319; elimination of, 57
*State and Federal Laws Relating to
  Nonpublic Schools,* 300
Stewart, Potter, 148
Strikes, teacher, 68–69
*Study of State Legal Standards for the
  Provision of Public Education, A,*
  300
Sufrin, Sidney, 106
Sullivan, Kathleen, 82–83
Sullivan, Neil, 87–88
Supreme Court, U.S., 74, 97, 102,
  127, 129, 130, 131, 132, 140,
  141–42, 146, 147–48, 149–50,
  151, 155, 268, 278, 282, 287,
  311, 316–17
*Swann v. Charlotte-Mecklenburg
  Board of Education,* 131
Sylvester, Peter, 287

Tabernacle Christian School, 278
Taft, Robert, 96
Taxes: double, for private-school
  parents, 289, 290; exemptions
  for private education, 287–88,
  289–90; level of, 103–4; to-
  bacco, 117
Teacher Corps, 100, 119
Teacher Standards and Practices
  Commission (Oregon), 84–85
Texas Education Agency (TEA),
  215
Texas Education Code, 213
Textbooks, selection of, 16, 56,
  74, 76–77, 78–79, 150, 195,
  212–18, 231–37
Thoburn, Rev. Robert, 292
Tinker v. Des Moines School District,
  74
To Teach As Jesus Did, 284

Today's Education, 51, 217
Torcaso v. Watkins, 147, 151
Transcendental Meditation (TM),
  155, 211
Treen, David, 117
Truman, Harry S., 96
Tunney, John, 137

Underwood, Kenneth, 231
Unfinished Stories, 19
Unionization, advantages of, 67–
  69, 75–76
Unions, role of, 56, 59
UniServe, 48, 66–67
United Federation of Teachers,
  50, 67, 68, 169
United Nations, 54
U.S. Catholic Conference, 101

Values clarification, 27, 30, 152–
  54, 274–75. *See also* Secular hu-
  manism
Vatican Council II, 280, 281, 298
Veterans' Administration, 133
Vocational Education Act (1946),
  109
VOTE (Vote of Teachers for Edu-
  cation), 62
Voucher plans, 267–70

War on Poverty, 122
Warren, Earl, 102, 129
Washington, D.C., school integra-
  tion in, 133
Washington Post, 138
Washington Star-News, 207–8
*West Virginia State Board of Educa-
  tion v. Barnette,* 74
Whisner, Rev. Levi, 278
White House Conference on Chil-
  dren and Youth, 1970 Report
  of, 121
White House Conference on Edu-
  cation, 98

351

White House Conference on Handicapped Individuals, 121
Wichita Collegiate School, 292–93, 296

Wilson, Jil, 173
Wisconsin v. Yoder, 317
World Council of Churches, 280